Yearbook of

ENGLISH FESTIVALS

Yearbook of

ENGLISH FESTIVALS

Dorothy Gladys Spicer

THE H. W. WILSON COMPANY

NEW YORK   1954

394
Sp4le

TO

KATHARINE SEYMOUR JACKSON GOODSELL

who loves
all English festivals
and
feast day foods

TO THE READER

Peruse with heede, then friendlie judge,
and blaming rash refraine;
So maist thou rede unto thy goode,
And shall requite my paine.

   —GEOFFREY WHITNEY. *A Choice of Emblems* ... 1586

PREFACE

I began this book the day I was convinced the British always mind their own business. If you live in one village nobody knows—much less, cares—what goes on in the next. If you want to learn about something, it is well to depend on yourself, because otherwise, nobody can tell you *where* anything happens, or *when*. This is fun. Once you become a sleuth in such matters, each hour is an adventure, each day a journey into the unknown.

Over a hundred years ago Washington Irving had much the same idea. He shrewdly observed that to really know the English, a stranger ". . . must go forth into the country; . . . sojourn in villages and hamlets; . . . visit castles, villas, farm houses, cottages, wander . . . along hedges and green lanes; . . . loiter about country churches; attend wakes and fairs and other village festivals."

This is what I did when writing this book. England has a vast wealth and variety of traditional customs—moving, picturesque, or humorous, as the case may be—which are celebrated at every season throughout the year. Such as:

A Pig's Face Feast, when Gloucestershire folk eat succulent roast pig (in small quantity, nowadays, alas!), to commemorate the wild boar feast Queen Matilda traditionally held over nine centuries ago, upon completion of their village church.

A "Clipping the Church" ritual in another Gloucestershire community, when parish youngsters join hands and "embrace" their church in rhythmic, swaying dance, in memory, some say, of an old Roman pastoral ritual to protect lambs from wolves.

An eight-hundred-year-old penance, called "Planting the Penny Hedge," to remind people that three wicked huntsmen once murdered a monk for sheltering a wounded forest beast.

A famous Goose Fair (the 659th to be held in 1954), kept ever since Edward I granted its Charter in 1284, and gooseherds, traveling for weeks from the provinces, "shoed" their birds' feet by coating them first with tar, then with sand.

And then there are the old games: Hurling the Silver Ball at Lent's beginning; Shrovetide pancake-tossings; Easter pace-eggings; Whitsun cheese-rollings; running after pretty girls at Hocktide, for forfeit payments of a penny or a kiss.

There are bequest sermons, such as the Lion Sermon, preached annually in a London church, to celebrate a pious merchant's miraculous deliverance from a desert lion.

And then there are old doles, such as one of bread and cocoa (once of cheese) to perpetuate a charity of twelfth century Siamese-twin sisters; or the twenty-one sixpences for twenty-one poor London widows who, on Good Friday, must "go and get them" by walking across a flat-topped tomb.

"To keep a custom you hammer the anvil still, though you have no iron," say the British. English people have forgotten the meaning of many old customs, yet they keep them up. Like the Yorkshire bell ringer who cannot tell why, on Christmas Eve, he tolls the church bell as many times as the years of our Christian faith; or the Lancashire man who does not know why his townsfolk bake small china dolls in their Wakes Feast pies; or the Staffordshire laborers who dance with reindeer horns at a village revel so old nobody knows when it began.

Every day in the year is a festival in some part of England. That is one thing which makes it a wonderful country.

To my descriptions of ancient festival customs I have added a few technical props, such as a regional map to show the geographic areas where more important events occur; notes on the Old and New Style calendars which exist side by side in some parts of England; a list of helpful books for additional background, and a glossary of festival terms that are not so familiar in American as British usage. I have included, also, various index classifications, to assist the reader in turning to any given ceremony and seeing at a glance *where, when, why,* and for *how long,* it occurs.

PREFACE

I have described the festivals in this book, not as an anthropologist would see them, but as a reporter who has spent many months of happy wandering from one village to another. My interpretation of festivals stems not so much from scientific findings as from traditions current among simple people with generations of forebears who have participated in similar ceremonies. Although I have attempted to check all data through reliable sources, a margin of error is always present in material of this kind which depends largely upon folk tradition as its basis. Such tradition is fluid. It often varies from person to person, place to place, year to year. Then, too, I am American; and although my roots, like those of the festivals about which I write, are deeply embedded in the England of eight or nine hundred years ago, the things I see and describe are through the eyes of one who belongs to the New World. Therefore, if errors inadvertently occur, I ask indulgence.

I wish I might thank individually the many kind persons all over England who have made this book possible through generous hospitality and sharing of cherished festivals and folkways with the stranger within their gates. I am particularly grateful for helpful information supplied by:

Mr. H. W. Kille, Hon. Secretary, West Somerset Branch, Somerset Archaeological . . . Society, on the Minehead Hobby Horse; Mr. P. Mitchell, Chairman, Wishford Oak Apple Club, on Wishford's Oak Apple Day ceremonies; Mr. W. Macqueen-Pope, historian of the Drury Lane Theatre, on Cutting the Baddeley Cake; Miss Christina Hole; Mr. Ralph Wightman; Mr. Morton Nance, Grand Bard of Cornwall, on the Helston Furry; the Reverend Canon C. W. Cooper, Rural Dean of Tetbury, on Avening's Pig Face Feast; Mr. James Gibson, and Mr. H. Watkinson, District Manager and Editor, *Horwich and Westhoughton Journal*, Lancashire, on Keaw Yed Wakes; the Reverend Gordon Hall, Rector St. Katharine Cree, London, on the Lion Sermon; Mr. T. Hemmings, Mayor of Ock Street Morris, Abingdon; Mr. C. J. Newman, Town Clerk of Exeter, on Lammas Fair; Mr. T. J. Owen, Town Clerk, Nottingham, on Nottingham Goose Fair and traditional brandy snap recipe; Mr. J.

Bright, Manager of Ye Olde Cheshire Cheese, Ltd., London; Mr. Alfred James Pugh, Alderman of Bebington Council, and Chairman, Bromborough Historical Society, Cheshire; Mr. Arthur Bakes, Chairman, Historical Committee of the Cheshire Rural Community Council; Mrs. Lilian Hayward, on the folk customs of Shropshire; Mr. E. J. Freeman, clerk of Sherborne Urban District Council; Mr. Henry J. Callendar, F.I.M.T.A., A.S.A.A., Town Clerk, City and County of Lichfield; the Reverend W. Warr, Rector, St. Mary of the Purification, Blidworth, on the Rocking Ceremony; Mrs. Ethel M. Abel, on the traditional Grasmere Gingerbread recipe; Mr. E. J. Hunter, Clerk Haxey Parish Council, on Throwing the Hood; Mr. Alexander C. Ross, D.P.A., Clerk of Whitby Urban District Council, on Planting the Penny Hedge; the Right Reverend Mgr. John H. Filmer, K.C.O.R., Master of the Guild of Our Lady of Ransom, on the Pilgrimage to the Chapel of Our Lady, Hastings Castle; the Reverend A. R. Ladell, Vicar of Church of St. Nicholas, Abbots Bromley, on the Horn Dance; Mr. F. W. Smith, Librarian, Dewesbury Public Library, on Ringing the Devil's Knell; Miss J. Royse, Castleton, on the Garland Ceremony; Mr. H. Gordon Jones, Hon. Secretary of the Biddenden Trust. I am also grateful to the Misses Bessie and Margaret Callow; Mrs. Frank Helliwell; Miss Emmie Allen, and many others too numerous to name, for their constant interest and their help in making contacts for me throughout England.

I also acknowledge indebtness for much material to the sources listed at the end of the book under *Some Helpful Books;* and to the British Museum Library, and County Libraries all over England, for placing their resources at my disposal. And last, but by no means least, I wish to thank Mrs. John K. Gieling for her preparation of the manuscript.

DOROTHY GLADYS SPICER

White Plains, New York
January 1954

CONTENTS

xiii

ENGLISH FESTIVALS

CONTENTS

ENGLISH FESTIVALS

xvi

CONTENTS

ENGLISH FESTIVALS

CONTENTS

xix

ENGLISH FESTIVALS

xx

CONTENTS

xxi

PART II

THE EASTER CYCLE

CONTENTS

xxiii

CONTENTS

PART III
FOR FURTHER REFERENCE

INDEXES

xxv

PART I

THE TWELVE MONTHS

JANUARY

Here we come a-wassailing
Among the leaves so green,
Here we come a-wassailing,
So far to be seen:

We are not daily beggars
That beg from door to door,
But we are neighbors' children
Whom you have seen before:

Call up the butler of this house,
Put on his golden ring;
Let him bring up a glass of beer,
And better we shall sing:

We have got a little purse
Made of stretching leather skin;
We want a little of your money
To line it well within.

Bring us out a table
And spread the table cloth;
Bring us out a mouldy cheese
And some of your Christmas loaf:

God bless the master of this house,
Likewise the mistress too,
And all the little children
That round the table go:

Good master and mistress,
While you're sitting by the fire,
Pray think of us poor children
Who are wandering in the mire.
            —*Old Wassailing Carol from Yorkshire**

* In olden times, little girls sang this carol on New Year's Day as they carried a holly bush adorned with ribbons, oranges and dolls about the neighborhood. Later, the custom was practiced throughout the week after Christmas, and a decorated box containing dolls, to represent Jesus and the Virgin Mary, was substituted for the bush. On receiving a penny, the children uncovered their box and exhibited the dolls.

3

New Year's Day

January 1

In many towns and villages of northern England the New Year, and sometimes Christmas also, is "let in" by a dark-haired man or boy, called "First-foot," or "Lucky Bird." Nobody should leave the house until First-foot arrives, thus establishing good luck to the household for the coming year. Most people agree that a woman, a squint-eyed, or a flat-footed person is unlucky. Light, or sandy-haired men are generally unpopular, since Judas Iscariot was thought to have had red hair!

First-foot often carries gifts into the house, such as something green (but not dead), a lump of coal, or a loaf of bread, so that the household may have good luck, warmth and plenty of food during the next twelve months. In Yorkshire's mining area I know a man who, on New Year's Eve, always wraps lumps of coal in bright blue, green or red paper, and leaves one piece at midnight with each of his cronies. From year to year, the recipients cherish the coals which, on no account, may be burned or cast aside. First-foot always is heartily welcomed with a glass of ale, a piece of Yule spice cake and a bit of cheese.

In many Staffordshire villages the family head (if dark-haired) leaves the house just before midnight, while church bells are tolling the old year out. Then, just as the chimes begin their joyous pealing, he returns, "bringing the New Year in" through the open front door, and "letting the Old Year out" by the back. All the women-folk are kissed, congratulations exchanged, healths drunk and little mince pies eaten. For Staffordshire, Shropshire, and some other counties claim that the Twelve Days between Christmas and January first mirror the coming year, and a person will have one happy month during the next twelve for each mince pie* he eats at a neighbor's home. It is small wonder then, that village wassailers, acquaintances and friends visit constantly from house to house during Yuletide, and that hospitality flows as freely as good wishes and

* In some parts of England plum puddings, rather than mince pies, are the rule.

congratulations. Nor is it surprising that small mince pies are as popular today as the huge seventeenth century Christmas pies which Herrick describes as needing protection by a special guard:

> Come, guard this night the Christmas-Pie,
> That the Thiefe, though ne'r so slie,
> With Flesh hooks, don't come nie
> > To catch it
> From him, who all alone sits there,
> Having his eyes still in his eare
> And a deale of nightly feare
> > To watch it.*

New Year's Day in rural England, as in many other countries, abounds in signs and portents. Each county has its own quaint sayings and folk superstitions to safeguard the family welfare for the next twelve months.

In Lancashire, Lincolnshire, and some other places, for example, people say it is unlucky "to give away a light from the house" on New Year's Day, while elsewhere it is generally thought that bad luck results from *taking anything* out of the house before *bringing something* in! To carry in *something green* means plenty of bread, but to carry in *bad news,* results in sure disaster!

In Cornwall, to pay out money on January 1 means you will be passing it out for the next twelve months, while in Devonshire a handsel, or gift, of something sweet, must go to the bees, if there is to be plenty of honey during the coming year. Of course, washing on New Year's Day may "wash a friend away," while sweeping towards the door instead of the hearth, takes out every bit of luck!

On New Year's Day every one does well to watch his ways. For the beginning of the year is the time for remembering old customs, old ceremonials and old superstitions, many of which—quite unknown to persons who do so—originated in the midwinter rites of pagan times.

* Robert Herrick. *Hesperides.* "Christmas Eve." 1648.

ENGLISH FESTIVALS

January 1

Allendale is a tiny community some fifteen miles southwest of Hexham. The village, which is built about a market place, is surrounded by magnificent Northumbrian scenery—pastoral toward the valley of the River Allen, bleak and forbidding toward the lonely moors. Against this dramatic backdrop, men and women have welcomed the New Year with ceremonial fires and dances for at least eight hundred and fifty years.

On New Year's Eve Allendale's townsfolk hurry towards the square to build a great bonfire. Meanwhile, a band of guisers dressed in all sorts of rag-tag fancy costumes makes village rounds and receives hospitality at different homes. Although all the performers are men, some dress in women's clothes. At each home, the men put on a rough-and-ready show in return for abundant New Year's cheer.

Shortly before midnight the guisers troop into the square, which already is filling with people from far and near. Quickly a procession forms. First comes the Braes of Allen Band, then blackened-faced youths (the number varies from year to year) supporting on their heads trays filled with tar lighted by a torch from last year's bonfire. Bringing up the rear are dancing townsfolk, who joyfully follow the long procession as it leaves the square and winds through the ancient village streets.

Now it is almost midnight. The burning tar is too hot to carry longer. The procession returns to its starting point and circles the bonfire from right to left. Suddenly the youths hurl the tar upon the huge pile, which bursts into flame against the black winter sky. The village chimes strike twelve. The band starts up a dance tune. Shouts of joy break from the crowd. Friends and neighbors congratulate each other and exchange good wishes for a happy New Year. Young and old dance deliriously about the flames. Allendale salutes the New Year. Not until the last ember dies do villagers

6

disperse to their own homes, or go "first-footing" to the neighboring farms scattered throughout the dale.

Even during the blackouts of the Second World War, Allendale observed its traditional ceremony. The bonfire, it is true, was lighted under an iron canopy, and candles, burning in darkened jam jars, were substituted for the trays of blazing tar. But in spite of wartime safety restrictions, the continuity of Allendale's ancient festival of fire remains unbroken from pagan to modern times.

SWORD DANCING AND MUMMERS' PLAYS, NORTHEASTERN COUNTIES

Usually in early January, sometimes between Christmas and the New Year

The Sword Dances, which with a few exceptions are found chiefly in the northeastern counties of Northumberland, Durham and North Yorkshire, are thought to have possibly originated in the folk dances of the Danes who occupied this part of England over a thousand years ago. The dances, similar to those of many other European countries, are traditional to the midwinter season.

The Sword Dancers appear sometimes at Christmas, sometimes at the New Year, to perform dances which folklorists think symbolize the conflict between dying winter with the quickening forces of spring. The dancers themselves—simple workingmen—are unaware that the theme they present is common to primitive people of every land. For centuries the men, their sons and grandsons, have made village rounds and presented a crude play, distinguished by stock characters such as the Fool, or Medicine Man, the Woman (a man, dressed in feminine attire), Beelzebub with his club, and a hobby horse. The beheading of the Fool, and his subsequent resurrection and restoration to youthful vigor, follow ancient folk rites which represent Winter's death and the resurgence of Spring.

The Yorkshire performers traditionally employ a long steel or wooden sword, while those of Northumbria (as the counties of Northumberland and Durham are called), generally use the short, flexible steel sword which closely resembles a workman's tool. The technique of the Northumbrian dance features highly complex, close formation, "stepping" or rapid tap dancing, and elaborate sets, ending with a locking of the short swords.

Some of the traditional Sword Dance teams which are well known are:

1. The *North Skelton and Lingdale Teams* of Yorkshire. Both of these groups are composed of ironstone miners who, when unemployed after World War I, revived their ancient county dances and presented them in various North Riding villages, to raise funds to support themselves and their families. The two teams, which were organized independently of each other, are active in the mining area of Cleveland.

The North Skelton dancers have no distinctive costume but generally dress informally in white or colored shirts or tunics.

2. The *Handsworth Dancers* of Yorkshire. There are eight men in this group from Handsworth, near Sheffield. Although costumes vary among all the dancers from time to time, the Handsworth dancers have long been distinguished by lambswool caps which are dyed red on one side and left white on the other.

3. The *Grenoside Dancers** of Yorkshire.

4. The *Plough Stots†* of Goathland and Sleights, Yorkshire.

5. The *Flamborough Head Dancers* of Yorkshire. The dance of this team of eight men from the fishing village of Flamborough Head is done rapidly and with great skill, in spite of the heavy fishermen's boots that are worn. The dancers link their wooden swords, which are held in the left hand, as they perform figures suggesting the operations of net making. The costume of the men usually includes blue jerseys and caps, in addition to the boots already mentioned.

6. The *Royal Earsdon Sword Dancers* of Northumberland. This team, composed of miners, is said to be one of England's most dis-

* *See* Sword Dancers, *Grenoside,* Yorkshire, p 177.
† *See* The Dancing Plough Stots, p23.

tinguished. The costume generally consists of white shirts and crimson jackets and breeches.

TWELFTH NIGHT AND TWELFTH DAY

January 5 and 6

Twelfth Night (also known as Twelfth Day Eve, Epiphany Eve, and Old Christmas Eve) has not been celebrated extensively since the mid-nineteenth century. For all that, many scattered reminders of the old revels, and the still older beliefs concerning the festival, have survived to modern times.

Ceremonies of cutting the Twelfth cake, wassailing fruit trees, caroling from house to house for goodies, belief in the miraculous blossoming of thorn or bush, of animals that kneel and bees that sing, are a few of many picturesque customs still associated with the season.

Before the calendar change of 1752,* Twelfth Night was celebrated on a gigantic scale. In those days, a Twelfth Night cake was universal. The cake, baked with a bean and a pea inside, was washed down with generous draughts from the wassail bowl, which brimmed with "lamb's wool," or ale, well seasoned with sugar, spices and roasted apple pulp. Friends and relatives assembled, to dine sumptuously and then cut the cake. Whoever found the bean in his portion was proclaimed king of the revel, while the person getting the pea was queen. In modern times the cake, as will be seen, still plays an occasional role in Twelfth Night festivities.

Robert Herrick vividly describes the Twelfth Night ceremony, as celebrated in his day:

> Now, now the mirth comes
> With the cake full of plums,
> Where Beane's the *King* of the sport here;
> Beside we must know,
> The Pea also
> Must revell, as *Queene,* in the Court here.

* *See* "England's 'Two' Calendars," p249.

9

Begin then to chuse,
(This night as ye use)
Who shall for the present delight here,
Be a *King* by the lot,
And who shall not
A health to the King and the Queene here.

Which knowne, let us make
Joy-sops with the cake;
And let not a man be seen here,
Who unurg'd will not drinke
To the base from the brink
A health to the King and the Queene here.

Next crowne the bowle full
With gentle lambs-wooll;
Add sugar, nutmeg and ginger,
With store of ale too;
And thus ye must doe
To make the wassaile a swinger.*

Wassailing the fruit trees is an ancient fertility rite, still practiced on Old Christmas Day in certain areas. As in olden times, the farmer and his helpers carry jugs of cider to the orchards. There, surrounding one of the best-bearing apple trees, they offer toasts to its health.

Some West Country folk who stubbornly adhere to the Old Style calendar, still maintain that Old Christmas Eve is the "true" anniversary of Christ's birth. In Cornwall and Devon, people still say that at midnight oxen, horses, and sheep fall on their knees in adoration of the Christ Child, while in Hampshire and Lancashire, the leaves are said to rustle on trees at twelve o'clock, just as the Holy Thorn bursts into bloom. Bees come singing from hives and

* Robert Herrick. *Hesperides.* "Twelfe Night, or King and Queene." 1648.

all living creatures rejoice in the Sacred Birth. For, as in Shakespeare's time:

> Some say that ever 'gainst that season comes
> Wherein our Saviour's birth is celebrated,
> The bird of dawning singeth all night long;
> And then, they say, no spirit can walk abroad;
> The nights are wholesome; then no planets strike,
> No fairy takes, nor witch hath power to charm,
> So hallowed and so gracious is the time.*

PILGRIMAGE TO THE HOLY THORN,† GLASTONBURY, SOMERSET

Old Christmas Eve, January 5

> And did those feet in ancient time
> Walk upon England's mountains green?
> And was the Holy Lamb of God
> On England's pleasant pastures seen?
>
> And did the Countenance Divine
> Shine forth upon our clouded hills?
> And was Jerusalem builded here
> Among those dark Satanic hills?
>
> —WILLIAM BLAKE, *Milton.*

Up and down England's West Country coast from Marazion, one-time outpost of Cornwall's tin mines, on north to Paradise, in Somerset, the story of how Jesus visited Britain recurs persistently and in varying guises,—in folk song and proverb, in place name and oral tradition. But one must tramp on up to Priddy, high in the Mendips, as I have done, to hear people speak reverently of Jesus, who "came with his uncle, Joseph of Arimathaea," during the "hidden years" ‡ about which the Gospels tell us nothing. In humble

---

* *Hamlet.* Act I, scene 1.

† From COUNSEL, Copyright 1953 by W. L. Jenkins. Used by permission.

‡ India, Italy, Egypt, Greece, and other countries, as well as England, have legends that Jesus visited them between the time when he was found in the Temple as a boy of twelve and his entry into the ministry at thirty.

11

cottages throughout these lonely windswept hills, once the center of
Roman lead mining operations, people draw close to their hearths
and speak of Jesus as the Beloved Friend, who recently passed this
way.

"Everybody up here knows He came to the lead mines from
Glastonbury with His uncle," said an old Priddy-born woman. Then,
a radiant smile breaking over her wrinkled, care-worn features, she
suddenly leaned forward, speaking confidentially:

"It makes us feel so *safe* to know our land is blessed:

> And did those feet in ancient time
> Walk upon England's mountains green?"

she quoted haltingly from William Blake's poem, *Milton*.

She stopped, groping for words.

"Please go on. How does the next line go?" I encouraged.

"Well, *you* ought ter know," said the old woman reprovingly.
"Surely, *you've* 'ad as much schooling as I!"

Her husband, sitting opposite in the worn rocking chair, continued the poet's thoughts in his own way.

"You know," he said dreamily, "when the rains come and you
look down the hills here, it's green all about. *This* is the spot!"

"Jesus came to Priddy," declared the plump postmistress. "And
on the way He stopped at Charterhouse," she added, referring to the
small hamlet some three miles back on the Mendips, once a thriving
lead mining center of both Britons and Romans.

At Paradise, close to Burnham-on-Sea, the Holy Visitors traditionally began their journey, according to people in the vicinity. A
farm woman left her green grocery untended to step up to the
corner and explain the very route.

"Jesus and His uncle landed right down at the bottom of that
road yonder," she said, pointing toward the sea. "They beached
their flat-bottomed boat on the sand tops (dunes) and sojourned
there awhile. Then they walked right up past here," she said, pointing to the grassy lane where we stood, "and went on to the 'Green

12

Hump.' That's Brent Knoll," she explained, indicating the large hill rising some miles distant above lush, cattle-dotted pastures.

"You know," she added wistfully, "one day *I* hope to make the whole journey."

At Glastonbury, where it is believed Joseph and Jesus eventually arrived, the thorn blossoms each Christmastide. On January 5 pilgrims from far and near go to Glastonbury to see this thorn which blooms in St. John's churchyard, in plain view of passers-by. Branches of the shapely tree, which has waxy white flowers resembling those of English hawthorn, are reverently cut and arranged on St. John's altar for the Christmas Eve service. Tradition says many cures have been effected on the faithful, by their touching it. For, according to Tennyson:

> . . . if a man
> Could touch or see it, he was healed at once
> By faith, of all his ills.

The Glastonbury Thorn is said to be an offshoot of the miraculous staff that Joseph of Arimathaea planted when journeying to Glastonbury. Traditionally, it blooms on Old Christmas Eve, January 5. Should the tree's blossoming vary by a few days in one direction or the other, then the fault is said to lie with the modern calendar. It was not until 1752 that England finally adopted the New Style calendar which already had been in use in Europe for some time. And many West Country folk believe that Christ was really born on January 6, Old Christmas Day, not on December 25 of the modern calendar.*

We are told that a zealous Puritan chopped down the original thorn during the Civil Wars. Be this as it may, throughout the centuries pilgrims have carried many other thorns, slipped from the original, to distant places.† At least three are in Glaston-

---

* *See* England's "Two" Calendars, p249.

† At least one slip of the Glastonbury Thorn was brought to the United States and was planted in the Cathedral Gardens, Washington, D.C. There, during the visit of the then Princess Elizabeth, in November 1951, the thorn, traditionally said to bloom only at Christmas and "for visits of royalty," put forth four blossoms.

13

bury—the one already mentioned, a smaller tree growing within the ancient Abbey's precincts, and the young grafting recently planted on Wearyall Hill, at the very spot where, it is said, Joseph thrust his staff into the earth. No less than six such trees exist in Herefordshire alone,* while other counties claim *their* thorns also, and hold special services to honor the Christmastide bloomings.

The Glastonbury Thorn is of Syrian origin and the story of how it traveled from Syria to a Somerset town constitutes an important chapter in the Glastonbury legend, "which is *truth*, not legend," according to a devout churchman with whom I talked.

As with all such living traditions, the Glastonbury story has many strands which sometimes merge, sometimes diverge widely. According to the popular English version of the legend, Joseph was a wealthy tin merchant who came to Cornwall in the course of extensive trading with the Phoenicians. Cornish miners still cherish the old song, "Joseph was a tin-man." On one of his trading voyages for tin in Cornwall and lead in the Mendips, he was accompanied by his great-nephew, the boy Jesus. Finally, they ". . . came in a ship of Tarshish to the Summerland (Summerset, or Somerset, the 'land where summer lingers') and sojourned in a place called Paradise," says an old record.

Paradise, as we have seen, is regarded by many as the starting point for the journey to Glastonbury, and from thence on up to the Mendips. Paradise is consequently closely identified with Celtic Glastonbury, once an island of the fens. It was to Glastonbury, then, after Jesus's Passion, that Joseph is thought to have brought his miraculous staff and the sacred chalice. There also, he is said to have founded the Wattle Church which later became the great Abbey; and there, in the Church of St. John, is his reputed tomb.

Thus, the Glastonbury Legend continues through the centuries, as a reality in the lives of England's West Country people. And Glastonbury is thought of as "the holyest erth of England," while

* Wormesley, Rowlstone, Dorstone, Colwall, Stoke Edith, King's Thorn, and Tyberton are among the Herefordshire places claiming to have, or to have had, their thorns.

14

the Thorn blooms each Christmas as a symbol of Christ's faithfulness to generations of believers.

> Bring me my bow of burning gold!
> Bring me my arrows of desire!
> Bring me my spear! O clouds unfold!
> Bring me my chariot of fire!
>
> I will not cease from mental fight;
> Nor shall my sword sleep in my hand,
> Till I have built Jerusalem
> In England's green and pleasant land.
>
> —WILLIAM BLAKE, *Milton.*

CUTTING THE BADDELEY CAKE, DRURY LANE THEATRE, LONDON

Twelfth Night, January 5

Each Twelfth Night, following the regular performance at Drury Lane Theatre, the cast assembles in the foyer (formerly in the Great Green Room), to observe the ceremony of "Cutting the Baddeley Cake." Attendants dressed in eighteenth century wigs and costumes ceremoniously carry in the cake, which is cut and served, together with wine, in memory of Richard Baddeley.

Richard Baddeley, who began life as a pastry cook in Lord North's service, later became—in the course of a long and checkered career—an excellent comedian at Drury Lane Theatre, as well as one of the original trustees of the Drury Lane Fund, which David Garrick founded. When the actor died, in 1794, he left a lengthy will, including a bequest of a hundred pounds, to be invested at three per cent interest. This sum was to buy a cake for His Majesty's Company of Comedians to eat every Twelfth Night, so the actor's name should always be remembered.

The ceremony has been observed since 1795. During the First World War, when sugar shortage prevented carrying out the bequest, the money was given to charity. From 1940 to 1946, also, when no company of His Majesty's Comedians was appearing at

Drury Lane, the terms of the old actor's will could not be carried out. But the ceremony was revived again in 1947, and will continue—it is hoped—for many centuries to come. The year 1954 marks the hundred and fifty-ninth year of the bequest of the pastry cook who became an actor.

Although some other playhouses—among them the Old Vic— now observe Twelfth Night Cake celebrations, these must not be confused with Drury Lane Theatre's Baddeley Cake, which represents a unique bequest to this theatre alone.

CUTTING THE TWELFTH CAKE, SADLER'S WELLS THEATRE, LONDON

Twelfth Day, January 6

On Twelfth Day Night the ceremony of "Cutting the Twelfth Cake" is observed at Sadler's Wells Theatre.

Following the regular opera performance, the house is emptied, and guests are readmitted by ticket.* Then follows a special entertainment feature, which may be, for example, a burlesque show in which the ballet appears in the singers' roles, the singers in ballet parts. Later, the Twelfth Cake is brought in, cut by some prominent stage celebrity, and served to the guests by members of the company.

In order to preserve the Twelfth Night Cake tradition in days of shortages and food restrictions, the Vic-Wells Association solicits from members advance "contributions or promises."

"WHAT AM I TO BUY FOR OUR TWELFTH NIGHT CAKE?" was a heading appearing in a recent pre-holiday Association *Bulletin*. Then followed an ancient recipe:—"Three pound of sugar; five pound of currants; nutmegs, seven; a race or two of ginger, four pounds of prunes, and as many of raisins o' the sun"—with a hint that these ingredients and "much more" were needed, including fat and eggs.

* Tickets are obtainable in advance by members of the Vic-Wells Association.

16

JANUARY

Throwing the Hood,[*] Haxey, Doncaster, Lincolnshire

Old Christmas Day, January 6

On old Christmas Day a curious sport called "Throwing the Hood" still is observed annually at Haxey, near Doncaster, Lincolnshire. The Haxey Hood Game is so ancient that nobody knows when it began. Some suggest possible Celtic or druidical origin; some say the sport is the forerunner of Rugby football. Local oral tradition, however, claims it started in the late thirteenth or early fourteenth century, with a whim of Lady De Mowbray, whose husband owned a large portion of the parish of Haxey. No written records exist of the sport before 1828. An account appearing in a Retford newspaper of 1865 gives the popularly accepted legend of the game's origin:

One Old Christmas Day Lady De Mowbray was riding horseback with her groom when a great gust of wind blew off the large black silk hood which, in the middle ages, was the gentlewoman's accepted winter headdress.

"Near the place," according to the newspaper, "were thirteen men who, seeing her Ladyship's predicament, started in pursuit of the hood, striving with all their might which should have the honour of restoring it to its owner. The wind was very fitful, and the chase long and exciting; but after much tumbling and jostling the most powerful man in the company succeeded in catching the hood, with which he returned to her Ladyship in triumph. Although a veritable son of Anak physically, he had not the courage to look at the Lady's brilliant, laughing eyes, so gave the hood to another man, who promptly presented it to her. The chase so pleased the Lady that she promised to give them each a broad piece of land for themselves and their successors for ever if they could invent and continue a similar game to be played every January 6. She also gave them the name of 'Plough-boggins,' presumably from the way they turned

[*] The author is indebted for much of the information in this account to Mr. E. J. Hunter, Clerk of Haxey Parish Council.

17

up the soil in their efforts to secure the fleeing hood. The meaning of 'boggined' is not clearly understood, though it seems to have tickled my Lady's fancy, for every time the hood changed hands, she cried out in delight to her manservant, 'See, John, it's boggined again!'

"Titles also she gave: 'My Lord,' to the man who presented the hood; 'Fool' to the giant who secured it but dared not restore it; 'His Lordship's Ploughboy' to one unlucky wight whose nose bore unmistakable signs of having done duty as a ploughshare; 'His Lordship's Servants' to the rest. All were to wear red jackets except the 'Fool' whose appearance was to be the more suitable one of a harlequin."

Preparations for the Haxey Hood Game, which, in rules and conduct have remained virtually unchanged through the years, start on Saint John's Eve (June 23). The "Lord"—a permanent official elected because of his knowledge of procedure—calls a committee meeting to make secret plans for the following Old Christmas Day. From among the attenders twelve men are appointed who are known variously as "Plough Boggins," "Plough Jags," or "Plough Bullocks."

On January 6 all village work stops promptly at midday. Men, women and children, landowners and laborers, householders and helpers, of the community's five parishes assemble at Haxey Church Green to await arrival of the Lord and his Boggins. Promptly at two o'clock the church bells ring out their welcome to the little band of men who, dressed like morris men and surrounded by crowds of admiring children, come up the street and pause at the "mounting stone" near the church gate. There the Lord orders one of the Boggins, known as the Fool, to pull off his cap, mount the stone and make a standard speech, which is familiar to generations of Haxey Hood attenders.

The Fool gives the program of the day, invites all who are present to join the games which will start shortly and begs the people

* From " 'Haxey Hood' Game," by Philip D. Taylor, past headmaster of Haxey Senior School. *Lincolnshire Magazine*, September-October 1932.

". . . to play upright and downstraight, not to kill themselves nor one another; it is to be hoose agin hoose, toon agin toon, if a man meet a man knock a man doon, but doant hu't im."

With these concluding words the Fool is knocked off the mounting stone, and the Lord leads his Boggins in procession to the field on the high point of Haxey Hill, at the boundary separating Haxey on the east from Westwoodside on the west. The Lord, who acts both as master of ceremonies and umpire, stands in the center of the field, his men around him, and invites the most distinguished guest present to throw up the first hood. There are several of these hoods (rolls of sacking measuring two feet long by three inches in diameter) which must be distinguished from the principal leather "Hood," of the same size and shape.

When the first hood is thrown up, the man who catches it tries to carry it off. It is unlikely he will, however, because he will be challenged by another player. In this case, the first man has to toss the hood into the air at once—toward a partner, if he is lucky. Should he be tackled by a Boggin, however, the hood is "boggined," which means it goes back to the Lord. He, in turn, throws up the hood again.

Throwing up the sham hoods is a rough free-for-all in which everyone participates; but these preliminary games are just "warming up" exercises for the big tussle with the leather Hood, beginning at half-past three.

When the Hood is thrown into the air men of the five rival villages surge forward, each group trying to push it toward their own men. A terrific struggle ensues, as stalwart farmers and laborers begin the "sway" or tug-of-war, amid the cheers and shouts of onlookers. At last, the "Sway-Hood" is captured and the victorious men carry it in triumphant procession to a public house of the village to which they belong. There the Hood remains in a place of honor until the following year—a coveted trophy which signifies the strength and prowess of the village men. The conquering heroes are rewarded with free beer and showered with congratulations and attentions.

In the evening the Boggins go about from house to house, singing and collecting money for the celebration. In olden times they used to pull a plough about the village streets. They would end by dragging it three times around the village green and then fighting to see who should keep it.

ROYAL EPIPHANY OFFERING, CHAPEL ROYAL, ST. JAMES'S PALACE, LONDON

Epiphany Day, January 6

A special Epiphany service is held annually in the Chapel Royal, St. James's Palace, in commemoration of the gifts of gold, frankincense and myrrh, which the Magi offered at Christ's birth.

Once the King of England bestowed the gifts with his own hand. During the Regency, however, the presents were made by proxy. In modern times the Lord Chamberlain (representing the monarch) presents three symbolic purses in the royal name, during the singing of the Offertory.

ST. DISTAFF'S DAY, OR ROCK DAY

January 7

Although St. Distaff's Day now is obsolete, it is noted here, since Plough Monday, the day's masculine counterpart, recently has been revived.

St. Distaff's, or Rock Day, was the traditional time for women to return to their spinning or other domestic duties, following the Christmas holidays. In olden times the chief sport of the men (who did not resume work in the fields until Plough Monday) was to burn the women's flax and tow. It was customary for the woman to retaliate by drenching their tormentors with pails of water.

20

JANUARY

BLESSING THE PLOUGH, CHICHESTER, SUSSEX

Plough Sunday, the Sunday following
Epiphany, or some Sunday thereafter

Chichester Cathedral observes the opening of the ploughing season with the traditional ceremony of Blessing the Plough.

Representatives of the Young Farmers' Club draw an ancient plough up to the chancel steps, placing the stilts toward the west. The young men, flanking the plough on either side, face the altar. Then the Bishop and Dean, laying their hands on the implement, invoke God's blessing on " . . . all who plough the fields, that the people of our land may be satisfied with bread."

This service survives from early days when the Church blessed the plough prior to the Plough Monday procession. Oxen, or farm boys known as "plough bullocks," drew the plough through the village streets. Some of these old rites still are observed in different parts of England.

BLESSING THE PLOUGH, BLUNHAM, DUNTON AND WRESTLING-
WORTH, BEDFORDSHIRE

Plough Sunday

The villages of Blunham, Dunton and Wrestlingworth, and possibly other places in Bedfordshire, observe Plough Sunday, or a day near that time, with a blessing ceremony similar to Chichester's. "The plough is a symbol of our work on the land," say the members of the local plough teams.

"May the Lord bless our going out and our coming in," respond the young farmers, who draw the plough up the chancel steps for consecration, and then read the lessons of the day.

21

PLOUGH MONDAY

First Monday after Twelfth Day, or Epiphany

Plough Monday next, after that Twelfth tide is past,
Bids out with the Plough, the worst husband is last.

wrote Thomas Tusser, in the sixteenth century.

From time immemorial, men resumed work in the fields on Plough Monday, just as farm women returned to domestic duties on St. Distaff's Day.

Plough Monday ceremonies were observed traditionally until the Napoleonic wars. Since then, rather self-conscious efforts at revival have been made in various parts of England.

At Haxey, as we have seen,* Plough Monday is still celebrated with the Hood Game. The day is observed chiefly in the northern and northeastern counties of Lincolnshire, Northumberland, York-shire, Norfolk, Cambridgeshire, Huntingdonshire, Northampton-shire, Leicestershire and Derbyshire.† In some communities plough boys, with blackened faces and white shirts, still drag about a plough through the village streets, in procession with such characters as a Fool who carries a whip with an inflated bladder on the end, the Bessy, or man-woman, and various other traditional characters. The men, who are variously known as Plough (or Plu) Stots, Plough Jacks, Jags, Bullocks, or Boggins, perform a Plough Play featuring singing, dancing, and a crude drama with minor incidents of a slaying and a resuscitation by a "doctor." These dramas have almost disappeared in recent years.

The performers collect coins for their entertainment. In bygone times the men used to plough up the front gardens of householders who refused to contribute in return for their dances.

In olden days the Lord Mayor of London and his aldermen customarily celebrated Plough Monday by visiting estates in the City

* *See* p 17 ff.
† E. K. Chambers. *English Folk Play.* p89 ff.

and witnessing ploughing matches. Now the Lord Mayor observes the day by resuming official duties after Christmas recess. Among other activities, he presides at the Guildhall over the Grand Court of Wardmote, where ward returns on the St. Thomas Day (December 24) elections are presented.

Plough Monday was, and still is, in many districts, the time when farm boys assemble to break the first ground in the New Year, with a wish of "God speed" to the plough and success to the harvest.

THE DANCING PLOUGH STOTS, GOATHLAND AND SLEIGHTS, YORK-
SHIRE

Plough Monday, the first Monday after Twelfth Day

On Plough Monday the Plough Stots of Goathland and Sleights perform traditional Sword Dances in northeastern Yorkshire agricultural hamlets. Formerly many villages in the area held Plough Monday festival, but now the custom is dying out. Sometimes a *Plough Play,* enacted on Christmas or Plough Monday, accompanied the dance; or, the traditional characters simply appeared and were introduced individually by a series of "calling on" rhymes.

The Plough Stots of Goathland and Sleights, accompanied by their fiddlers, dance through their own and neighboring villages. The teams usually consist of eight men, two of whom are Fools, or Toms, who pass around money boxes and perform antics while their comrades dance. The dances consist of many intricate movements which are executed with precision and restraint. Swords are held in the right hand. In one figure they are interlaced and formed into a hexagon, which is so firmly constructed it can be held aloft in a single dancer's hand. To conclude the spectacle, the geometrical figure is undone as each performer takes back his own sword.

The performers are farmers, workmen and young men, to whom dancing is a hobby. The Sword Dance, as already noted, is traditional to midwinter. The morris on the other hand, although confined to no special season, usually accompanies Easter and May Day festivities or is associated with summertime activities.

COMMEMORATION SERVICE FOR "GIVING OF CAKES AND ALE," BURY ST. EDMUNDS, SUFFOLK

The Thursday following Plough Monday

On the Thursday following Plough Monday, Bury St. Edmunds commemorates the "Giving of Cakes and Ale" with a religious service which has been observed for over four hundred and fifty years. Nowadays, local almshouse residents receive a shilling apiece, in place of the cakes and ale originally given. Some people claim that this service, which never has been omitted since its establishment, represents the country's oldest charity.

ST. HILARY'S DAY

January 13

According to tradition, "St. Hilary's is the coldest day of the year." St. Hilary, fourth century Bishop of Poitiers, has given his name to the terms of Britain's law courts and universities. Law Courts' Hilary term begins on January 11, since St. Hilary's is the saint's day nearest this date.

WASSAILING THE APPLE TREES, CARHAMPTON, SOMERSET

Old Twelfth Night, January 17

Wassailing, or drinking to the health of the fruit trees to ensure a good crop, is practiced in Carhampton, Somerset, and some other West Country villages. Roughly speaking, this old ceremony flourishes chiefly in cider-producing districts of the rolling valley between Exmoor Forest and the Quantock Hills, and of the yet wider valley which lies between Exmoor to the north and Dartmoor on the south.

Traditionally, wassailing should take place on Old Twelfth Night; but in recent times many places seem to prefer the date of February 13, since this is the season when the sap rises in the trees.

In Carhampton, village men carrying lanterns and a pail of cider (supplied by the orchard owner), make rounds of the neighborhood orchards at night. One man has a gun, which he fires through the branches at conclusion of the ceremony, "to scare away evil spirits."

The men gather around a favorite apple tree. Floating on the cider bucket is a piece of toast, which they place in the fork of the tree, "for the robins." This offering is supposed to keep the birds from eating the buds. In each orchard visited the men pour some cider about the tree's roots and sing a rousing wassail song:

> Old apple tree, old apple tree,
> We've come to wassail thee—

or possibly the older version:

> Here's to thee, old apple tree
> Whence thou mayst bud, whence thou mayst blow!
> And whence thou mayst bear apples enow!
> Hats full! Caps full!
> Three score bushels full
> And my pockets full, too!
> Huzza! Huzza! Huzza!

"Way Down in Somerset," "Under the Old Apple Tree," and "Little Brown Jug," are other songs popular at wassailing ceremonies.

Originally the wassailing ceremony was an old fertility rite, performed to ensure health to the fruit trees. The robin's gift and the cider libation were offerings to the vegetation spirit which watched over the tree. But nowadays the old meanings have been forgotten, and the custom continues more as a lark than anything else.

ANNIVERSARY OF ST. WULSTAN, WORCESTER CATHEDRAL, WOR-
CESTERSHIRE

January 19

On January 19, Worcester holds a memorial service in the ancient cathedral crypt, to commemorate St. Wulstan's death, in 1095.

The crypt, which is the cathedral's oldest portion, is one of England's most beautiful sanctuaries. Wulstan, one of the few Saxon
bishops to retain his see after the Norman conquest, built a great
Norman cathedral upon the site of St. Oswald's more humble edi-
fice. Although the original cathedral suffered greatly from fire in
the twelfth century, the crypt was preserved in its original austere
beauty, a fitting tribute to the cathedral's founder.

EVE AND DAY OF ST. AGNES

January 20 and 21

St. Agnes, patroness of maidens, always has been popular among
North Country farm girls. Many of the old charms and incantations
generations of fun-loving British girls have practiced on St. Agnes's
Eve and Day bear some resemblance to America's favorite Halloween stunts and ceremonies.

For centuries, English girls have held that the feast of St. Agnes,
fourth century Roman virgin who suffered persecution under Diocletian, was a propitious time for looking into the future. By fasting
all day, and eating at night a salt-filled, hard-boiled egg (shell and
all) a girl dreams of her lover, who appears and offers her water!
A raw red herring, swallowed bones and all, produces a like result;
while saying a *Paternoster* and pulling pins out, one by one from
a row, and then going to bed, is certain to evoke visions of a future
husband. As Ben Jonson says,

> And on Sweet Agnes' night,
> Please you with the promis'd sight—
> Some of husbands, some of lovers,
> Which an empty dream discovers.

26

JANUARY

January 25

On January 25, St. Paul's Cathedral holds an annual musical service, to commemorate its patron saint's conversion to Christianity. A rendering of Mendelssohn's "Saint Paul" is a feature of the event.

From early times St. Paul's Day has been as important to the countryman as to his music-loving city cousin, although for a different reason. In rural lore, upon January 25 depends the weather of the entire year!

The *Shepherd's Almanack* for 1676 states that sun on St. Paul's means a good year; rain or snow foretells indifferent weather; a mist means want, and thunder twelve months of wind and death. Another prediction is that

> If Saint Paul's day be faire and cleare
> If doth betide a happy yeare;
> But if by chance it then should rain
> It will make deare all kinds of graine;
> And if ye clouds make dark ye skie,
> Then neats and fowls this yeare shall die;
> If blustering winds do blow aloff,
> Then wars shall trouble ye realm full oft.

Anniversary of King Charles the Martyr, London

January 30

London churches observe memorial services to honor Charles I, on January 30, anniversary of his execution in 1649.

One of the most impressive ceremonies takes place at the foot of the equestrian statue of Charles I in Charing Cross. Choristers attire themselves in nearby St. Martin-in-the-Fields, and then go in procession to the statue. After an appropriate service, wreaths are laid at the foot of the royal martyr's monument and the old prayers, once included in the prayer book, are read.

27

Another memorial service is held at the shrine of Charles I in the Church of St. Andrew by the Wardrobe, on Queen Victoria Street. Other London churches observing the anniversary are St. Mary-le-Strand, Strand; St. Alban the Martyr, Holborn; St. Saviour's, Hampstead; Whitechapel Parish Church.

DICING FOR MAID'S MONEY, GUILDFORD, SURREY

Usually the last Thursday in January

Each year towards the end of January, Guildford's mayor and magistrates conduct a strange ceremony called "Dicing for Maid's Money," in the sixteenth century Guildhall's stately council chamber. Once dicing for money was a favorite English pastime, in which great fortunes were won and lost. Today an annual dicing competition for the modest sum of eleven pounds nineteen shillings is a unique event which brings together Guildford's officials and citizenry, in accordance with terms of an ancient will.

Today the dicing contestants are two humble maidservants, carefully selected from a score or more applicants by the Guildford Municipal Charity Trustees. Represented among the sixteen trustees are a doctor, a gunsmith, a builder, an accountant and a number of merchants and tradesfolk. These men administer the will of one John How, who on January 27, 1674, established a fund of "four hundred pounds," to be invested and the proceeds given as an annual charity to a local "maid," or a young unmarried woman, according to seventeenth century usage of the word. She must have served faithfully in the same position for at least two years. The will further stipulates that two servants should throw dice for the gift (originally considered sufficient for a dowry) and that "the maid which throwest most on the said dice at one throw, or to whom the lot falleth," receive the money.

Throughout the years, in the presence of mayor, trustees and townsfolk, the two candidates have taken turns in shaking two yellowed dice in a hide dice box—silver banded and bottomed—which for over a century has been dedicated to this particular use. The women toss the dice in the middle of the long council table. After a breathless pause, the maid who throws the highest number is proclaimed recipient of the coveted charity.

For many years the one who lost was retained as an aspirant for the following year. But not always! For history records that a certain John Parsons, (possibly influenced by How's bequest) established another charity, nearly twenty years later.

John Parsons bequeathed the sum of "six hundred pounds," to be given to "a poor young man who has served an apprenticeship of seven years in the same town (Guildford)," but who, at the time of application for the money could swear before a magistrate that he possessed less than twenty pounds. If no suitable candidate was found, the entire sum was to go to a maid who had served one household satisfactorily for at least three years.

For a long time, no apprentice has appeared for John Parson's charity. Consequently, the Town Fathers decreed that the bounty should go to the loser of the Maid's Money. By this strange coincidence—since Parson's charity was larger than How's—the loser of the Maid's Money often receives a slightly more substantial gift than the winner!

Curious about the women who receive these seventeenth century charities, I visited the offices of the Guildford Municipal Charity Trustees. There I was shown the Maid's Money receipt book, which has been in use annually since 1776. Running down the neatly written records, I was gratified to note that all recipients of Maid's Money in recent years (when both the meaning of the word maid, and the original purpose of the bequest as a dowry have been forgotten) have been older women, each one of whom has faithfully served in the same family for approximately eighteen years. And this in times when the average Englishman shakes his head and sighs, "Help isn't what it used to be. The old-fashioned maidservant just doesn't exist!"

29

FEBRUARY

Down with the Rosemary, and so
Down with the Baies and miseltoe:
Down with the Holly, Ivie, all,
Wherewith ye drest the Christmas Hall:
That so the superstitious find
No one least Branch there left behind:
Nor look how many leaves there be
Neglected there (maids trust to me)
So many Goblins* you shall see.
—ROBERT HERRICK. *Hesperides.* "Ceremonies upon
Candlemas Eve." 1648.

ST. BRIDE'S DAY

February 1

People in the Midlands say that dew gathered on St. Bride's Day
will beautify their features and make them youthful.

February 1 has always been an important day in English weather
lore. The old Worcestershire saying that

> If February Calends be summerly gay,
> 'Twill be wintery weather on the Calends of May

is typical of a rural superstition that a mild and bright St. Bride's
Day portends a cold spring.

CANDLEMAS DAY

February 2

Candlemas, the feast to commemorate the Purification of the
Virgin Mary as well as of Christ's Presentation in the Temple, gets

---

* Reference is made here to the widespread seventeenth century superstition that
unless every leaf and berry of the Christmas decorations is removed by Candlemas Eve
(February 1), dire misfortune will follow—not only *goblins*—even death to someone
in the family!

its name from olden times when candles were blessed in the churches and then lighted and carried in procession. Until the Reformation Candlemas was an important holy day of the English Church. Some people see in the Christian festival earlier pagan rites to Ceres. For at this season the goddess was thought to carry burning torches, to light her search for Proserpina, who was in the nether world of darkness.

In popular tradition, February 2 is associated with weather lore and customs of various sorts. It has always been considered bad luck to leave up the Yuletide greens after Candlemas Eve, when they should be removed and replaced with box. In early times a brand, kindled from the Yule-log of the previous year, was lighted on Candlemas Eve and kept burning until sunset. Then the flame was extinguished and the charred stick was preserved to light the Christmas log of the coming year.

The farmer has always regarded February 2 as an important date. More proverbs, indeed, are said to exist about this day's weather than of any other:

> If Candlemas Day be fair and clear,
> There'll be five winters in the year

and

> When Candlemas Day is fine and clear,
> A shepherd would rather see his wife on her bier

are two popular sayings showing that a fair Candlemas augurs no good.

In Norfolk, Cheshire and some other counties, people say winter is half over by Candlemas. Any farmer does well, therefore, to review his food stocks for man and beast. For, according to Norfolk lore,

> The farmer should have, on Candlemas Day,
> Half his turnips and half his hay.

Once Candlemas was popular for cattle, horse and general merchandise fairs. Today many such events have been discontinued, although Reading, in Berkshire, still holds its annual February 2 fair.

31

A number of other towns,* continue their fairs on February 12, *Old Candlemas Day*.

In many parts of England February 2 is important in land tenure customs. In the Lake District, especially, Candlemas is regarded as the accepted time for beginning and ending farm tenancies, as well as for closing the farmer's fiscal year.

ROCKING CEREMONY, ST. MARY OF THE PURIFICATION, BLIDWORTH, NOTTINGHAMSHIRE

Feast of the Purification, February 2, or the nearest Sunday

Blidworth's parish Church of the Purification holds a charming Rocking Ceremony on the afternoon of the Purification Feast, when it falls on a Sunday, otherwise on the Sunday nearest the feast. The child chosen for the service is the boy last christened before the feast. If possible, he is also a first-born child.

The ceremony is in allusion to the Feast of the Purification, when Jesus was presented in the Temple, and symbolizes the "dedication of child life to God." A first-born infant is preferred for the rite, since, in the ancient Jewish ritual the child was presented to God and "bought" back by the parents for five shekels.

Holding the baby in his arms, the vicar rededicates the boy before the altar. Then he lays the baby in an old fashioned wooden cradle (flower-decorated and surrounded by lighted tapers) and rocks it back and forth about twelve times. After the singing of a hymn and the *Nunc Dimittis,* the Song of Simeon,† the vicar returns the child to its mother.

The cradle featured in the ceremony is very old and was presented to the church, in 1922, by Eliza Poynton. The origin of Blidworth's Rocking Ceremony is unknown, although the fact that the church is dedicated to St. Mary of the Purification doubtless has something to do with the rite. Some say the ceremony began in the

* *See* Devizes and Dorchester. p38.
† Luke 2:29-32.

thirteenth century. For about a hundred years the Rocking was discontinued. It was revived in 1922, however, and has been observed ever since.

CEREMONY OF BLESSING THE THROAT, ST. ETHELREDA'S CHURCH, LONDON

St. Blaise's Day, February 3

On the Day of St. Blaise, Patron of Throats, three services* are held in St. Ethelreda's small thirteenth century chapel in Ely Place, Holborn, to bless those who suffer from diseases of the throat.

Persons afflicted with such ailments, or those hoping to remain immune, kneel before the priest, as he places beneath the chin two consecrated candles, tied together in the form of a St. Andrew's cross. As the priest touches the diseased area, he pronounces the benediction, "May the Lord deliver you from the evil of the throat and from every other evil."

St. Blaise, in whose memory the service is performed, was a fourth century Bishop of Sebaste, in Armenia. The saint was noted for many miracles, including that of saving a boy who was choking to death on a fish bone, by simply touching his throat. After this miracle, the saint became special patron of all throat sufferers.

In 316 A.D., when Blaise was tortured to death by having his flesh torn to bits with a sharp iron comb, the wool-combers adopted him as their guardian. For centuries, leading wool centers, such as Bury St. Edmunds, York and Guildford, celebrated their patron's feast with pageants and processions. St. Blaise was represented wearing his bishop's mitre and black robe, and carrying a prayer book and wool-filled comb.

As England's great wool trade declined, the pageants of the past died out, remaining only as colorful background to today's religious observance of St. Blaise's Day.

* Services are held at 1:15 P.M., 6 P.M. and 8 P.M.

HURLING THE SILVER BALL, ST. IVES, CORNWALL

*Feast Monday (Monday following Feast
of St. Ia,) which is the Sunday nearest
February 3*

St. Ives celebrates Feast Monday, the day after the Feast of St. Ia, the town's fifth century patron, by Hurling the Silver Ball,* an ancient game once played by adults of the parishes of St. Ives and Lelant but now continued mainly as a children's sport.

Hurling, often described as a kind of "hand football," is played with the so-called "silver ball," which is made of cork, silver encased, and is about the size of a baseball. The ball, which is dented and worn and believed by many to be very old, is held in safekeeping during the year in the town clerk's office.

Feast Monday is a general holiday. Promptly at half past ten in the morning, the mayor tosses the silver ball against the side of the parish church, which is dedicated to St. Ia. The ball bounces out among the milling crowd of school children. Without a moment's hesitation, they toss the ball back and forth from hand to hand. At twelve noon the game stops, officially, although sometimes, as in 1952, an excited child throws the ball into the water. That year, the town clerk told me, the ball was not recovered until five o'clock in the afternoon! The one who has the ball in his possession when the game stops returns it to the mayor and receives a prize of money or a medal. Sports events in the afternoon and a municipal ball at night complete the day's festivities.

Ia (or Eia), the missionary saint after whom St. Ives is named, was supposedly a nobleman's daughter. She was martyred, in 450, on the River Hayle and was one of over a hundred Celtic saints, including her brothers Uny and Erth, said to have reached Cornwall miraculously. The holy ones, after whom parishes and churches

* St. Ives, St. Colomb Major and Minor are, to my knowledge, the only three towns in England where the game survives.

throughout the county are named, have given rise to the boast that Cornwall has more saints than heaven itself!

St. Ia's journey was perilous, according to legendary accounts, one of which states that the intrepid missionaries crossed the Irish Sea by sailing eastward "an eighteen Myles" in a millstone boat! On Cornwall's wild and rocky coast the little band made safe landing at Pendines, where St. Ives now stands. It is in memory of this event that the town holds its annual Feast Monday sport.

BLESSING THE WATER, ST. MARY'S ABBEY, EAST BERGHOLT, SUFFOLK

St. Blaise's Day, February 3

St. Mary's Abbey celebrates St. Blaise's Day by blessing water and sending it throughout the world, to those who suffer from throat maladies.

BLESSING THE SALMON NETS, NORHAM-ON-TWEED, NORTHUMBERLAND

February 13-14

Just before the salmon season opens, Norham-on-Tweed annually observes a modern benediction service which doubtless replaces a more ancient ceremony.

At this service, which is held shortly before twelve on the night of February 13, all net fisheries along the Tweed are blessed. Fishermen and village folk from both the English and Scottish sides of the river assemble at Pedwell fishery. The vicar pronounces his blessing and offers prayers for safe-keeping. Then, just before midnight, the first boat of the season is launched. The vicar of Norham, from his place in a fishing coble, conducts a similar service at Berwick-on-Tweed.

35

St. Valentine's Day

February 14

The St. Valentine who gave his name to the fourteenth day of February doubtless is one of the best loved and least known saints of the Christian calendar. And although nobody seems to know just who he was or when he lived, lovers of many lands have honored him for over seventeen centuries.

Although we are accustomed to think of *one* Saint Valentine as patron of lads and maidens, there seem to be *three,* each linked with February 14. One was Bishop of Umbria; the second a Roman priest. Both these men were martyred toward the end of the third century. The third Valentine we know little about, except that he lived in the first century and was slain for his Christian faith. Legend traces the origin of choosing valentines to early Roman practice when, on February 13 at the annual feast of *Februata Juno,* youths drew from urns slips inscribed with the names of girls.

In England and Scotland the custom of chance name-drawings on Valentine's Eve continued far into the Middle Ages, despite Church disapproval. Wherever young people gathered together, names were written on slips and these slips placed in a receptacle. Each boy drew a name—a "valentine," it was called—and the girl whose name was inscribed was regarded, as in Roman times, as his sweetheart for the year.

Samuel Pepys, writing in his *Diary,* frequently refers to this custom in seventeenth century England. In his day the custom of choosing valentines was both popular and costly, to judge from the diarist's rueful entry of February 14, 1666-7 that, " . . . I am . . . this year my wife's Valentine, and it will cost me five pounds!"

In England, as in the United States, Valentine's Day always has been a popular time for young people to practice love charms and divinations. Throughout the centuries, there have been many variations of the saying that a young girl would marry the first bachelor encountered on the fateful day; that at midnight, Valentine's Eve, a visit to the village graveyard would result in the lover's appearance, especially when a certain chant was sung while running twelve times about the church; that sleeping on bay leaves, sprinkled with rose water and slipped under the pillow, would induce the future husband to appear in a dream!

Now most of England's charming old Valentine customs have died out—the anonymous presentation of gifts on the loved one's doorstep; the "Valentine buns," once so famous in Leicestershire; the pretty ceremony of "valentining," by children of Oxfordshire, Worcestershire and Norfolk, who went from door to door singing ditties such as this:

> Good morrow to you, Valentine;
> Curl your locks as I do mine,
> Two before and three behind.
> Good morrow to you, Valentine.

Gone are most of these old customs. But London still observes Valentine's Day in urbane manner, with parties in fashionable hotels and the sending of love missives and telegrams. And in the provinces Valentine's Day is associated with weather lore. In Warwickshire, Norfolk, Staffordshire, and many other places, there is a saying that, by February 14, "every good hen, duck and goose should lay," while in other places people declare that on May Day snow will drive into the house as far as the sun shines in on Valentine's Day!

Valentine Fair, King's Lynn, Norfolk

February 14

King's Lynn Valentine Fair, usually known as "Lynn Mart," is one of England's oldest charter fairs. Eight centuries ago merchants from all parts of Britain gathered here to buy and sell at this ancient fair. According to its original charter, the fair commences on St. Valentine's Day and continues for six full days of pleasure and trading.

Today, as for generations past, the fair opens with traditional ringing of a hand bell. The Mayor of King's Lynn then reads the old Proclamation, which says in part that the "Mart or Fair, to be holden this year, doth begin on this present fourteenth day, at twelve o'clock at noon, and shall continue for the space of six days from henceforth next following, with all the ancient and accustomed Liberties and Privileges as far as the same will now apply."

People attending the mart are warned to forbear from selling or to ". . . show forth Wares, in the Lord's Day," and further, ". . . all such persons as may be justly suspected of evil behavior, so avoid this borough and the Liberties thereof."

Although Lynn Mart is by far the most important Valentine fair, others are held at Biggleswade, in Bedfordshire; Bath, in Somerset, and Wymondham, in Norfolk. The February 14 fair at Devizes, in Wiltshire, is known as "Old Candlemas," rather than as "Valentine Fair." Dorchester, in Dorset, still calls its fair "Old Candlemas Hiring Fair," because servants for the surrounding communities once were engaged at this event.

MARCH

Pleasure it is
To hear, I wis,
The birdès sing.
The deer in the dale,
The sheep on the vale,
The corn springing;
God's purveyance
For sustenance
It is for man.
Then we always
To him give praise,
And thank him then.
—WILLIAM CORNISH.* *Pleasure it is.*

ST. DAVID'S DAY

March 1

March 1, celebrated throughout England by the Welsh with special services and processions, honors St. David, sixth century patron of Wales, whose emblem is the leek.

In London, as elsewhere, Welshmen observe the custom of wearing leeks or daffodils. For they say that St. David, when leading his army to victory against the Saxons, commanded his men to put leeks in their hats to distinguish the Welshmen from the enemy. In accordance with this tradition the Welsh Guards hold an impressive ceremony in which officers, noncommissioned officers and men are presented with leek emblems.

St. David's Day is not famed for Welsh association alone. In rural communities there is an old time saying that fleas appear on

* William Cornish (or Cornysshe), who died in 1523, was Master of the Chapel Royal for Henry VII and Henry VIII. During his tenure of office, Cornish composed music and participated in court pageants.

March 1, and the best way to keep them out of the house is, logically enough, to shut all the windows! In Devonshire and Gloucestershire people call fleas "the black soldiers," who are trying to get inside. Shrewsbury, in Shropshire, has a saying that the Devil himself appears and "shakes a bag of fleas at everybody's door," while West Sussex people have a simple formula for ridding themselves of the nuisance. All that is necessary is to rise before sunup, throw open the window and cry out lustily, "Good morning, March!"

ST. CHAD'S DAY

March 2

St. Chad, patron of medicinal springs, lived in the seventh century and was Bishop of Mercia, with see at Lichfield. Lichfield Cathedral, like many other cathedrals and churches throughout England, is dedicated to this saint, while numerous holy wells and springs bear his name.

In olden times St. Chad's Day was considered propitious for sowing beans and peas. A threadbare Norfolk rhyme admonishes the farmer to:

> Sow beans and peas on David and Chad,
> Be the weather good or bad.

ST. PIRAN'S DAY

March 5

St. Piran, jovial patron of Cornish miners, was one of the most popular Celtic saints to arrive miraculously from Ireland upon the coast of Cornwall. The saint's oratory, founded fifteen hundred years ago upon the dunes of Perranporth, once was buried deep in the sands.

Formerly, tinners revered St. Piran so greatly that they refused to work on his anniversary; for Piran, they claimed, had revealed to their forefathers many valuable secrets about the mining of tin.

ST. PATRICK'S DAY

March 17

Just as Welshmen celebrate St. David's Day by wearing the symbolic leek, so the Irish pay tribute to Patrick, their country's patron, by the traditional "wearing of the green." The Irish Guards of the British Army observe the day by placing the shamrock in their caps. The shamrock, sacred to the saint, commemorates the legend that, when preaching to the heathen, he plucked the little plant with its three leaves growing from one stem, to illustrate to unbelievers the Trinity's mystic nature.

Throughout London flower vendors sell shamrock and oxalis on St. Patrick's Day. Parades and special festivities honor the Irish saint who, according to tradition, freed his island from snakes and converted the heathen to Christianity.

ST. BENEDICT'S DAY

March 21

St. Benedict, who founded monasticism in the Western world, died on March 21, 543. The day is important in determining the Easter date, which always is reckoned as the first Sunday following the paschal full moon of the vernal equinox (March 21). Probably this is why St. Benedict's Day is responsible for so much popular weather lore. In Surrey people say that wherever the wind is at noon on March 21, there it will remain for the next three months. Other parts of the country have a current rhyme that

> If peas are not sown by Benedick,
> They had better stay in the rick.

THE TICHBORNE DOLE, TICHBORNE, NEAR ALRESFORD, HAMPSHIRE

Lady Day, March 25

Every year, on Lady Day, Tichborne villagers gather about the hospitable columned porch of Tichborne House, to receive a gift of flour. This ancient bounty, established by Lady Mabella Tichborne, dates back to 1150. For nine centuries the lord of the house of Tichborne has distributed the charity, originally of bread, now of flour. For, according to ancient family prophecy, the Tichborne name shall cease, should the original bequest be altered.

At the annual ceremony, prayers are said for Lady Mabella's soul. Then the priest blesses twelve sacks of flour which are placed on the porch, in readiness for distribution to the village poor. Men, women and children, each carrying a pillow case or sack, gather about the porch to claim their portion of the gift: a gallon of flour for every adult, half as much for every child.

One old villager, recipient of the dole since boyhood, had forgotten the occasion for the gift, but knew it had something to do with the Tichborne family. A young woman, living on the estate in an army hut—now one of the village council houses—knew all about the charity, but remarked: "The flour isn't very good. It's heavy. But then, you know, these days every little helps!"

Family tradition says that the dole was instituted when Lady Mabella, wife of Sir Roger de Tichborne, lay dying. The wheat crop had failed. Hunger was sweeping across the countryside. Village people were in want. Lady Mabella earnestly begged her husband for lands sufficient to provide an annual bread bounty to all the neighborhood poor who should apply for it, annually, on Lady Day. Sir Roger's answer was to angrily snatch up a blazing stick from the fire, declaring that his wife might have as much land for the charity as she could crawl across before the flames burned out.

The dying woman, bedridden for years, prayed God for strength. Then she ordered servants to carry her from the house to the fields bordering the estate. There, Lady Mabella, aged and infirm though she was, miraculously managed to crawl across twenty-three acres of land, before Sir Roger's brand sputtered and finally died. Declaring that God had heard her prayers, the sick woman then claimed the lands she had traversed to provide the dole for her parish poor. With her last breath she then uttered the famous prophecy of the fall of the house of Tichborne, should her heirs ever cease to observe her dying bequest.

To this day the fields across which Lady Mabella made her last painful journey are known as "The Crawls." For eight hundred years the Tichborne family has controlled the estates and carried out the original bounty, in more or less modified form.

APRIL

Summer is icumen in!
Loudly sings the cuckoo,
Groweth seed,
And bloweth meade,
And springeth wood anew.
Sing, cuckoo!
Ewe bleateth after lamb.
Low'th after calf the cow,
Bullock leapeth,
Buck he verteth.
Merrily sing, cuckoo!
Cuckoo! Cuckoo!
Well singest thou, cuckoo!
Nor ever cease thou now.
—*Medieval Song**

APRIL FOOL'S DAY

April 1

The old custom of sending people on "fool's errands," a popular pastime on April 1 in early eighteenth century England, now is confined chiefly to children. Nobody seems to know just when or why the first day of April was dedicated to foolishness and to playing pranks on one's neighbors. As noted in *Poor Robin's Almanack* for 1760,

> The first of April, some do say
> Is set apart for All Fool's Day;
> But why the people call it so,
> Nor I, nor they themselves do know.

The custom of April-fooling may have originated with the calendar change,† when the New Year started on January 1, instead

* Freely adapted from a manuscript, dated about 1240, of Reading Abbey, now in the British Museum.
† *See* "England's "Two" Calendars," p249.

44

of the old date of March 25. Originally New Year festivities lasted until April 1, when presents were exchanged and formal visits made. When the year was set back to January 1, people claimed that mock presents were exchanged and formal visits made, in order to show up the foolishness of those who had forgotten the calendar change!

Wherever boys indulge in April fooling, victims are sent on "fool's errands" up to twelve o'clock, noon. Any attempt to make a fool of one after that hour, may be met with the answer,

> Up the ladder and down the wall,
> You're the greatest fool of all.

In most of the North Counties the name "April Gawk" (the gawk is a cuckoo) is given to anyone who is duped, but in Yorkshire "April Noddy" is the name applied to the unfortunate victims of the day's pranks.

Placing the Quill in the Hand of John Stow's Statue, St. Andrew Undershaft, London

Some time near April 5

Either just before, or just after, April 5, anniversary of John Stow's death, in 1605, London's Lord Mayor, sheriffs and local officials attend service at the church of St. Andrew Undershaft. There, gathering about the statue of John Stow, famous London historian, they remove an old white quill pen from the marble hand, and replace the quill with a new one.

The curious ceremony takes place in the dimly lit corner of the church where John Stow, a worshipper of many years standing, lies buried. Surrounding the Lord Mayor and his officials are a group of London school boys and girls, who compete annually in a John Stow essay contest. The school whose pupil has the winning essay receives the coveted prize of the old quill, which is carefully preserved in a case.

John Stow, who was born in 1525, began life as a humble tailor. Later, he became a historian. He is particularly revered for his work entitled *Survey of London and Westminster*. For had this book never been written, our historical knowledge of London previous to the Great Fire of 1666 would be scant indeed. It is in recognition of John Stow's unique contribution to Londoners, that the placing of the new quill in the hand of his statue has become an annual event.

LETTING THE "WHITE BREAD" MEADOW, GRANTHAM, LINCOLNSHIRE

Old Lady Day, April 6

On Old Lady Day, people of Grantham still let by auction an ancient piece of ground, known as the White Bread Meadow. While the bidding is under way, a boy runs a distance of fifty yards and back again to the starting point. The person whose bid for the property is unchallenged before the youth returns is appointed tenant for the year.

Money obtained from the transaction provides for a charity of one loaf of white bread for each household in Grantham's Eastgate section.

CANDLE AUCTION, TATWORTH, NEAR CHARD, SOMERSET

The Saturday following Old Lady Day (April 6)

The hamlet of Tatworth, in Somerset, is one of a few English communities still to observe the old custom of "selling by candle." Annually, on the Saturday following Old Lady Day, some six acres of valuable watercress growing land are let to landowners or tenants who, according to terms of an ancient deed, are qualified bidders. The bidders gather behind locked doors, in a room illuminated solely by a candle stuck to a board.

The custom of selling by candle has died out, save for a few local survivals. One popular method is to light the taper, marking it with a pin an inch below the flame. The bidding begins with the lighting and continues until the candle burns down to the pin, which then drops out. The simple plan acts as a check upon rival bidders, and gives sufficient time for thought before making an offer higher than the one previously presented.

ST. GEORGE'S DAY

April 23

April 23, the day of St. George, England's patron saint, is celebrated by wearing the rose and raising his flag (banner of the Church of England), which is a red cross on a white background. St. George, who was made England's patron about 1344, and later became the country's military protector, was an officer in the Roman Army under Diocletian. Refusing to abandon the Christian faith, George reputedly was martyred on April 23, about the year 300. He became the warrior hero of the Middle Ages and the ideal of the Christian soldier.

St. George's anniversary is marked by many observances. In St. Paul's Cathedral, in London, the Order of St. Michael and St. George holds its annual service. Members wear the traditional scarlet-lined blue mantles at a ceremony to commemorate the Order's dead and to welcome new members.

In Windsor Castle's beautiful Chapel of St. George there is a similar service, embodying all the pomp and ceremony of bygone days. Edward III dedicated this Chapel to the saint in 1348, when appointing him patron of the Order of the Garter. During the reign of Henry VII, the King's spurs became the choristers' special perquisites at the Windsor installations and feasts of St. George's Day. An entry in the King's "Privy Purse Expenses" for the year 1495 contains the note: "Oct. 1. At Windsor. To the children for the spoures."

Once St. George's Day was famous for its fairs, celebrated in many different parts of England. Today only a few such events are held, notably at Bewdley, in Worcestershire; Penrith, in Cumberland; and Hatfield, in Hertfordshire.

47

St. George's Court, Lichfield, Staffordshire
St. George's Day, April 23

The Ancient Court of the View of Frank Pledge and Court Baron of the Burgesses within the manor of Lichfield is held annually at noon, in the city's guildhall. This court, presided over by the town clerk, as steward of the manor, has been observed without interruption, since Norman days. A special jury appoints high constables, commoners, pinners* and bailiff, hears complaints and imposes fines (amounting to not more than a groat†) upon all absent burgesses. Many persons attending court wear a rose, red for Yorkists, and white for Lancastrians.

The mayor of Lichfield finally proposes a toast, which emphasizes the keynote of all ceremonies in honor of St. George:

"To the immortal memory of St. George, the Patron Saint of England."

Hobby Horse Parade, Minehead, Somerset
May Day Eve, April 30–May Day, May 1

The sailors of Minehead's old waterfront keep alive the ancient custom of welcoming the spring with their hobby horse on "Warning Eve" (as they call May Day Eve), and on the first of May. The custom has existed from the beginning of time, the sailor men claim, while a certain local tradition says Danish invaders were frightened away, long ago, by a glimpse of Minehead's hobby horse parade.

Although the fantastic, beribboned creature which annually greets the spring at Minehead is called a hobby horse, it bears no resemblance whatever to a horse, either wooden or alive. Perhaps its original pattern has altered somewhat through the years, but this is pure guesswork.

---

* Pinners, pinders, or pound-masters. Officers of the manor whose duty it is to impound stray cattle or other animals in the community.

† A *groat* is fourpence, or approximately a nickel.

Promptly at midnight on May Day Eve, the hobby horse, accompanied by a number of uncostumed attendants, a man with a drum (claimed to be over a century old), and an accordionist, issue from the Golden Lion and start making rounds. The hobby horse is made over a stout wooden frame of between seven and eight feet long. The frame is borne on the shoulders of a man whose body is concealed by a curtain of canvas-like cloth, and whose head is covered by a ferociously painted tin mask and tall dunce cap which rise from the center of the frame. The curtain is painted all over with innumerable colored polka dots and bears across the side the legend, "The Sailors' Horse." A slit in the canvas makes it possible for the man inside to reach out his hand for contributions from spectators. The tall peaked cap and the entire top of the structure are covered with hundreds of fluttering rainbow-colored ribbons which vibrate with the prancing and careening of the hobby horse. A rope tail trails along from behind. Once a cow's tail was attached to this rope. This gave rise to all sorts of unauthorized legends concerning a ship, wrecked long ago off the mainland, a dead cow that was washed ashore, and the story that tax collectors cut off the creature's tail, spliced it to the rope and thrashed tardy persons into paying their debts!

As the hobby horse cavorts about, performing grotesque antics to the delight of onlookers, the musicians play both modern and traditional tunes, including an old folk melody known as "Soldiers' Joy."

In olden times the hobby horse parade was a rough-and-ready performance. The retinue included two fantastically costumed teazers, or club men, called "gullivers," who did not hesitate to enter peoples' homes, demanding reward for their antics and emphasizing their demands with the clubs. Hobby Horse, in those days, was also armed. He carried a pair of wicked looking snappers with which he could catch a man and hold him until a contribution was forthcoming. The unlucky victim who refused to "pay off" was often "booted" ten times into submission, or soundly chastised with the cow's tail. Such practices as these have fortunately long since disappeared.

On May Day morning the hobby horse and his attendants always "go to Whitecross (a crossroads to the west of town, where a Maypole used to be erected), and it's got to be by five o'clock in the morning," an old sailor told me. When I asked him why he shook his head. "Oh, I don't know," he said. "It's just tradition."

As a matter of fact, the old man had his time mixed. From time immemorial it has been customary for Hobby Horse and his companions to go to Whitecross at six, not five in the morning. There they dance, play, and collect contributions before returning to town. The party usually shares the money received. In the old days the performers spent it on beer, as, indeed some of them doubtless do nowadays. My old informant hinted that the collection was for the hospital, but probably little of it ever gets that far.

On May Day afternoon the little troupe goes to the nearby picturesque village of Dunster, to visit the castle on the hill and pay respects to the lord of the manor. The ceremony of "bringing in the spring" reaches its climax in the evening when everyone gathers in Dunster's quaint square with its seventeenth century Yarn Market. There, to the accompaniment of his musicians, Hobby Horse performs all his capers, which include shimmying, cavorting, bowing to spectators and shaking the hundreds of flying streamers.

Minehead sailors claim that the idea of Padstow's hobby horse, which is described below, was stolen from them by the crew of a visiting Padstow ship.

Regardless of this accusation, Padstow is the only other West Country town to have a similar May Day ceremonial. Although the beginning of both customs is shrouded in mystery, there are many who believe the performances originated in ancient fertility rites, observed through the ages to welcome spring's return.

APRIL

HOBBY HORSE PARADE, PADSTOW, CORNWALL
May Day Eve, April 30

Padstow's hobby horse, which is thought to be one of the oldest folk survivals in England, is quite different in appearance from Minehead's. As in Minehead, however, its origin is lost in antiquity, and the horse is the focal point of all the May Day ceremonies.

Padstow, formerly a thriving shipbuilding center in the days of wooden sailing vessels, now is a sleepy fishing port which bursts into life once each year with the coming of the Hobby Horse.

Petroc, the Irish seventh century missionary saint, is said to have founded Padstow, which is picturesquely situated on the Camel estuary. Padstow is imbued with tradition. According to one legend, the boy Jesus, accompanied by his great-uncle, Joseph of Arimathaea, landed at Jesus Well, a little way down the estuary, when the Holy Visitors were on their way to Somerset.* Another story is that St. George set on shore not far from Padstow, in the bay which now bears his name, and that when his horse stamped, water sprang forth. Many Padstow citizens have been baptized at this holy well, as anyone will tell you.

Although nobody knows when Hobby Horse first appeared, Padstow citizens assert that once he saved the town from French invasion, an event which is variously dated as occurring some time between the fourteenth and the nineteenth centuries! The legend states that enemy ships were sighted while Padstow's men were away at sea. The women hurriedly donned their red cloaks and carried Hobby Horse out to Stepper Point, not far from St. George's Well. The French were so terrified by sight of the grotesque mask and snapping jaws, that every man turned and fled!

The Padstow Hobby Horse is indeed a terrifying sight. The Old 'Obby 'Oss, as he is popularly called, is made over a heavy round black wooden frame, which measures about six feet in diameter and is supported on a man's shoulders. The frame is covered with a black

* *See* "Pilgrimage to the Holy Thorn," p 11.

51

canvas curtain, which hides all but the man's feet and white-trousered ankles. He slips his head inside a ferocious-looking monster mask which rises from the center of the frame. The snapping jaws, studded with nail teeth, are manipulated by a string within. The hideous mask, painted in white and red, is surmounted by a slender black dunce cap, striped in the same colors and adorned at the peak with a ribbon-tied horsehair "plume." From the front of the frame, or body, projects the minor head of a horse, also grotesquely painted. It has a beribboned horsehair mane and also a tail.

For years there have been hobby horse quarrels and discussions, which have resulted in splitting the townsfolk into two main factions, those who support the Blue Horse and those who fancy the Black. The result is all very confusing to the stranger, but as far as I could learn the Blues represent the town's teetotaler group which contributes its funds largely to local charities, while the Blacks use their May Day contributions for purposes of jollification. "Why, last year," a member of the opposing group grumbled, "the Black 'Oss collected twenty-seven pounds, only to drink it all away!" Be this as it may, the Blues try to preserve the original folk flavor of the ceremony, while the Blacks introduce many details which make up in popular appeal what they lack in authenticity.

I arrived in Padstow on May Day Eve, to find doorways and houses decorated with branches of sycamore or "may," and the little square, which is surrounded by small shops and vine-covered dwellings, fluttering with excitement. With the aid of stout arms and sturdy ropes, a forty-foot Maypole was slowly swung into position in the center of the square. Although not the traditional Maypole, it was a beautiful sight. The pole was wound in yellow and red, and adorned with paper-wrapped hoops hung with great bunches of flowers and greens. In addition, there were twenty-two garlands of pink, white, purple and orange paper flowers. Strings of British flags and red and white pennants, attached to ropes at the center of the pole, were carried to the upper story windows of corner houses. The base was covered with sycamore branches and massed with cowslips and bluebells which village children had gathered from the hills and woods.

Children were all about. Suddenly I felt myself gently prodded from behind. I turned to find myself confronted by a five-year-old boy, with miniature six-shooter and Hopalong Cassidy suit which he "got sent" to him! Five pretty little girls immediately "adopted" me and took me up the hill to see the "original" Maypole at the top of Cross Street. No paper decorations or pennants were there. The pole was covered with green leaves. Near the top a large horizontal hoop, wound with green garlands, supported long ropes of foliage, each with posies of blue, yellow and pink wild and garden flowers attached to ends of varying lengths.

Padstow's May Day festivities begin officially at midnight. The tiny square before the Golden Lion (headquarters of Black 'Oss and his gang) is jammed with townsfolk at five minutes of twelve. My village host grasps me firmly by the elbow and guides me through the crowd, his electric torch lighting our course across the uneven cobblestones. It is pitch black, save for moon and stars. The church clock starts striking. A hushed expectancy comes over the crowd. At the stroke of twelve, the doors of the Golden Lion are suddenly flung open, and as with a single mighty voice everyone bursts into the traditional *Morning Song*:

> Unite and unite and let us all unite
> For summer is a-come in to-day,
> And whither we are going we will all unite,
> In the merry month of May.

The singers surge up the hill and through Padstow's streets and lanes, pausing now and again to serenade one or another householder by name:

> Arise up, Mr.——and joy you betide,
> For summer is a-come in to-day,
> And bright is your bride that lies by your side,
> In the merry morning of May.

53

Arise up, Mrs.——and gold be your ring,
For summer is a-come in to-day
And give to us a cup of ale the merrier we shall sing,
In the merry morning of May.

An hour later, as I gratefully crawl under a big down "puff" in the village home where they "never turn a stranger away," the words and melody of the spring song still echo through the chill starry night:

Now fare you well, and we bid you all good cheer,
For summer is a-come in to-day,
We call once more unto your house before another year,
In the merry morning of May.

Next day I rose early and was out "in the merry morning of May," along with most of Padstow's junior population. Boys and girls in stiffly starched white blouses and summer frocks were rushing about, intent on their own childish business. Many a wee lad had a big bunch of tulips, bluebells and cowslips pinned across his chest, while little fair-haired girls wore enchanting chaplets of pale yellow primroses. Men and women had posies pinned to caps or dresses. Even pets came in for their share of decoration. One lively brown and white pup sported a huge bunch of cowslips under his chin. Down by the quays barkers were doing a brisk business in dripping ice cream bricks and long brilliantly colored "ice" suckers. Pennants were fluttering, musicians were tuning up, and everywhere bands of "colts" or miniature hobby horses were parading up and down Padstow's lanes and alleys.

The colts were charming, being replicas of their elders' Old 'Obby 'Oss fitted to the slender shoulders of seven- and eight-year-old children. Each colt was accompanied by his followers, including a little boy with rattling collection box. So intent were the colts upon a "proper" procession, that often their treasurer failed to see the pennies bystanders proffered. As the little ones paraded, they chanted again and again the *Day Song* refrain, which like the *Morning Song,* begins:

> Unite and unite and let us all unite,
> For summer is a-come in to-day.

Promptly at eleven, loudspeakers began to blare and Black 'Oss emerged from the Golden Lion accompanied by his teazer and painted pirate band. I barely glimpsed the theatrical looking group, as I hastened to the more modest Blue 'Oss headquarters on a side street, squeezed in between two small tobacconist shops.

Out came 'Oss, accompanied by three accordion players, a drummer and the man with the collection box. The men wore white trousers, red knitted jerseys and flat topped white caps, decorated with bunches of cowslips and tulips. Hobby Horse was terrifying as he lunged and cavorted, careened and gamboled, to the lively accompaniment of the traditional tune and to words possibly not so old. After the preliminary four verses, similar to those of the *Morning Song,* the tempo of the music changed to a mournful dirge. The horse sank down swooning. His attendants dejectedly surrounded him, chanting wth great emphasis:

> O! where is St. George,
> O! where is he O?
> He is out in his long-boat on the salt sea O.
> Up flies the kite and down fall the lark O.
> Aunt Ursula Birdwood she had an old ewe
> And she died in her own Park O.

With the last word up bounded the horse to cavort down the street or make a playful gesture toward a pretty girl in the sidelines. Then Aunt Ursula Birdwood, the "man-woman," appeared. Aunt Ursula was a stocky man who wore a tight-fitting green frock and orange-lined black straw hat trimmed with garden tulips. "It was once a London fashion hat," his wife explained. Long stockings "to 'ide 'is 'airy legs" and long white gloves completed the costume. Aunt Ursula, obviously intended to represent a not-too-virtuous woman, went through all sorts of broad play with 'Oss, musicians and bystanders.

The music, singing and dancing continued, meanwhile, through many verses which brought in all kinds of confused references to spring, the young men of Padstow who "might have built a ship and gilded her with gold," and the young women who ". . . might have made a garland with the white rose and the red" and to the men who were away in France. Every now and then, however, the verse about Saint George was repeated and the horse swooned on the ground as if overcome with exhaustion, but with the last line he always once more bounded into life.

The Padstow ceremony is intensely moving, in spite of its broad horseplay. Does 'Oss, who suffers ritualistic death and then is resurrected, represent some ancient fertility rite connected with driving out winter and bringing in the spring? Or is he, perhaps, connected in origin with the horse cult of the early Britons? Whatever the origin of the hobby horse festival, it brings joy to the heart and a lilt to the spirit, "For summer is a-come in to-day."

MAY

Remember us poor Mayers all,
And thus we do begin
To lead our lives in righteousness,
Or else we die in sin.

We have been rambling all the night
And almost all the day,
And now returnèd back again
We bring you a branch of May.
—*Medieval May Carol.*

MAY DAY

May 1

The old English customs of planting May trees, weaving garlands and playing games on the green in early spring, probably originated in the *Floralia,* the April flower festival of the Romans. In Britain, as in every other country, the May Day rites symbolized awakening of life in early spring and renewal of the vegetation spirit's blessings.

In medieval times, young people wandered into the woods at night, returning at dawn with garlands and flowering branches for decoration of homes and churches. The Mayers carried about garlands from house to house and sang spring carols, in return for gifts.

Modern English May Day customs are largely revivals of old practices which fell into general disuse before the Reformation. Breaking the continuity of the original tradition has altered the observance of the day. Then too, since the war, many of the old customs have died, alas, along with the elderly villagers who practiced the arts of garland-weaving and posy-making the younger generation has never learned.

57

Puritan leaders were largely responsible for the original break in May Day customs. Philip Stubbes, Puritan author of Queen Elizabeth's reign, wrote scathingly, in his *Anatomie of Abuse,* about the idolatrous nature of the May Day practices:

"Against May, Whitsonday, or other time, all the young men and maides, old men and wives, run gadding . . . to the woods. . . . The chiefest jewel they bring from thence is their May-pole, which they bring home with great veneration as thus. They have twentie or fortie yoke of oxen, every oxe having a sweet nose-gay of floures placed on the tip of his hornes, and these oxen drawe home this May-pole, which is covered all over with floures and hearbes, bound round about with strings, from top to the bottome, and sometimes painted with variable colours, with two or three hundred men, women and children, following it with great devotion. And thus beeing reared up, with handkerchiefs and flags hovering on the top, they straw the ground rounde about, binde green boughs about it, set up summer haules, bowers and arbors hard by it. And then they fall to daunce about it, like the heathen people did at the dedication of the Idols, *whereof this is a perfect pattern, or rather the thing itself."*

Some of the English May Day ceremonies that have been revived since such outbursts of Puritan disapproval no longer are held at the original time. After Charles II was restored, and with him, many of the May Day pleasures previously banned, May 29, the "Merry Monarch's" birthday, was widely chosen as the time for crowning Queens, dressing Maypoles and once more welcoming the spring. In some places, May Day still is observed according to the Old Style calendar, while in others the festival is celebrated at Whitsun, Midsummer, at local wakes,* or fairs, or some other time when uncertain English weather is likely to be warmer and more settled than on the first of May.

* *See* "Glossary of English Festival Terms," *Wake.* p270.

MAY

DECORATING THE ROOD SCREEN, CHARLTON-ON-OTMOOR, OXFORD-
SHIRE

May Day, May 1

Atop the lacy, fifteenth century Perpendicular rood screen in
Charlton-on-Otmoor's village church, is a box-leaf cross which
stands five feet high. Each May Day a smaller cross of spring
flowers is laid over the background of the shining box.

"I always take the cross to the rectory to be done," said a farmer
proudly. "There two village women and a boy do the decorating."

For generations the custom of decorating the Charlton cross has
been almost a religious rite, observed not only on May Day, but at
Michaelmas and other village holidays as well.

"My great-grandmother decorated the cross for many years,"
said the farmer's wife. "She lived to be a hundred and nine, and
died little over forty years ago. People picked primroses, violets,
bluebells and other spring flowers and brought them to the rectory
for her to use. There she sat, her stick beside her, the flowers in her
big white apron. It took nearly 'alf a day for her to do it.

"In the old days," continued the farmer's wife, "men used to
carry the big church cross through the village streets, stopping and
singing at each door."

"They don't do that any more," interrupted the farmer. "Nowadays the children go about in twos and threes, singing the May Song
and carrying smaller crosses made of box and flowers. Then they
bang hard on the door, expecting a threepence for their effort." The
man's kind eyes crinkled at the corners. "They're crafty now, those
children are! They used to go about in crowds. Now they go in
twos and threes, so as to get more money."

"What do they use it for?" I asked.

"Oh, nothing in particular, just for pocket money."

When asked to repeat the May Song, the farmer and his wife
had to confer at length. The woman kept leaving the room to con-

sult the neighbors. The son out in the garden was asked to fill in an elusive line here and there. Finally the song was pieced together, bit by bit, in the form given below, although the farmer stoutly insisted "the last verse 'ad ought to come first."

> A May garland I have brought you,
> And at your door I stand.
> It looks very nice
> And smells very sweet
> And it came from the Lord's right hand.
>
> Good morning, ladies and gentlemen.
> We wish you a happy May
> We've come to show you our garland
> Because it's the first of May.

BRINGING IN THE MAY, WILTON, SALISBURY, WILTSHIRE

May Day, May 1

Bands of children "bring in the May" in Wilton by carrying through the streets sticks with flower garlands, which are known variously as "posies," "May blobs," or "tissty-tossty balls." As groups of boys and girls go from house to house, they sing short traditional rhymes such as the following, and receive in return gifts of pennies or goodies:

> Good morning, Missus and Master,
> I wish you a happy day;
> Please to smell my garland,
> Because it is the first of May.

"May blobs," "Mary blobs," or "tissty-tossty balls," are made by snapping off the heads of primroses or other spring flowers and leaving only a short piece of stem. Each flower is tied at short intervals to a long piece of string and the two ends are then fastened together.

Dorsetshire children play a charming divination game with the balls by tossing them back and forth with the rhyme,

> Tissty-tossty, tell me true,
> Who shall I be married to?

The children then repeat the letters of the alphabet while still tossing the ball. The letter which is spoken as a child misses the ball and drops it, indicates the initial of the future mate.

Children play a similar game to foretell their life span. After repeating the couplet that follows, they call out successive numbers, starting with one and continuing until the ball is dropped:

> Tissty-tossty, four and foarty,
> How many years shall I live hearty?

Of course, the number that is spoken as the ball falls, clearly shows the years of "living hearty."

In some Sussex villages, such as Anstye, old men until recently have made the May posies and carried them about the streets on top of long poles. The men who knew the art have died, villagers tell me, and the custom has been abandoned.

WELCOMING THE MAY, MAGDALEN TOWER, OXFORD, OXFORD-SHIRE

May Day, May 1

One of the country's most beautiful ceremonies is the annual song service from the top of Magdalen Tower to "Bring in the May."

At six in the morning, robed choristers of the Magdalen Church School ascend the hundred and forty-five steps to the Tower, to welcome the May with the hymn of thanksgiving and praise which begins: *Te Deum Patrem colimus.* This old Latin hymn, which has come down through the centuries, was ". . . composed by Benjamin Rogers, Doctor of Musique of the University of Oxen, 1685."

After the song service listened to by hundreds of spectators, standing in the streets below the Tower, crowding Magdalen Bridge, or sitting in boats on the river, the church bells ring out joyously. The ancient May Day tradition is continued by the appearance of the morris men, who generally perform near the bridge, then in Radclyffe Square and Broad Street, and finally, in the open space before the Martyrs' Memorial. In former days the morris dancers included among their characters the Lord and Lady, Jack-o'-the-Green, and the Chimney Sweeps. Today the famous Headington Morris Team, and the Oxford Morris Men, are the chief performers at the celebration.

Originally, a Requiem Mass for the soul of Henry VII was sung each May Day morning from the top of Magdalen Tower. After the Reformation, however, the musical ceremony we know today was substituted for the older service.

MAY FAIR, BOSTON, LINCOLNSHIRE

About May 1

Boston's famous May Fair, authorized by Charter from Henry VIII, opens in the Market Place on or about May 1, and continues for a week. At twelve o'clock noon the town clerk, in the presence of mayor and civic officials, formally opens the fair from the balcony of the assembly rooms, by reading an ancient proclamation.

The May Fair is a fun fair, characterized by side-shows, roundabouts and other forms of popular entertainment. The mayor, aldermen and city councillors, in ceremonial attire, customarily participate in the first round of amusements.

MAY QUEEN OF LONDON FESTIVAL, HAYES COMMON, KENT

The Saturday following May 1 (or on the same afternoon, should May 1 fall on a Saturday)

London keeps up her May Day tradition with a public May Festival, held in the suburbs, in Hayes Common, near Bromley, Kent,

62

usually at two o'clock in the afternoon. Each of the elementary schools celebrates the first of May by electing a Queen with appropriate ceremonies.

The festival is a gay affair, which starts with a procession of May Queens from the various schools. The Queens are attended by maids of honor, pages and other retainers. When the procession arrives at the Common, the Prince of Merrie England (usually the Queen of the preceding year, who is now dressed in boy's costume) chooses the May Queen of London from among all the lesser queens. The lesser queens then pay tribute to the new Queen of London, and the festival ends with traditional Maypole dances and songs. The ceremony is a pretty one, since the young queens, who range from twelve to fourteen, are fresh and charming in their white frocks, gay ribbons and flowers.

MAY FESTIVAL, ELSTOW, BEDFORDSHIRE

Early in May

A charming May Festival has been held each year on Elstow Green, since the May Day revival in 1925, after a lapse of many years.

Although the Elstow Festival is not "traditional" in the technical sense, it is reminiscent of early English May games and ceremonies and, as such, is worthy of note.

The participants in the festivities are children from Elstow County Primary School, who form a May Day procession from the school to the Green. The May Queen in white frock and long train is drawn to the Green in a flower-decked carriage accompanied by her train bearers, maids of honor, the Queen of the previous year, the Jester, Hobby Horse and other May Day characters. During the ceremonies, small children wearing flowers and colored dresses twine the Maypole in traditional country style.

MAY FAIR, HEREFORD, HEREFORDSHIRE

Some time during the first week in May

People think that this ancient fair, once called St. Ethelbert's, or the Nine Days' Fair, originally was held by Charter from Henry III. The May Fair, once under the jurisdiction of Hereford's Bishop, now consists of a cattle fair, held in the Market, and a pleasure fair, in "High Town," the center of the city. Like most very old fairs, the May Fair formerly was noted as a hiring fair, when farm help was engaged for the surrounding countryside.

EVE OF THE FINDING OF THE CROSS

May 2

On the eve of the finding of the "true Cross," in 326, by St. Helena, mother of Constantine the Great, popular superstition attributes supernatural power to mountain ash and witchen tree. Formerly, people thought that branches of these trees, when gathered on the eve, were a protection against witches' power and evil forces.

Since St. Helena, according to one tradition the daughter of Coel, Duke of Colchester (later a King of the Britons and the legendary original of Old King Cole), is supposed to have been born in Colchester, Essex, the anniversary holds special significance for people of that city. Colchester's ancient coat-of-arms represented the Cross, surmounted by three crowns.

FURRY DAY, HELSTON, CORNWALL

St. Michael's Day, May 8 (except when this date falls on a Sunday or Monday)

The ceremonies of Helston's Furry Day (or Flora Day, as it is often incorrectly called) consist chiefly of presentations of the processional dance known as the Furry, and the singing of the "Hal-an-tow," in honor of "the Summer and the May, O." The festival is celebrated on May 8, Feast of Saint Michael, Helston's patronal saint.

There are many speculations regarding the origin of the word *furry*. According to Mr. Morton Nance, Grand Bard of Cornwall, its derivation is from the old English word *fery*, meaning feast day of the patron saint. Gradually *fery* degenerated into *furry*.

"Nowadays people think the word 'unrefined' and call the dance *flora*, after a term which arose in the eighteenth century. There is absolutely no basis for the explanation that *flora* comes from the Roman *Floralia*, the festival to honor the goddess Flora," says Mr. Nance. "There was no town of Helston when the Romans were in Cornwall. Their influence was superficial."

The popular explanation that *furry* is a corruption of the old Cornish word *fer*, meaning a fair, is also incorrect. The Furry celebrates the feast of Helston's patron saint. Two centuries ago, however, people evidently mixed the May day and feast day celebrations, with the result that features of both now appear in Furry Day festivities.

The people of Helston tell various legends about the origin of their Furry Dance. But aside from the one indisputable fact that it "is so old it has always existed," there seem to be two or three favorite versions of the story. One is that the dance celebrates the town's deliverance from a "fiery dragon,"* which appeared over Helston many centuries ago and dropped a mammoth stone on the very spot where Angel Inn now stands. In support of this theory (doubtless invented to explain the presence of a megalith) an immense stone was split up in 1783, and used for building purposes. A portion of the stone has been built into the west wall of the Angel Hotel, where it is pointed out with pride.

A second, and more picturesque, version of the story is that the Furry commemorates St. Michael's victory over the Devil. Helston, or "Helleston," gets its name, so some inhabitants say, from the huge granite stone that once lay at the mouth of Hell. The Devil

* One source suggests that the appearance of a large meteorite may account for this legend.

tried to steal the stone away, but on his way through Cornwall St. Michael intercepted him. After a fierce fight, the Archangel forced the Devil to drop his burden and flee for his life. As in the first story, the stone fell into Angel Yard, and part of it later was built into the wall. In celebration of their patron's victory, the people of Helston through the centuries have danced through each other's houses as an expression of their joy and gratitude.

Yet a third popular account of the Furry's origin is that the fight between the Archangel and the Devil occurred not in Cornwall, but on St. Michael's Mount in France. The saint, apparently getting rather the worse of the fray, escaped to his Mount in Cornwall. The Devil, angry because his opponent had slipped away, at once pried loose the lid of Hell and hurled it after his disappearing foe. The Devil's aim was faulty for, instead of hitting the saint, the stone hit Helston! The Archangel was unharmed, however; the people of Helston unhurt. Their joy knew no bounds. They joined hands and danced and sang through streets and houses in expression of thanksgiving for deliverance.

These are just a few of the many legends which have sprung up through the years to explain the origin of a custom so ancient that it has no real explanation.

The Helston Furry begins at seven o'clock in the morning, when dancers, officials and town band meet at the guildhall in the center of town and dance up Meneage Street, then up and down many of the town's hilly thoroughfares, through certain specified gardens and houses, and finally back to the guildhall. There, the group is invited to a well-earned breakfast, as guests of the Flora Day Association.

While the first dance is going on, Helston's youths are in the woods cutting boughs of fresh sycamore for the Hal-an-tow ceremony, thought by many to be the festival's oldest feature. *Faddy,* the old Cornish word for sycamore, is the name originally given to this dance, because the young people returned from the woods in a processional morris, waving sycamore branches and singing a May carol.

Today the boys assemble at St. John's Bridge at half-past eight and, as in olden times, perambulate the town with swaying branches. The band accompanies the group with the charming, monotonous melody of the "Hal-an-tow," or Furry song, traditional to Helston. At stated points the procession stops and sings the enchanting old song that tells of Robin Hood and Little John who figured in English May Day revels of long ago. Then follows a rollicking chorus which, according to some, may be derived from a popular medieval seamen's chantey. The song continues, with an amusing verse about the Spaniards (possibly in reference to the Spanish Armada) who shall eat the grey goose feather* and the English who shall "eat the roast." There are references to Saint George and, in the last verse, to Aunt Mary Moses, whose name, authorities claim, was substituted during the Commonwealth for that of an unpopular monarch. It has been suggested by Mr. Morton Nance that the "Hal-an-tow" is of possible Elizabethan, rather than more ancient, origin:

> Robin Hood and Little John,
> They both are gone to the Fair, O,
> And we will to the merry green wood
> To see what they do there, O,
> And for to chase, O,
> To chase the buck and doe.

> *Chorus:*
> Hal-an-tow, Jolly rumble O
> For we are up as soon as any day, O,
> And for to fetch the Summer home
> The Summer and the May, O,
> For Summer is a-come, O,
> And Winter is a-gone, O.

> Where are those Spaniards
> That make so great a boast, O?
> For they shall eat the grey goose feather
> And we shall eat the roast, O,
> In every land, O,
> The Land where e'er we go.

* Grey goose feathers were affixed to the butt-ends of the shafts used by English yeomen in their longbows.

(Repeat Chorus)
As for that Good Knight, St. George,
St. George he was a Knight, O,
Of all the Knights in Christendom
St. George he is the right, O,
In every land, O,
The land where e'er we go.

(Repeat Chorus)
God bless Aunt Mary Moses
And all her power and might, O,
And send us peace in Merry England
Both day and night, O,
And send us peace in Merry England
Both now and evermore, O.

(Repeat Chorus)

The "Hal-an-tow" died out in about 1820, when it acquired a bad name because of drunkenness and license on the part of the dancers. Thanks to the efforts of the Old Cornwall Society, this traditional part of the celebration was revived about thirty years ago, and nowadays the dancers visit public buildings rather than public houses. The boys end their dance at ten o'clock at the old grammar school.

At the secondary modern school playground adjoining the grammar school, some five hundred white-clad school children wait with their teachers to begin the Children's Dance at about ten-fifteen. This wholly modern feature, introduced into the festivities a few years ago, is gay and full of charm, but not traditional. Each small girl wears a pretty white frock and chaplet of lilies-of-the-valley; each small boy a posy of lilies pinned to his blouse.

The three dances are subordinate to the main event of the day— the noonday performance of the traditional Furry Dance. Promptly at the stroke of twelve, fifty, seventy, or more couples headed by the mayor and town officials assemble at the guildhall. The men wear morning coats, silk hats and lily-of-the-valley boutonnieres; the women garden party hats, long gloves, light summer frocks and lily-of-the-valley corsages. The dance begins with the formation of a

long line, men on the left, women on the right. The master of ceremonies counts off the participants into pairs, who progress through
the cobbled streets of Helston, with various steps. The moving line
advances for possibly three miles or more, pausing at certain doors
to pound knockers and ring bells, then dances through houses and
gardens, sometimes just about the gardens.

The twelve o'clock dance originally was intended for the gentry.
The men in cocked hats, the women in fine silks, must have presented a picture of taste and elegance as they danced in and out of
old houses and through stately gardens. In the eighteenth century
the gentlemen wreathed their hats with garlands of flowers and
now, in the twentieth, they wear high silk hats.

The last dance of Helston's Furry Day belongs to the people,
rather than the privileged few. It starts at five in the afternoon.
Anyone who wishes joins in. Then the dancers celebrate at the huge
pleasure fair at the end of town, or munch "fairings" of gingerbread
or sweets purchased from hucksters stationed along the streets,

> For summer is a-come O,
> And winter is a-gone, O.

CHESTNUT SUNDAY, HAMPTON COURT, MIDDLESEX

About May 8

At this date, or a little later, according to the season, thousands
of Londoners visit Bushy Park to enjoy the beauty of the triple
Chestnut Avenue. This majestic avenue, planted by William III,
measures more than fifty yards in width and over a mile in length.
Here and there among the chestnuts are beautiful limes, which add
the fragrance of their blossoms to the soft spring air.

BEACONSFIELD FAIR, BEACONSFIELD, BUCKINGHAMSHIRE

May 10

This ancient fair still is held each year on its original site, at
the Old Town cross roads. Although the fair now is chiefly an

69

amusement event for young people of the surrounding communities, it was once the famous cattle fair of the entire district.

The date of the old fair has been juggled about a good deal since it was established. Since the late nineteenth century it has been held on its present May 10. In 1269, the fair occurred on the Vigil of the Ascension; in 1551, on the Vigil and Morrow of the Purification; and toward the end of the eighteenth century, February 13 and Holy Thursday were proclaimed the proper fair dates.

GARLAND DAY, ABBOTSBURY, DORSETSHIRE

Old May Day, May 12

On Garland Day, boys and girls of the charming Dorset fishing village of Abbotsbury still carry garlands from door to door and receive small gifts, in return for "bringing in the May." Later, their wreaths are laid at the base of the War Memorial.

Once Garland Day was an important festival, marking the opening of the fishing season. The wreaths were blessed at a special children's church service, then carried to the water's edge and fastened to the bows of fishing smacks. The rest of the day was devoted to singing and dancing on the sand. At night, however, the fishermen rowed out to sea, tossing the garlands to the waves and offering prayers for preservation from harm and an abundant mackerel harvest.

Legend says the annual ceremony survives from pagan times, when sacrificial offerings were thought necessary to propitiate the gods of the sea. Abbotsbury's May garlands are woven nowadays by a local woman and her helpers who are regarded as "official" village garland makers, and through whose efforts the unique custom survives. Some garlands are fashioned from cultivated flowers, others of early spring blossoms gathered by the children from the lush meadows and fragrant hedgerows surrounding the picturesque hamlet.

Each garland is made over a frame through which a stout broomstick is inserted. A "crown" of fragrant garden blossoms surmounts the top. Two young people lift the garland between them, each supporting an end of the broomstick as they go about the village.

"I couldn't do it less than five or six hours to make they," declared a village woman, inviting me into her tiny cottage and pulling out old photographs, to show me how the garlands looked fifteen years ago when *she* made them. Lovely they must have been, too, but different from today's May garlands. Even to look at the aging photographs, however, was almost to sniff the fragrance of the roses, cowslips, lilies and sweet wood violets, which typify Abbotsbury's lovely rite of "bringing in the May."

MAY FESTIVAL, ICKWELL, BEDFORDSHIRE

About mid-May

Ickwell's traditional May Festival includes a procession of flower-crowned girls, carrying floral hoops, who accompany their May Queen and her attendants to Ickwell Green. Following the ceremony of Crowning the Queen, the Maypole is plaited and old English country dances and games performed.

ST. DUNSTAN'S DAY

May 19

In southern Devon there is a saying that should mid-May frost ruin the apple crops, it would be because of a pact St. Dunstan once made with the Devil!

Dunstan was a West Country lad who finally became a bishop; but before that happened, he raised barley for beer, like any other Devonshire farmer. One year the cider apples were so plentiful that Dunstan feared he might be put out of business. Just then, along came the Devil with an offer. He would kill all of the apples with frost, in return for Dunstan's soul.

The young man thought over the bargain with care, then finally agreed—but on condition that the apple trees suffer frost only on the three days of May 17, 18 and 19. If this ever happens, Devon-

71

shire people will shake their heads and declare that the Devil, not St. Dunstan, is to blame!

MAYORING DAY, RYE, SUSSEX

May 23

It is an old custom for the new mayor of Rye to toss shiny heated pennies to village children, from the balcony of the George Hotel. Following his election, crowds of boys and girls gather in the streets beneath the balcony and impatiently await the mayor's appearance.

"This is a traditional practice," an old townsman told me. "But sometimes," he added shrewdly, "the mayor can't afford the pennies! He may spend as much as forty pounds, if he's rich; and, as you know, the office of mayor is largely honorary." Then, with a reminiscent chuckle, the old man went on to explain how hard it is to lift a red-hot penny. "Grown-ups, as well as children, grab for them," he added.

Until 1949, Rye's Mayoring Day was observed on November 9. By the Representation of the People Act of 1948, Mayoring Day in Boroughs was altered from November to May.

ROYAL OAK DAY, HOSPITAL, CHELSEA, LONDON

Royal Oak or Oak Apple Day, May 29

The old and disabled soldiers of the Hospital, Chelsea, London, pay tribute on May 29 to the memory of Charles II, who, in 1682, founded the institution as a home for aged army men.

Impressive commemorative ceremonies* are held annually on the parade grounds in the Hospital's center court. On three sides stand the fine old Christopher Wren buildings; on the fourth, a broad expanse of lawn stretches out to a pleasant vista of grass and trees. The statue of Charles II, decorated knee-high in oak branches, re-

---

* The year 1954 marks the two hundred sixty-second ceremony.

72

calls the monarch's traditional escape by hiding in an oak tree, following the Battle of Worcester.

The Royal Scots Band, in colorful uniforms and tall bearskin caps, was playing stirring music as I arrived at the parade grounds. Old pensioners, dressed in three-cornered hats and brilliant scarlet coats (today replacing their somber dark blue winter uniforms), wore many distinguished service medals across their chests. Each man had a sprig of oak in his buttonhole. The old men were inspected by the Chief of the Imperial General Staff and then passed before Charles II's statue in military parade, heads erect, steps often faltering, backs sometimes bent. Some three hundred and fifty old soldiers were represented, ranging between fifty-six and ninety-five years of age. A number of veterans, too feeble to march, patiently sat on the sidelines and followed with dimming eyes the moving line of scarlet coats.

This is a gala day, for each old man holds open house for relatives, friends and distinguished guests who make hospital rounds following the marching, the speeches and the military music. For each there will be plum pudding and double beer today. Congratulations are extended, cameras click. Tomorrow some of the journals will carry pictures of the pensioners in their brave red uniforms and sprigs of oak.

I visited the old men, along with the other guests. In the long dormitories, each pensioner has a cubicle opening into a wide corridor. Dark curtains are drawn across the windows and doors are closed when privacy from passers-by is desired. A chest outside each door accommodates worldly possessions. Food is brought to the dormitories and served from numbered metal plates and mugs. Each corridor has two large stone fireplaces, which are now occupied by faultlessly polished stoves. Enormous teakettles make possible the "cup o' tea" the men prepare for themselves. Above the fireplaces are thirty-one notches; below, a wooden peg which is moved along day by day to mark the passage of time.

Each old soldier reveals himself in the arrangement of his meager belongings in the cubicle that represents his tiny kingdom. Here are toilet articles, books and souvenirs. On the walls are ranged his "pin-up" girls. Chief among them, in 1952, was the winsome face of the Princess Elizabeth.

Most of the old soldiers are talkative. One proudly demonstrates his "three-speed" wooden leg, which performs some astonishing tricks. A smiling nurse pins oak leaves to the bosom of an eighty-five-year-old veteran, the entire left side of his chest smothered by medals. A picturesque white-bearded man watches benignly from under his cockaded hat the clumsy efforts of the curly-headed little boy on his lap, who struggles to attach an oak sprig on the fourth button down. Founder's Day is a gala occasion to these aged army men of the Royal Hospital, who, having served their country with honor, have found a well-earned haven of rest.

Anthem Service, Cathedral Tower, Durham

Oak-Apple Day, May 29

On May 29 Durham Cathedral holds a unique service from the tower, but the service, as we shall see, bears only a slight association with Oak-Apple Day. Immediately following evensong, choristers and lay clerks mount the steps to the central tower to sing three anthems, one to the south, one to the east, and one to the north sides of the tower. The western part is excepted because, tradition says, a choir boy once fell to his death from this point.

The song ceremony is said to have originated on October 17, 1346, when the monks of Durham stood on the tower, chanting prayers for victory and watching the progress of the Battle of Neville's Cross. In breathless anxiety they witnessed the conflict raging below, little over a mile away. When word finally came that the English, led by Queen Philippa, had routed the Scots and that David II, the Scottish leader, had been captured, the monks broke into a grateful *Te Deum*.

74

Legend says that the Abbot of Durham promised prayers of thanksgiving would be chanted from the same spot each year if God attended the monks' petitions for help against the invaders.

The custom of singing from the tower was discontinued for a time. When it was finally revived, it was as a ceremony in recognition of the Restoration.

GARLAND DAY, CASTLETON, DERBYSHIRE

Royal Oak Day, May 29

Each year, on May 29, Castleton observes the unique ceremony of the garlanded May King, which is of ancient origin and which has no parallel in other parts of England.

Castleton in olden times was a strong Royalist center. As in some other places, the town's May Day festivities were transferred to May 29 in recognition of the restoration of Charles II, and many reminders of Cavalier sympathies appear throughout the celebration.

Castleton is an isolated Peak village, lying in the valley of the Hope. High above the town are hills riddled with curious caverns and lead and spar mines, which once were worked by the Romans. On Castleton's overhanging precipice the Britons camped and William Peveril, the Norman, built his mighty Peveril Castle in 1068.

Against this ancient setting the Garland, or May King, his attendant, who leads his horse, and his consort (a man dressed in female costume) annually ride forth on horseback, at the head of a group of musicians and girls, who perform a processional dance similar in character to the Helston Furry.*

The King presents an extraordinary appearance. He is dressed in a blue velvet Cavalier coat, breeches and boots. Over his head and shoulders, however, is the "garland," an immense beehive-shaped wooden frame †, covered with greenery and wild and cultivated flowers, which usually include bluebells and peonies. Into the top of

* *See p64 ff.*

† People of Castleton claim that originally the garland frame was made of lead taken from the local mines.

the garland is fitted a special bouquet, called the "queen" or "quane," which is mounted on a short thick pole, twelve to fourteen inches long. The "queen" consists of choice garden flowers, such as tulips, or a combination of cultivated flowers.

Within living memory the history of the queen has changed. Once the flowers were specially grown for it. Before World War I, it was customary after the day's ceremonies to present the queen to one of Castleton's leading ladies, whose husband always paid a guinea for the compliment! Since the war, however, the queen has been dedicated to the War Memorial in the market place. For probably sixty years this unique posy has been fashioned by the skilled hands of Mr. Ellis Eyre, an expert in the art, who now has a younger assistant, Bob Nall, in training for the traditional making of the queen.

The King's costume, like the queen on his garland, has also undergone changes with the passing years. The original dusty-red coat and black hat, trimmed with lace and fur, dated back to 1720. Although worn for many years, they were snipped into so often by souvenir-hungry visitors who coveted bits of the Garland King's ribbons and lace as mementos that the tattered garments finally were given to Castleton's Douglas Museum. The present Royalist costume was substituted for the traditional one.

The Garland King's young "consort" is also dressed in a blue velvet Royalist-style costume. Over a curled auburn wig, he wears diadem and veil, and over the shoulders a shawl. This costume was bequeathed by the will of a former Castleton resident, to be worn in the annual ceremony.

The procession starts from the public house or hotel where the garland is made for that year. Since Castleton boasts six hotels, each takes its turn in the honor. The King and Queen on horseback lead the parade. The Castleton Silver Band follows, playing the Garland theme. Then come the dancing girls who replace the traditional morris men of forty or fifty years ago. "Probably the girls were considered more attractive than the men," said a local informant in trying to explain the change.

The words of the garland song, which are mere doggerel, expressed in Derbyshire dialect, refer to Castleton's ancient feud with Bradwell (Bradda), a nearby mining village:

> Aw dunno kno, an aw dunno care,
> What they are in Bradda,
> An old cow's yead (head)
> On a lump o' bread,
> An a puddin' bak'd in a lantern.
> La, la, la, la, la, la,
> La, la la, la, lum.

Castleton's men used to claim that Bradwell's people were descended from convicts who had to work in the lead mines, while Bradwell's men retaliate by saying Castleton's inhabitants were descended from slaves!

In former times when the morris men danced it was customary for the bell ringers, armed with sycamore boughs, to "sweep away" any onlookers who blocked the path of the oncoming procession.

The group stops at each hotel, where local children make a circle and perform a charming dance, in which men and women sometimes participate. After playing the traditional dance tune, the band continues with modern airs while the Garland King and his retinue receive refreshment. The dancing ends at the Maypole, erected on the site of the old Bull Ring, in front of Castleton Hall. This feature of the ceremony is a modern innovation introduced between forty and fifty years ago. Among the figures performed about the maypole are the Single and Double Plait, the Barber's Pole, Spider's Web, Threes, and *Amo Amas*.

The traditional Garland theme* played at each stop is said to be a corruption of the Helston Furry. Over a century ago, when lead mining was the area's leading industry, Jeremy Royse of Castleton

* *See p67.*

77

employed between two and three hundred Cornish lead miners, to cut the second tunnel in Speedwell Mine. The men brought with them some of their own dances and songs, including the beloved Furry, which in turn was transferred to the indigenous Garland ceremony.

At sunset the King and Queen turn toward the parish church. They ride into the churchyard and stop beneath the fifteenth century church tower, which has all pinnacles except one decorated with sycamore.*

A little group of Castleton citizens assist in removing the garland from the King's head. After carefully taking out the queen, which later is laid on the War Memorial, six or seven stalwart men, who are prepared with stout ropes, stand on the south side of the church tower and slowly hoist the immense garland to the center pinnacle. There the garland remains until the flowers fade.

For nearly three hundred years the Garland ceremony was organized by the bell ringers. Since World War I, however, when so many of the men went into service, arrangements have been handled by a local committee of interested village people, who wish to preserve the ancient ceremonial.

As already suggested, the origin of the Castleton Garland ceremony is obscure. Many different theories have been advanced, ranging all the way from a local allusion to its possible connection with druidical observance† to a suggestion that it stems from the same ritual source as a fourteenth century Arthurian poem of "Sir Gawain and the Green Knight."‡

---

* In olden days, when the oak was the most plentiful tree in the area, oak branches were used, but since Napoleonic times, when so many oaks were felled that the trees became scarce, sycamore branches have been substituted.

† The Druids were thought to have held an annual flower festival at which, every seven years, a maiden was sacrificed.

‡ "A Re-Examination of the Castleton Garlanding," by Michael M. Rix, *Folk-Lore*, June 1953, p342-344.

PRESERVATION OF WOOD-CUTTING RIGHTS, WISHFORD, SALISBURY WILTSHIRE

*May 29 (except when the day falls on a
Sunday, when certain ceremonies are
held on the Monday following)*

Every year Wishford's inhabitants enact a curious ceremony to reestablish their ancient claim to wood and pasture rights in the Grovely Forest. The celebration commemorates a Royal Charter of March 15, 1603, which set out the Wishford rights to collect firewood and to pasture cattle for as long as these rights should be asserted annually. As a matter of fact, according to Wishford inhabitants, these rights already "had . . . existed time out of mind," when the charter was granted, and were probably of Saxon origin.

At dawn of May 29, everyone treks to the forest to cut down green oak branches. When the people of Wishford return they bring back boughs to decorate every cottage in the village. In addition, there is an immense oak limb, known as the "marriage bough," which the men drag after them.

In the forenoon, a delegation of villagers visits Salisbury Cathedral, where they lay oak branches at the foot of the high altar and utter the historic shout:

> Grovely! Grovely! Grovely!
> And all Grovely,
> Unity is strength.

Later, the "marriage bough" is decked out with bright ribbon streamers. Then, as with Castleton's garland, the branch is hoisted up to a pinnacle of the parish church tower. This is "to bring luck to the marriages celebrated during the year," Wishford people say.

By noon, the festivities are well under way. The Wishford Oak Apple Club, acting as committee of arrangements, oversees a procession with standard bearers carrying a huge banner decorated with the oak symbol and the Grovely legend, and a colorful fancy dress parade. The procession forms at the Town End Tree, circles about the village, and finally ends in a field where the judging of costumes is conducted. A festive luncheon follows, with appropriate toasts and speeches. The remainder of the day is given to folk dancing, merrymaking and a pleasure fair. The village children dance about the Maypole and the White House team of morris dancers comes from Oxford to add special gaiety to a happy celebration which has survived through many generations.

JUNE

Shepherd, shepherd, leave decoying,
Pipes are sweet on Summer's day,
Whilst your lays we are enjoying,
We to Flora homage pay.

Then with flow'ry garlands 'twining,
Lightly trip it o'er the sward,
Gladsome hearts know no repining
Beauty brings its own reward.
—HENRY PURCELL (1658-1695)

SICK CLUB PROCESSION, STOKE ABBOTT, DORSETSHIRE

The first Friday in June

Stoke Abbott's Sick Club holds an annual procession and celebration for which the entire village turns out. Members of the club parade through the streets, following their leader, who carries an ancient silk banner.

The afternoon is devoted to all sorts of festivities, including sports and contests in the open; at inns and taverns people play the traditional games of Skittles and Shove-ha'penny.

Club processions or "walks" such as Stoke Abbott's are reminiscent of the picturesque trade or guild processions of early days. Later on, ceremonial walks to church (usually celebrated during Whitsun) became popular among benefit clubs, especially in Dorset, Berkshire, Somerset and other southern counties.

ST. BARNABAS'S DAY

June 11

St. Barnabas's Day once was a great feast throughout England. Churches were decorated with garlands of sweet-scented flowers;

81

fairs were held in many villages. Now the day is remembered chiefly for its quaint weather lore, which has come down through the centuries.

> Barnaby bright, Barnaby bright,
> The longest day and the shortest night

is a familiar rhyme, which certainly holds true for *Old* Barnaby Day,* falling as it does, on June 22.

> When St. Barnabas smiles both night and day,
> Poor Ragged Robin blooms in the hay,

is another saying, true of this time of year, when every damp meadow and overgrown ditch is adorned with the ragged loveliness of this humble wayside beggar.

For some reason Sussex children used to call the ladybug (lady-cow, or ladybird) Bishop Barnabee. A favorite fortune telling game among little girls was to place the insect on the back of the hand and then flip the little creature off with the rhyme:

> Bishop, Bishop Barnabee,
> Tell me where my wedding shall be,
> If it be tomorrow-day,
> Ope' your wings and fly away!

Macclesfield still holds Old St. Barnaby Fair. Formerly, this was such an important event to people from surrounding hamlets that all other dates were reckoned from the fair. "She's eighteen, come Barnaby," was typical of the way country folk computed ages.

MAY DAY FESTIVITIES, SHILLINGSTONE, DORSETSHIRE

Some time in June

For centuries, Shillingstone celebrated May Day on June 9 by dancing round a Maypole, said to be the tallest in all England. In olden times the pole was garlanded with flowers. In addition to

* *See* "England's 'Two' Calendars," p249.

82

the country dances, there was a May fair, with picturesque booths, coconut shies, tempting merchandise and all sorts of fairings.

Shillingstone's historic Maypole disappeared long before World War II; but the ancient tradition of the season is continued by annually decorating with wreaths of spring flowers another pole, which is set up on the village green. Nowadays there is no dancing to welcome the May, but the garlands remain up until they wither.

ELECTION OF THE "MORRIS MAYOR" OF OCK STREET, ABINGDON, BERKSHIRE

The Saturday nearest June 21

England's strangest election takes place in Abingdon's Ock Street, on the Saturday nearest June 21, when people vote for the "Morris Mayor." The pavement is the polling booth; an old soap case, the ballot box. Only residents of Ock Street may vote. And just to see no cheating is done, an Abingdon policeman guards the polls!

The old custom was revived in 1950, after a lapse of eleven years, as Tom Hemmings, sixty-three-year-old nephew of Henry Hemmings, the late eighty-nine-year-old "Mayor," was voted in by a majority of one hundred nineteen ballots. For well over a century the Hemmings family has claimed first place among Abingdon's famous morris men. As a boy, Tom Hemmings and his father danced before King Edward VII.

Following the election the dancers "chair" their Mayor, carrying him shoulder-high in a flower-trimmed rocker. They are preceded by a dancer who carries a black-horned ox head, which is wreathed with flowers and mounted on top of a tall pole. The procession parades the length of long Ock Street—which it may not leave— and then returns to its headquarters, "The 'appy Dick." But on the way there are many stops for refreshment from a certain apple-wood chalice, silver-bound, and decorated with a silver heart. According to tradition, this "glass" must be filled at the Warwick Arms, The Cock and Tree, The Crown and Thistle, The White Horse, and each of Ock Street's many other public houses; for if this is neglected the pub has no luck during the coming year! When I asked if his party did not get pretty gay before the night ended, the "Mayor" explained, "Oh no, there are so many of us, each man gets *only a tiny drop!*"

Abingdon's custom of parading Ock Street with black ox horns is said to have started in 1700, with a black-ox-roasting on Abingdon Bury. As the people gathered to eat the animal, a dispute arose concerning possession of the horns. The result was a fight between the two sides of town, the East represented by the Vineyard, the West by Ock Street. Finally, to make the fight really official, chalk lines were drawn at the foot of the Vineyard and outside Ock Street's Cock and Tree Inn. The winners were to be those who managed to drive their opponents over these lines. The weapons used in the ensuing battle were said to be torches, sticks, stones and bare fists. Ock Street won the horns, over the Vineyard. The traditional apple-wood drinking cup, according to one of my informants, "was made from a piece of the wood used to sock 'em." A member of the Hemmings family, moreover, was said to have participated in the dispute, and that is why the family has sustained an interest in the morris dancers throughout the years.

Abingdon has long been famous for its morris dance team, which ranks among the best in England. The six dancers are dressed in white shirts and wear the jingling bell pads and the customary "high-low" hats, ornamented with flowers, feathers and ribbons. The men are accompanied by an accordionist, sometimes by a drummer, and a Fool wth a bladder attached to a string. The Morris Mayor carries a coin collection box, suspended from his neck by a scarf or cord. Among the dances in the performers' repertoire are such old fashioned favorites as "A-Nutting We Will Go"; "The Curly-Headed Ploughboy"; "Jockeys to the Fair"; "Maid of the Mill" and "Sally Luker."

People say that morris dances—thought to have originated with the Moors and to have been brought to England in Edward III's reign—were performed in Abingdon three or four centuries ago.

JUNE

It is probable that these dances formed a part of the entertainment at the Feast of the Brotherhood of the Holy Cross, previous to the dissolution of the monasteries. Abingdon's first authentic mention of the morris dances is found in the churchwardens' accounts of St. Helen's Church for the year 1560, when the sum of one shilling was "payde for two dozsins of Morres belles," and seven years later, when eighteen pence was "payde for setting up Robin Hoodes Bower."

A madrigal of 1660 gives this description of the morris:

> Harke, harke, I hear the dancing
> And a humble Morris prancing,
> The bagpipes and the Morris bells
> That are not farre hence us tells;
> Come, let us goe thither
> And dance like friends together.

Rose Festival, St. Alban's Cathedral, Hertfordshire

June 22

St. Alban's Cathedral annually holds a Rose Festival on the anniversary of the martyrdom, in about 303, of St. Alban, Britain's first Christian martyr. In memory of a legendary incident in the saint's life, local school children gather roses and carry them in procession to St. Alban's Shrine,* where the flowers are dedicated at a special service. Later, women parishioners make the flowers into a solid carpet, which remains in the chapel throughout the week.

* The original gold- and gem-encrusted shrine disappeared in 1539, with the dissolution of St. Alban's Benedictine Monastery, which Offa, Saxon King of Mercia, founded about 793. Now, only the supporting marble pedestal remains. This remarkable fourteenth century masterpiece was shattered, people say, into over two thousand fragments. The pedestal, however, was rebuilt, bit by bit, and now occupies its original position in the center of St. Alban's Chapel. Aside from its fine sculptures, the pedestal is interesting because of the "healing holes," where many miraculous cures reputedly were effected, and the small niches where medieval pilgrims once placed votive offerings.

According to tradition, the shrine was built when an angel, appearing to King Offa in a vision, commanded him to find the saint's bones, which were buried in a forgotten tomb, and to place them where they might be venerated by the people. Offa found Alban's bones in Verulamium and subsequently built the shrine and monastery to house them.

85

Legend says that Alban was a Roman soldier, stationed in Verulamium, the thriving fourth century Roman-British town which occupied the site of the present St. Albans. Alban once sheltered Amphibalus, a persecuted Christian priest. The young soldier, who was converted and baptized, hid the priest while the Romans pursued him.

When the Roman soldiers finally came to his house demanding Amphibalus' arrest, Alban dressed himself in his guest's robes and offered himself in his place. At the same time Alban confessed that he, also, was a Christian. The Romans immediately tortured Alban and dragged him off to execution, on the hill where the cathedral now stands. Tradition says that roses, tumbling over a stone wall, were the last sight Alban looked upon before he was beheaded. In memory of this fact, people instituted the Rose Festival.

MIDSUMMER, OR ST. JOHN'S EVE

June 23

The festival of John the Baptist, the only Christian saint whose day commemorates the anniversary of birth, rather than death, superseded the pagan Feast of Beltan, held at the summer solstice.

On Midsummer Eve, bonfires once blazed from crags and hilltops all over England, in memory of the Druid Baal fires. Cattle driven between the fires were considered immune from disease throughout the year. Boys and girls joined hands and leapt through the embers, to symbolize growth of corn and abundant harvest.

Today, Midsummer fires still are lighted on Whalton hilltop, in Northumberland, and on the rugged moorland heights of Rough Tor and Brown Willy, in Cornwall. As in olden times, the villagers dance for hours about the blazing piles, stopping only when the last spark dies.

The Druids foretold the future, not only with fire, but with charms and incantations, some of which survive to modern times. Such popular Midsummer rites as sowing hempseed in the churchyard at midnight, dropping melted lead into water, or sticking a

86

black velvet cushion full of pins and then hanging it at night in a right-foot stocking—all for the purpose of glimpsing one's future mate—doubtless originated in early Druid divination practices.

Because of the supernatural forces which seemed to surround Midsummer Eve, rural people began to associate the night with superstitious belief in fairies, spirits and ghosts of the past. In Somerset, some claim that King Arthur's knights still ride silver-shod horses about Cadbury Castle,* while Sussex folk declare that the "beasts of the field go down on their knees at midnight," and "fairies dance in the Pharisees' † rings," on Tarberry Hill, at Harting.

Of Roman origin is the widespread Midland custom of well-dressing, often—but not always—performed on Midsummer Eve. This custom is said to go back to the ancient *Fontinalia*, the festival when people tossed garlands on the streams, and sought to propitiate the well spirits with flower offerings. Seneca referred to this custom (described below in its modern version) when he wrote:

"Where a spring rises, or a river flows, there should we build altars and offer sacrifice."

WELL-DRESSING FESTIVAL, BUXTON, DERBYSHIRE

June 23-27

Buxton has two wells of which it is justly proud. One is Upper Buxton's Well, in the Market Place; the other St. Anne's, in the Crescent. Every year hundreds of sick persons come from far and near to drink the curative waters and receive treatment in this beautiful Peakland resort. Starting on Midsummer Eve, there is an annual Blessing of the Waters ceremony, when Buxton's inhabitants

---

* Cadbury Castle (a British hill-fort of some thirty acres in area), near Sparkford, is claimed by many to be the legendary Camelot, where King Arthur held court. William Camden (1551-1623), British historian and antiquary, writes of a silver horseshoe which, in his day, was found at Cadbury Castle; so possibly the legend of silver-shod horses originated in fact.

† In Sussex dialect, *Pharisee* means *fairy*.

give special thanks for benefits their wells have brought them. Local artists decorate both wells with traditional flower mosaic pictures, representing a biblical theme, like the Pool of Bethesda, or illustrating a scriptural text, such as, "Man goes forth to his work and to his labour, until the evening."

Ceremonies start with an early-afternoon procession to the wells. Following a red-and-gold-uniformed band and young people's choir, comes the imposing Mace Bearer, resplendent in high silk hat and black uniform, and carrying the city's handsome silver mace. Next come local officials, the Mayor in his crimson fur-trimmed robe and gold chain of office, the Sheriff in gown and wig, and the officiating clergy.

Grouping themselves about the well, they hold a simple and impressive religious service. After appropriate Scripture readings and hymns, the waters are blessed and the Lord's Prayer and the national anthem are rendered. After the ceremony, the procession goes to the concert hall, in Pavilion Gardens, where Buxton's mayoress crowns a charming Festival Queen—actually, a May Queen—accompanied by ladies-in-waiting, attendants in long white frocks and tinsel crowns, and a multitude of pages and dancers. The festival ends with winding the Maypole on the terrace.

Buxton's first well-dressing took place little more than a century ago, when the Duke of Devonshire gave Upper Buxton a fountain, thus enabling townsfolk to draw water close at hand instead of fetching it from a distance. So grateful were the inhabitants, that they celebrated the event with merrymaking and rejoicing. Today's festival carries out the original tradition of thankfulness for the blessing of water.

In many Midland families, the art of making flower mosaics as well decorations has been handed down from father to son for generations.

JUNE

Well-dressings are observed in various Derbyshire towns and villages, including Tideswell,* Bakewell, Hope, Youlgreave,† Stoney Middleton‡ and Tissington.§ Since dates vary considerably from year to year, it is always wise to check the time of celebration before attending.

CEREMONY OF THE "FRESH PLUCK'T ROSE," MANSION HOUSE, LONDON

Midsummer Day, June 24

London's Lord Mayor annually receives a "Fresh Pluck't Rose" from the churchwardens of All-Hallows-by-the-Tower, in accordance with an old custom. Tradition claims that in the fourteenth century Lady Knollys, wife of the famous soldier Sir Robert Knollys, had a bow window erected in Seething Lane, without first asking permission of the City's authorities. The City consequently imposed an annual fine, or Quit Rent, to consist of "one Red Rose fresh pluck't from the garden." The ceremony, which lapsed for a time, was revived in 1924 by the Reverend P. B. Clayton. Since this date each Lord Mayor has received a rose in payment of the ancient fine.

SUMMER SOLSTICE SERVICES, STONEHENGE, WILTSHIRE

Midsummer Day, June 24

Each year several hundred people gather at Stonehenge, to witness the Midsummer Day sun rise and shine upon the Altar Stone of the so-called Druids' Circle.

* Revived in 1946. In 1950, the service was held at the end of June. In that year the principal screen, erected on the site marking the old village fountain, depicted the parish church.

† Held on Saturday nearest June 24 (1951). In 1829, spring water was piped to five public taps in the little village. All five are decorated for the well-dressing. Processions visit each one and services of prayer and thanksgiving are held in gratitude for the gift of water.

‡ Held August 5, 1950. *See* p 110.

§ Held on Ascension Day, 1951. *See* p229.

A "modern" Druid Order, founded in the fourteenth century and calling itself the Church of the Universal Bond, conducts the Summer Solstice dawn services. Druid Bards, dressed in white and purple robes, file into the Circle about an hour before dawn and perform their rites before the altar stone. Viewed from this point, the sun rises directly over the Hele Stone, some two hundred and fifty feet distant. According to tradition, this imposing megalith was brought from Ireland by the Devil.

As the sun appears over the horizon and shines upon the altar stone, the Chief Druid recites a prayer and consecrates the "sacrament," which is placed before him, surrounded by seven candles. He then sips wine from a silver cup. Each member of the Order, in turn, pours out and drinks a little wine, while facing the sun.

Spectators at the ceremony usually present a mixture of students, cyclists, hitchhikers from London, couples in evening dress, and a few youths, perhaps, who manage somehow to camp all night within the Circle, even though the official gates are closed.

Formerly the ceremony took place on June 21. Recently the date has been changed to Midsummer Day. The Stonehenge ceremony as it exists today is a revival, not a survival, of what once was an old folk observance.

WINSTER WAKES SUNDAY, DERBYSHIRE

The Sunday following Midsummer Day (June 24)

The old Norman market town of Winster annually celebrates its Wakes Feast* on the Sunday following Midsummer Day. Hundreds of visitors flock to the village to see the morris dancers perform. The morris men accompany the traditional King, Queen and Jester through the streets. Each dancer holds a white handkerchief, which he swings and throws with perfect timing, in unison with his comrades.

* See "Glossary of English Festival Terms," *Wakes Week*. p270.

90

Wakes Cakes, made from a traditional recipe,* and home-brewed ale or wine, are the festival foods Winster inhabitants offer to all visitors. In the words of an old local rhyme:

> At Winster Wakes there's ale and cakes,
> At Elton Wakes there's wenches,
> At Bircher Wakes there's knives and forks,
> At Wensley Wakes there's trenches.

RUSH-STREWING, WINGRAVE, NEAR AYLESBURY, BUCKINGHAMSHIRE

The Sunday following St. Peter's Day (June 29)

Each year, on the Sunday after June 29, the inhabitants of Wingrave cover the floor of their parish church with grass or hay, in fulfillment of an ancient bequest. Originally, rushes were used in the ceremony, which started many years ago on a dark and bitter winter's night. A woman lost her way in the fields outside Wingrave. She would have died of cold except for the sound of the village church bells, which finally guided her back to safety. Upon her death, the woman gratefully left a field to the parish church, stipulating that rushes should be cut from the land annually and strewn over the floor, as a thank-offering.

The custom of rush-strewing, which still is observed in a number of communities, originated in times when church and dwelling floors were made of earth. Since this surface was damp, cold and hard on the feet, rushes were used as a substitute for carpeting.

THE RUSH SERMON, ST. GILES'S CHURCH, FARNBOROUGH, KENT

The Sunday following St. Peter's Day (June 29)

A memorial Rush Sermon, so-named after a sixteenth century parishioner who reputedly was found dead in a bed of rushes, is preached annually in St. Giles's Church. Before the man died he

---

* For recipe, see Dorothy Gladys Spicer, *From an English Oven*, p58-59.

prepared a will, dated 1566, in which he bequeathed a sum of money for the sermon and specific benefits for the parish poor.

STREWING THE CHURCH WITH HAY, BRAUNSTONE, LEICESTERSHIRE

The Sunday following St. Peter's Day (June 29)

Braunstone is another parish to benefit from an old will, which provides an annual covering for the floor of the church.

On the Thursday preceding Feast Sunday (the Sunday following St. Peter's Day), a certain piece of ground known as "Clerk's Acre," in Holme Meadow, is mown. The parish clerk, who traditionally must fetch in the load of hay, spreads it by hand over the sanctuary floor. Any hay that happens to be left over is the clerk's perquisite.

JULY

Under the greenwood tree
Who loves to lie with me,
And tune his merry note
Unto the sweet bird's throat,
Come hither, come hither, come hither:
Here shall he see
No enemy
But winter and rough weather.

Who doth ambition shun,
And loves to live i' the sun,
Seeking the food he eats,
And pleased with what he gets,
Come hither, come hither, come hither:
Here shall he see
No enemy
But winter and rough weather.
—WILLIAM SHAKESPEARE. *As You Like It.*

CEREMONY OF DRINKING THE HEALTH OF SIR FRANCIS DRAKE, PLYMOUTH, DEVONSHIRE

Some time during June or July

Plymouth's city fathers assemble on a day in June or July to drink two toasts to Sir Francis Drake, their town's most distinguished citizen and one-time Lord Mayor. One toast is to the great man's memory, the other to his heirs, so that" . . . the descendants of him who brought us water, may never want for wine."

This custom commemorates Drake's continuous interest and effort in behalf of improving Plymouth's water supply. He contracted with the Corporation of Plymouth to bring the river Meavy to the town by constructing a watercourse some twenty-five miles in length.

93

This watercourse was built between December 1590 and April 1591. The despatch with which the task was accomplished doubtless gave rise to the legend that he rode to the upper banks of the Meavy, muttered a few magic words and then galloped back, a stream of water rushing behind his horse's heels. Plymouth people declare that Sir Francis brought their city the softest and purest water in the entire world!

Another legend illustrative of the city's great faith in Sir Francis's ability relates that he whittled a stick into Plymouth Sound, transforming every chip into a man-o'-war!

HAY-STREWING CEREMONY, GLENFIELD, LEICESTERSHIRE

The second Sunday following St. Peter's Day (June 29)

Glenfield, like Braunstone, observes its ancient Feast Day by strewing the floor of the parish church with hay.

VINTNERS' PROCESSION, THE CITY, LONDON

The Thursday following the Feast of the Translation of St. Martin (July 4)

On the Thursday following July 4, the Worshipful Company of Vintners of the City holds its annual procession. Starting from Vintners' Hall, in Upper Thames Street, the procession goes to the churches of St. James Garlickhythe, Garlick Hill, and St. Michael Paternoster Royal, in College Hill. The Vintners' colorful ceremonies have survived for over seven hundred years.

Two wine porters, dressed in top hats and white smocks, and carrying nosegays and besom brooms, lead off the procession. The porters still go through the motions of sweeping the road before the advancing dignitaries, who include a magnificently gold-and-black-liveried beadle, officials such as the stavesman, swan-warden and bargemaster, and the members of the Company of Vintners. The members—some dressed in traditional brown and mauve robes, some

94

in conventional morning attire—all carry herb and flower nosegays, which they sniff from time to time.

Both broom-men and nosegays commemorate an era when London's streets were filled with offensive garbage. The refuse had to be swept away, to prevent Company officials from slipping or soiling their fine robes of fur or velvet. The nosegays were smelled of frequently in those days, since the stench of the streets was otherwise unbearable.

According to court order of 1205, it was decreed that "... wine porters should sweep the roads with full besoms that the Master and his Wardens and Brethren ... slip not on any foulness in our streets." Furthermore, the aforesaid Master, Wardens and Brethren were to be provided with "... a nosegay of fine herbs, that their nostrils be not offended by any noxious flavours or other ill vapours."

The Company of Vintners was once one of the wealthiest and most influential of all livery companies. Today it has the right to export and import all spirits from and to the Port of London, or anywhere within the three-mile limit.

RUSHBEARING, MUSGRAVE, WESTMORLAND

July 6

Musgrave celebrates its annual Rushbearing with a charming floral procession, followed by an afternoon of village sports and country dances in the open.

Village girls, wearing pretty white frocks, weave elaborate flower garlands and carry them in procession to the parish church. There the young people cover the floor with rushes and fasten the garlands against the walls. Following a religious service, the entire community then gives itself over to gaiety and sports.

The gradual evolution of the original rushbearing custom into a floral festival is interesting. Rushbearing, which many people think began over a thousand years ago, is still carried out in a number of small communities.* The Westmorland Lake towns of Musgrave,

* Wingrave, p91; Farnborough, p91; Braunstone, p92; Old Weston, p98.

Ambleside, Grasmere and Warcop are particularly tenacious of the old custom which, until the mid-eighteenth century, was observed widely.

As the necessity for rush-strewing decreased with the invention of various kinds of floor coverings, the original ceremony, especially in the Lake towns, became little by little a floral festival, similar to the traditional May Day celebrations. Sports, songs, garland-weavings, folk dancing and processions all characterized these later rush-bearings.

In modern times rush-bearings and hay-strewings generally come in July and August, usually at any time between the Saturday nearest St. Anne's Day (June 26), and the Saturday nearest St. Oswald's (August 5).

St. Becket's Day

July 7

St. Becket's festival is little noticed nowadays, except in the Stogumber district, along western Somerset's Quantock foothills.

Thomas of London, better known as Thomas à Becket, was assassinated in Canterbury Cathedral, December 29, 1170. Two years later he was canonized. On July 7, 1223, the saint's relics were translated from the crypt to the magnificent shrine at the cathedral's east end.

"Bawming the Thorn," Appleton Thorn, Cheshire

Early in July

Appleton Thorn claims to have received its name from the ancient thorn which grows in the village and is protected by an iron railing. This aged tree, say the inhabitants, was slipped of Glastonbury's Holy Thorn.* Since "bawming" in Cheshire dialect means "adorning," villagers annually hold a pretty ceremony, called Bawming the

* *See* Glastonbury Thorn. p 11.

Thorn, to honor the sacred tree. The school children weave wreaths and garlands, which they carry in procession to the old tree. There, they decorate both tree and surrounding railing with floral offerings and then dance in honor of the thorn.

St. Swithin's Day

July 15

St. Swithin, Winchester's ninth century bishop, is held responsible for the weather of the forty days following his anniversary! There are many legends to explain the superstition. One is that the saint's last words to his fellow monks were, "Lay me where the feet of passers-by tread and the rains of heaven fall." Consequently, the brothers buried their beloved bishop outside the cathedral church.

About a hundred years later, according to one version, the friars decided to remove Swithin's body from its humble grave, and inter it more fittingly within the church. On July 15, the day set for the translation of the relics, a terrific storm arose, continuing for forty days. Believing that the storm indicated the saint's displeasure, the monks built a shrine in the churchyard, over the original place of burial. On July 15, 971, however, St. Swithin's remains finally were placed in a splendid tomb within the church, this time without disturbance by the elements.

Many weather rhymes and predictions have developed from the legend of St. Swithin. One of the best known, perhaps, is this verse of 1697, from *Poor Robin's Almanack:*

> In this month is St. Swithin's Day,
> On which, if that it rain, they say,
> Full forty days after it will,
> Or more or less, some rain distil.
> This Swithin was a saint, I trow,
> And Winchester's bishop also,
> Who in his time did many a feat.

HAY-STREWING, ST. SWITHIN'S CHURCH, OLD WESTON, HUNTING-
DONSHIRE

St. Swithin's Day, July 15

On parish Feast Day, Old Weston holds a hay-strewing in
St. Swithin's Church, to fulfill the terms of a curious will. A woman
of the parish once left a field to the church, on condition that the
tenant farmer should provide enough hay to cover the sanctuary
floor on St. Swithin's Day. The bounty was given, not so much for
the sake of the church, we are told, as to muffle the squeaking of the
parishioners' new boots, which were worn on this day!

LAMMAS FAIR, EXETER, DEVONSHIRE

The Tuesday before the third Wednesday in July

Lammas Fair, now scarcely more than a formality, always opens
at noon of the Tuesday before the third Wednesday in July.

The ceremonies which accompany the opening predate the Norman conquest.

Two sergeants-at-mace, starting from the guildhall, proceed
down High Street, accompanied by two men playing the fife and
drum. The sergeants carry a long pole, from which is suspended a
large stuffed white glove, decorated with flowers and ribbons. The
sergeants proclaim the fair at the four ancient gates of the city,
before returning to the guildhall, where the mayor announces
the event. According to the words of the historic Proclamation,
". . . Lammas Fair taketh its beginning from Twelve of the clock
of this present day and doth continue until Friday next Twelve of
the clock at noon of the same day (that is to say) two whole days
and two half days, making in the whole three days."

The glove, ancient symbol of the Crown's protection of the peace,
is hoisted up before the guildhall, where it remains for the fair's
duration.

The Lammas Fair proclamation contains many quaint clauses regarding the rights and powers of persons who come to buy or sell. Such persons are guaranteed against ". . . any molestation, arrests, attachments or other troubles whatsoever within the City of Exeter," save for ". . . Treason, Murder, Felony, Routs, Riots . . . or any acts whatsoever against His Majesty's peace, Crown and dignity." Persons are prohibited from selling goods except within the Fair and its precincts, or from placing ". . . any wares open in their shops out of the said Fair within the length and reach of any man's arm upon pain of the forfeiture of all such goods, wares and merchandizes so sold or set to sale or hanging in any house or shop within the reach of any man's arm as aforesaid." Furthermore, a Court of Pie Powder * originally was arranged at the guildhall. Both the mayor and the city officials were prohibited from dealing with any misdemeanors which could be handled by this court.

Once Exeter's Lammas Fair ranked as one of the West Country's most important fairs. Today it remains simply a historic link between the Exeter of Saxon and of modern times.

ST. MARGARET'S DAY

July 20

In modern England the festival that marks the martyrdom of St. Margaret of Cremona is remembered chiefly in weather prophecy and legend. The rains, often starting at this season, are called "Margaret's floods."

Legend says that while Margaret was in prison awaiting death, the Devil visited her as a dragon and swallowed her alive. Immediately, however, the dragon burst open, leaving Margaret unhurt.

---

* A Court of Pie Powder was attached to every Fair and Market of olden times, to render justice in all commercial disputes and injuries incident to the event. The term Pie Powder is derived from the French *pied poudré*, meaning "dusty footed," since plaintiffs came to Court from the Fair, their feet covered with dust. "Dusty foot" was the term popularly applied to medieval itinerant merchants. The description of Vanity Fair in Part One of *Pilgrim's Progress* gives an accurate account of a seventeenth century Court of Pie Powder.

A quaint custom, probably originating in this devil myth, grew up between the Somerset villages of Langford Budville and Thorne St. Thomas. The church bells of the first parish used to ring vigorously on Midsummer night, "to drive the Devil over to Thorne." Their rivals, the people of Thorne St. Thomas, retaliated by ringing their bells on St. Margaret's Day, to return the Devil to Langford!

St. James's Day

July 25

Popular tradition connects the day of the martyrdom of St. James with the opening of the oyster season. According to the well-known eighteenth century satirical poet:

> July, to whom, the Dog-star in her train,
> Saint James gives oysters, and Saint Swithin rain.*

An old saying that "He who eats oysters on Saint James's Day will never want for money," may mean that only those with money can afford them!

St. Christopher's Day Blessing, Church of St. Michael Paternoster Royal, London

July 25

On St. Christopher's anniversary, automobiles line up on College Hill outside the Church of St. Michael Paternoster Royal, so their occupants may receive blessings and prayers for protection from the hazards of the road.

St. Christopher, the third century saint who reputedly carried the Christ Child across the stream on his shoulders, is patron of all who travel.

* Charles Churchill. *Gotham.* 1764.

100

JULY

RUSHBEARING, AMBLESIDE, WESTMORLAND

The Saturday nearest St. Anne's Day, July 26

Ambleside, like Musgrave, observes its Rushbearing mainly as a children's festival, in which flowers and rushes are essential to the "bearings," or wooden frames on which many unique and beautiful designs are woven, and carried like standards.

During the ceremonies, the boys and girls take their bearings in procession to the market square, where they sing *The Ambleside Rushbearers' Hymn*, written by the Reverend Owen Lloyd (1803-1841), a former Ambleside curate and a friend of William Wordsworth:

> Our fathers to the House of God,
> As yet a building rude,
> Bore offerings from the flowery sod,
> And fragrant rushes strew'd.
>
> May we, their children, ne'er forget
> The pious lesson given,
> But honour still, together met,
> The Lord of Earth and Heaven.
>
> Sing we the good Creator's praise,
> Who sends us sun and showers,
> To cheer our hearts with fruitful days,
> And deck our world with flowers.
>
> These, of the great Redeemer's grace,
> Bright emblems here are seen!
> He makes to smile the desert place
> With flowers and rushes green.*

After singing in the square, the bearings are lifted and carried in procession to Saint Mary's Parish Church, where the children arrange them and attend a special service.

The annual ceremony, which commemorates, as a modern children's festival, the feasting and rejoicing of former days when

* Sung to the tune *Irish*.

fresh rushes were gathered and laid down on the church floor, is delightfully represented by a large mural in the rear of the church. The painting, which is by Gordon Ransom, depicts the events of the festival in four scenes—the Procession, the Hymn, Lifting the Bearings, and Placing the Bearings in Church.

According to Lakeland tradition, each boy and girl receives a piece of gingerbread on leaving the church after the service.

The bearings remain in the church over Sunday. On the Monday following, sports events are held and the children have a gala tea.

WAKES WEEK, ECCLES, LANCASHIRE

The last week in July

Eccles Wakes Week, famous in Elizabethan days for robust amusements, such as bull baiting, cock fighting and donkey racing, now is mainly a children's holiday. An outstanding feature of the event are the gala processions of children from various churches and Sunday Schools. Arrayed in their Sunday best, the boys and girls march through the streets, each group carrying its own special banner or insignia.

Eccles Cakes,* for which the town is famous, are the traditional Wakes Week treat, even though present shortages of essential ingredients greatly restrict their production at other times of year. The round pastries are made of flaky puff paste, filled with a delectable combination of currants and brown sugar.

* For recipe, see Dorothy Gladys Spicer, *From an English Oven,* p54-55.

AUGUST

Harvest home! harvest home!
We've ploughed, we've sowed,
We've reaped, we've mowed,
We've brought home every load.
Hip, hip, hip, harvest home!
—*Old Harvest Home Song*

LAMMAS

August 1

People think that Lammas, with its tradition of thanksgiving for the wheat harvest, originated in the early Anglo-Saxon rite called *hláfmasse*, or loaf mass, when priests consecrated loaves made from the first ripe wheat. To the Saxons, bread blessed at this ceremony held special potency against evil forces. This belief is proved by a fragmentary charm which has come down through the ages, to advise people to ". . . take from the hallowed bread which is hallowed on Lammas Day, four pieces, and crumble them on the four corners of the barn."

There are many who see the origin of Lammas in the Lamb Mass, once held on August 1, at the Cathedral of St. Peter in Vinculis, at York. On this festival each cathedral feudatory offered a lamb at High Mass.

Today, in rural churches throughout England, a sheaf of wheat and a loaf of bread (made, in olden times, from wheat of the first field to be reaped) are offered at the annual harvest thanksgiving.

The clergyman blesses both grain and loaf, with prayers for "weather to prosper the harvest, . . . bread for all the people, for . . . unity in labor," and "peace in our land and in all the world."

Formerly, Lammas was celebrated with numerous fairs. In modern times, the dates of many of these fairs have been changed to later in the season. This change is due, doubtless, to the Bank Holiday, which falls on the first Monday in August and is the accepted time for all kinds of trips and excursions.

In many places, Lammas is a popular term or rent day.

FLITCH OF BACON TRIAL, GREAT DUNMOW, ESSEX

August Bank Holiday Monday (First Monday in August) every second year (1955, 1957, etc.)

The Flitch, or Gammon, of Bacon Trial of Little Dunmow was a solemn event in fifteenth century England. Today, the ceremony, which is held in Great Dunmow every other year on the first Monday in August, is a farcical trial of married couples who swear to perfect conjugal happiness before a mock judge and jury, consisting of six spinsters and six bachelors.

Some think the custom originated with Robert Fitzwalter, a favorite of King John. Fitzwalter is said to have promised a flitch of bacon to any husband who could swear before the head of Dunmow Priory and assembled villagers that, for a year and a day, he had never repented his marriage.

History shows that claimants for the handsome prize were few in pre-Reformation days. Only three husbands seem to have qualified for the flitch!

The first recorded award was made in 1445 to Richard Wright, laborer of Bradbury, Norfolk. William Langland, however, writing in the *Vision of Piers Plowman*, about 1362, made the first reference to the custom in English literature:

Many a pair since the Pestilence have plighted themselves together
And the fruit that they bring forth is foul speaking,
Jealousy and joylessness and jangling in private.

They have no children but cheating and chopping themselves to pieces,
Though they go ride to Dunmow, unless the devil help them
To fetch the Flitch, they will fail to get it;
Unless both be foresworn, the bacon is another's.*

According to an interesting theory which I found recorded in notes † in the Little Dunmow parish church of St. Mary the Virgin, the flitch award may have originated in the ancient custom of "handfasting" or trial marriage for a year and a day. If the man and woman did not repent of their association in that period, the church formally recognized their union with legal marriage. The gammon was given as a reward and encouragement to handfasting couples, "to live together in harmony and to seek the church's formal blessing on their union, later on."

By the eighteenth century, winning the flitch was made more difficult because *couples,* rather than *husbands alone,* became applicants. Persons who swore solemnly to the authenticity of their claim before prior and townsfolk had to kneel down on two sharp-pointed stones in the churchyard. Later the couple was seated in a thirteenth century chair ‡ still preserved in the parish church and carried triumphally through the village. The last award was made on June 20, 1781, when Thomas Shakeshaft, of the parish of Wethersfield, weaver, and his wife came to demand the prize and received a gammon of bacon. The pair "knelt down on two bare stones," within the church, according to one account, and took the oath. Since the Shakeshaft year, the custom has been revived only in jocular vein in many parts of England and for many occasions.

Today's claimants take their oath before the mock jury. The farcical trial is conducted with many gay quips and great general hilarity. The flitch goes to the couple judged to be the happiest. The entire proceeding is a parody of the ancient custom. Little Dunmow Trial, suspended in 1939, has since been revived, and now is

* William Langland. *Vision of Piers Plowman.* Passus. ix, lines 195-203.

† Written by "G.I.R." in a lecture made to the Essex Archaeological Society.

‡ The "prior's chair," which has been variously dated from the twelfth to the mid-thirteenth centuries, is thought by some to be the end of a series of church stalls.

held in Great Dunmow on August Bank Holiday Monday rather than on Whit Monday, as formerly was the case.

Flitch trials are held in many places besides Great Dunmow. At a recent ceremony at Marlow, Buckinghamshire, a live pig was put up as the prize for the couple judged to have the happiest marriage, while at West Wickham, Kent, a couple took home a seven-pound piece of bacon which a Canadian packing firm flew across the Atlantic, accompanied by an additional five pounds to be divided between the two couples who were runners-up.

DOGGETT'S COAT AND BADGE RACE, RIVER THAMES, LONDON

August 1

"Waterman's Derby," known as Doggett's Coat and Badge Race, is held on the Thames, annually, on August 1. The racing course is approximately the distance of four and a half miles, between Old Swan Pier, at London Bridge, and Cadogan Pier.* Six young watermen who end their apprenticeship on this day row against the tide at the time when it runs strongest. The winner receives an orange coat and a badge (imprinted with the Hanoverian white horse), in addition to a ten-pound prize, and a pair of new breeches. Each of the other contestants is awarded six, five, four, three, or two pounds, respectively, according to the order of his arrival at the goal.

The contest originated in 1716 with Thomas Doggett, famous comedian and joint owner of Drury Lane Theatre, who wanted to commemorate the "happy accession to the throne of George I," on August 1, 1714.

When Thomas Doggett died, in 1721, he left a legacy, providing continuance "for ever" of the race he had established. According to the will, he left ". . . five pounds for a Badge of Silver weighing about twenty ounces and representing Liberty to be given to be rowed by Six young Watermen according to my Custom eighteen shillings

---

* Before 1875, the course ran to the Old Swan Inn, Chelsea. After the demolition of the Inn (now marked by Swan House, Cheyne Walk), the race terminated at Cadogan Pier.

for Cloath for a livery, whereon the said Badge is to be put, one pound one shilling for making up the said Livery and Buttons and appurtenances to it and thirty Shillings to the Clerk of Watermens Hall. All which I would have to be continued for every yearly, in Commemoration of his Majesty King George's accession to the British Throne."

The Fishmongers' Company, to which the actor belonged, now administers the terms of the will. An interesting painting of the first winner of the race may be seen in the Watermen's Hall in London.

PILGRIMAGE TO THE SHRINE OF OUR LADY, HASTINGS CASTLE, HASTINGS, SUSSEX

First Wednesday in August

The annual Catholic procession and pilgrimage to the crumbling shrine of Our Lady in the ruins of Hastings Castle dates back only to the beginning of the century. The chapel of St. Mary's, however, which is the pilgrimage objective, was a Catholic shrine before the Reformation.

The picturesque procession includes richly-vested clergy with church banners, surpliced choir boys, Children of Mary in white veils and blue cloaks, and little girls with light frocks and handfuls of fragrant posies. To the accompaniment of hymns of praise, red-sashed men of the Blessed Sacrament Guild bear, shoulder-high, the flower-adorned image of Our Lady of Ransom from the Church of St. Mary Star-of-the-Sea, up the hill to the ancient shrine.

The colorful pilgrimage, which now is observed each year, originated with Mr. Lister Drummond, who once saw a curious photograph of the ruined chapel on the hill. In the photograph, a trick of lighting revealed a statue of Our Lady. This circumstance immediately suggested to Mr. Drummond the idea of annually escorting a statue of the Virgin to the shrine, and of holding Catholic devotions in the chapel as in bygone years.

OLD ST. JAMES'S DAY

August 5

There are many who claim the oyster season begins on this day, rather than on July 25 (St. James's Day, New Style). The following verse from an old rhyme entitled *Oyster Day* proves it!

> Greengrocers rise at dawn of sun—
> August the fifth—come haste away!
> To Billingsgate the thousands run—
> 'Tis Oyster Day! 'tis Oyster Day!

RUSHBEARING, GRASMERE, WESTMORLAND

The Saturday nearest St. Oswald's Day (August 5)

Grasmere claims it is the *only* community where the rushbearing tradition has remained unbroken from ancient to modern times. The poet Wordsworth was largely responsible for keeping the custom alive in the mid-nineteenth century. Today the ceremony continues with much of its early charm.

On the Saturday nearest August 5, Feast Day of St. Oswald, Grasmere's patronal saint, boys and girls assemble in the peaceful churchyard where Wordsworth lies buried. As at Ambleside, the children carry flower garlands and rushes, which are woven into bearings of traditional designs. Such subjects may be chosen as St. Oswald's Hand, for example; a serpent on a pole; Moses in a basket of rushes. In addition, there are ecclesiastical emblems, such as crosses, triangles, crowns and many intricate symbols. A group of girls carries the "rush sheet," a locally-made piece of homespun linen, which is heaped with rushes.

Led by the vicar and a standard bearer with St. Oswald's banner, the children form in procession and perambulate the village before going to the church. While marching, the boys and girls sing *The Rushbearers' Hymn* * to the accompaniment of the village band.

* See also *The Ambleside Rushbearers' Hymn*, p 101.

During the church service which follows, everyone sings the traditional *Hymn for Saint Oswald*, which begins:

> As break of dawn on heathen gloom,
> Thy Saints, O Christ, like Oswald shine;
> A living light that scorns the tomb,
> And glows within a shrine.
>
> By him up-reared, the Cross far threw
> Its shadows on Northumbrian sod,
> A folk that only idols knew
> Stretched forth their hands to God.

and ends with this charming verse:

> To Thee, we keep these festal hours,
> Fragrant with rush from vale and mere;
> Thy sun wakes colour in our flowers,
> By Thee Thy Saints shine clear.

After the ceremony, during which rushes are strewn over the floor and garlands and bearings arranged at the altar and against columns and walls, each child receives a shiny new penny and a piece of Grasmere's famous gingerbread. The gingerbread shop is conveniently located just outside the churchyard!

The recipe for this traditional sweet—which is in reality a very rich ginger-flavored shortbread, with chopped candied orange peel added—is jealously guarded by both shops and housewives. After waiting almost two years, I finally obtained the following recipe which I have converted to American measurements:

Grasmere Gingerbread

(Traditional Recipe from Mrs. Ethel M. Abel)

> 1 cup butter
> 1 cup brown sugar (or more, if softer
>   gingerbread is desired)
> 1/4 tsp. salt

½ cup finely chopped candied orange
   peel, floured (or more, if desired)
1 tbsp. corn syrup
4 cups flour
1 tsp. soda
1 tsp. cream of tartar
1 tbsp. ground ginger

Cream together butter and sugar. Add syrup and mix thoroughly. Sift together flour, salt, soda, cream of tartar and ginger. Gradually work into the first mixture, together with the floured orange peel. The dough should be of a consistency to press lightly with the hand into a shallow baking tin.

Bake about an hour in a slow oven (275°F.) and cut into small squares or "fingers" while still warm.

The difficult part about Grasmere Gingerbread comes at the very end, for my informant sternly adds that it must "be kept a month before eating!"

As is customary at rushbearings in other parts of England, Grasmere devotes the Monday following to sports, Maypole dancing and a festive tea for the children.

WELL-DRESSING, STONEY MIDDLETON, DERBYSHIRE

August 5, or thereabouts

The Peakland village of Stoney Middleton celebrates one of Derbyshire's most colorful well-dressings. The date varies from one year to another. In 1949, it was held on July 30; in 1950, on August 5. This ceremony, like Buxton's, is an expression of thanksgiving for the two wells which supply the inhabitants with an unfailing source of pure water.

Mr. Ben Milner, a local laundry motor-van driver, is the well-dressing leader. In his spare time on winter evenings, Mr. Milner makes the preliminary sketches for his flower pictures. These plans he enlarges to blueprints on the back of wallpaper strips, which he hangs up in his living room.

Anyone in the village may assist Mr. Milner. Among his staunch helpers are the vicar, a quarryman, a local boot and shoe factory manager, a builder, and many others, including housewives and children. Stoney Middleton's well-dressing is a community affair.

A few days before the ceremony everyone goes out to woods and fields to gather the mosses, cones, flowers and lichen needed for the pictures, which represent such biblical scenes as the Good Samaritan, or Elijah being fed by the ravens.

The committee installs itself in the courtyard of Moon Inn, where large wooden boards are set up on trestles. Wet clay, applied to the boards, is smoothed down and leveled off.

Then Ben Milner lays down his blueprints and marks off his drawing on the clay with a tailor's tracing wheel. His assistants press in tiny birch or alder cones, beans or small leaves, to make the outline clear. The next step is to apply tree buds and mosses, green dock seeds and lichen, to make a mosaic frame for the picture. Last of all, comes the "petalling," an exact and tedious task, since each fresh petal must be inserted into the clay, like the overlapping scales of a green pine cone. Villagers gather thousands of flowers from fields and gardens. Each one contributes his choicest rose, his bluest larkspur. Everyone likes to lend a hand to the "filling in," which is like fitting together the missing parts of a jig-saw puzzle.

Ben Milner oversees the entire job. The finished pictures glow with color, like rich stained glass. When completed, many pairs of stout arms carry the pictures to the wells near the parish church, and there hoist them up into position. The boards must be handled with great care at this stage, because the clay cracks with the slightest jar, and then the work is ruined.

Stoney Middleton's well-dressing is a labor of love, in which every villager hopes to participate.

ENGLISH FESTIVALS

CRANHAM FEAST, CRANHAM, NEAR PAINSWICK, GLOUCESTERSHIRE

The second Monday in August

Each year Cranham, a tiny Gloucestershire hamlet composed of scattered farms and a square-towered church built on Norman foundations, celebrates its annual Feast Day. The church stands high on a hill, looking out over miles of blue-misted farm lands, rich with ripening grain, brilliant with wild flowers, and sweet with haunting songs of skylark and robin.

Feast Day starts Sunday night with a special service in the church, which has a pair of sheepshears cut into its ancient tower, and a churchyard whose yellow lichen-splotched stones rise crookedly among tall buttercups and crimson sorrel.

Monday is characterized by parades of local clubs and benefit societies, led by a brass band, and an evening feast at "Ye Royal William," which is tucked away in Cranham Woods beneath the earthwork known as Kimsbury Castle. After eating roast deer meat or other festive foods, the real fun starts with bowling for pigs, coconut shying, and dancing with pretty girls.

TAN HILL FAIR, NEAR DEVIZES, WILTSHIRE

St. Lawrence's Day, August 10

Tan Hill Fair, which is held every year on St. Lawrence's Day, once was an important event to shepherds from miles about. People say that this fair, which is held on the highest peak of the Wiltshire Downs, miles from the nearest village, originated in pagan times. As far back as anyone remembers, salt beef and beans have been Tan Hill's "fairings," or traditional fair-time foods.

MITCHAM FAIR, SURREY

August 12, 13, 14

Mitcham, proud of its ancient Fair charter which Sir Walter Raleigh, one-time citizen of the town, obtained from Queen Elizabeth, appoints a Charter Mayor to open their Fair with an enormous symbolic key.

Throughout the year, the "Chartered Fair Key of Mitcham" is kept locked up in the Town Clerk's office. The cherished relic is an extraordinary four-foot affair, cut out from wood, then gilded and gaily decorated.

At the opening ceremonies the Charter Mayor makes a speech, in the course of which he uses the key "to unlock the joys of the Fair." Then come the usual processions, more speeches and preliminaries, and the event is ready for three days of popular enjoyment. Brightly painted roundabouts*, shooting galleries, dart throwing and side shows—all are features of this ancient pleasure fair which draws annually crowds of trippers and holiday makers from many parts of England.

St. Bartholomew's Day

August 24

St. Bartholomew's Day, once an important fair day throughout England, now has fallen into general obscurity except for a few old folk customs and a good deal of entertaining weather lore.

Children of Sandwich, in Kent, still run to St. Bartholomew's Chapel on this day, to receive free gifts of currant buns. People say the custom originated in the twelfth century, when free food was distributed to the Canterbury pilgrims.

St. Bartholomew, as will be recalled, was the Apostle who was flayed alive, then crucified, head downward. His symbol became the knife, in allusion to the instrument of this torture. People claim Bartholomew was a simple husbandman, the son of a water drawer. Probably this is why popular fancy associates him with water.

> St. Barthelmy's mantle wipes dry
> All the tears that St. Swithin can cry

suggests that St. Bartholomew, whose feast day falls forty days after St. Swithin's, may deliver the countryside from wet weather.

* *See* "Glossary of English Festival Terms." p267.

113

KEAW YED WAKES FESTIVAL, WESTHOUGHTON, NEAR BOLTON, LANCASHIRE

The Sunday on or after St. Bartholomew's Day (August 24)

The cotton mill and coal town of Westhoughton annually celebrates its Wakes Week Festival (called in local dialect "Keaw Yed") on the anniversary of St. Bartholomew, its patron saint. The festival, which is about four hundred years old, dates back to the time when Westhoughton was a mere hamlet, with a chapel on the site of the present nineteenth century parish church, of St. Bartholomew. In those days, Westhoughton's mother church was at Deane, Bolton.

In early times the Wakes was predominantly religious in character. Today, merrymaking, feasting and secular amusements are the main features of the celebration. According to Whittle's *History of Lancashire*, it is recorded that ". . . there used to be a grand rush-bearing, which was carried on by the people here similar to those at Bury, Whalley, and other mother churches, accompanied by a procession of pipe and tabor, and the richest household plate fixed upon a cart filled with rushes, for the church at Deane. The horses were bedizened with ribbons, the old rushes from the pews were interred annually, and fresh ones procured in September (St. Augustine's tide)."

In 1948 and 1949, local authorities tried to revive the religious aspect of Westhoughton's Wakes by a church vigil on St. Bartholomew's Eve and a rushbearing, with schoolchildren as the principal attraction in a long procession led by the vicar and choir, which walked round the town and finally ended at the church with special services. The old custom of giving each child "rush money," at the close of the sermon (so they might enjoy some of the material joys of the day) was also revived. By the following year, however, the festival once more had lapsed chiefly into jollification and the traditional rushbearing was discontinued.

114

The Keaw Yed (meaning cow's head in Lancastrian dialect) is typical of the merriness and tongue-in-cheek good humor which characterize any real northern "do." The mere mention of the words produces a gusty guffaw and a torrent of amusing anecdote from any Westhoughton resident. When asked how the town's patronal feast ever got such a nickname, my informant said with twinkling eyes and solemn face:

"Our annual Wakes commemorates the time when the farmer's cow got her head stuck in the fence. So the farmer, unable to budge the head, dispatched the farm boy to the house for a saw. With this, he calmly sawed off the poor creature's head, because he was too stupid to saw the gate!"

"It makes a good laugh," he added. "And our parish church tower is decorated on the four sides with a cow's head cut into the stone."

Because Lancashire folk enjoy a joke and have an eye to business, too, local hotels before the war portrayed the legend of the farmer and his cow in tableaux.

"It used to bring in hundreds of visitors to our town from out-lying areas," according to a newspaper editor.* "We can afford a good laugh at our expense, provided we're making some money out of it!"

"Actually there is a far more probable story of the name 'Keaw Yed,' " he continued. "About the time of the Napoleonic wars (1815) some of the well-to-do are believed to have donated a cow to be publicly roasted and given to the poor. Bonaparte was burned in effigy, and the distribution took place. There was apparently some rivalry between two sections of the district, the 'Lower Siders' (from Daisy Hill, a village in the present urban district) and the 'Chapel Moorers' who lived in the vicinity of the chapel, now the town center. The relic of the feast—the head of the cow—became a sort of battle standard and the two factions had what is known in Lancashire as a 'real dust up' before the Chapel Moorers eventually

* Mr. H. Watkinson, assistant editor and manager of Horwich and Westhoughton *Journal.*

won the day, the victors then being scornfully dubbed 'Keaw Yeds' by their Daisy Hill rivals."

Lancashire people know how to cook and love to eat good food, so, as might be expected, there has from early times been no lack of tasty Wakes Week fare. Harland and Wilkinson, writing *Lancashire Folk Lore,* in 1882, state that ". . . at the annual feast, or Wakes, there is a singular local custom of making large flat *pasties* of *pork.*" Another writer, of the early twentieth century, declares this to be ". . . a recent innovation, not more than forty years old at most. Previous to that, many people made furmoty porridge, made from new wheat, sweetened and very palatable."

"Furmoty porridge" has not been seen in the editor's day, but pork pies have. Recent shortages, he explained, made it impossible to get the real thing nowadays, the only kind he has heard about having come from tins! Many people compromise by making chicken pies, or pies made with a combination of chicken and beef, and inside they often bake a tiny china doll about one inch long—why he has never discovered.

Brandy snaps are another delicacy as typical of Westhoughton Wakes as of Nottingham Goose Fair, Abbots Bromley's Wakes, and many other festival occasions. These paper-thin wafers are rolled up while warm into small hollow cylinders which are crisp and delicious with tea or without.

Keaw Yed Wakes weekend is a great holiday and still draws big crowds from surrounding towns. Everybody is "imbued with the idea of making merry," according to my informant, and people look forward from one year to another to eating brandy snaps and feast-day pasties!

PLAGUE SERVICE, EYAM, DERBYSHIRE

The last Sunday in August

Each year the people of Eyam hold an open air service in Cucklet Dell, outside their village, in memory of the plague victims of 1665.

A procession consisting of clergy, standard bearers, choir and band, forms in early afternoon at Eyam's parish church, which has existed since the year 1150. Singing, the little group slowly marches along the rutty, limestone-walled road, which zigzags through the meadows and pastures leading toward the Dell. Hundreds of people, including villagers, cyclists, hikers, parents with babies in "prams," and tourists with clicking cameras, press back from the narrow road to let the procession pass. Then they, too, drop into line and reverently follow up the steep roadway to the sanctuary in the hills.

"Cucklet Church," with sky for roof and natural rock for pulpit, is the spot where the procession halts. The clergy and musicians take their places in the center of the Dell; worshippers seat themselves quietly on the grassy slopes which rise in a natural amphitheatre from the central plateau.

On the sunny August day I attended the service, I thought that the congregation—numbering about three thousand—must be very much like the multitude that gathered on the Mount over nineteen hundred years ago to listen to the words of Jesus. Rarely have I witnessed a more reverent group. Now and then a mother rose to soothe a restless baby, a wild bird burst into song, or a mongrel pup gently nuzzled his master's shoulder. No disturbing sight or sound marred the beauty of the simple sermon which recalled the purpose of the gathering:

While the Great Plague raged in London, Eyam, cut off though she is from the rest of England by the rugged Pennine Hills, eventually fell victim to the dread disease. People think the germ may have arrived in a box of clothes from London. Be that as it may, the plague soon swept the village with unrelenting fury. Although death wiped out family after family, the heroic selflessness of Eyam's people will never be forgotten.

The inhabitants, inspired by their Vicar Mompesson, preferred isolation to seeking outside help and thus endangering neighboring hamlets. Consequently, everyone agreed to having medical and food supplies left at a point well outside the village, where they could be collected and brought back.

117

Mompesson helped his rapidly dwindling flock tirelessly, exhorting his people to steadfastness, encouraging them to fight. Eventually, however, the disease became so virulent that the vicar, fearing infection to surviving villagers, refused longer to hold services in the parish church. Instead, he led them up into the hills to this spot, south of Eyam. Here, where hundreds pay annual tribute to the plague victims and the thirty-five lone survivors, Mompesson preached nearly three hundred years ago.

> O God of our forefathers, mighty and holy;
> To Thee did they cry in their hour of need;
> Thy pity extend to the poor and the lowly.
> O hear us and help us, for mercy we plead.*
>
> With dark clouds around them, Thy countenance hiding,
> They trusted in Thee, to Thy Word they gave heed;
> May faith never fail, though we see not Thy guiding,
> O hear us and help us, for mercy we plead." *

Thus sing three thousand voices, led by the village band.

* *The Plague Hymn*

SEPTEMBER

September, when by custom (right divine)
Geese are ordained to bleed at Michael's shrine.*
—CHARLES CHURCHILL (1731-1764)

BARNET FAIR, HERTFORDSHIRE

September 4, 5 and 6

Barnet's three-day fair is famous for its trading of horses, cattle and sheep, as well as for the variety of its "fairings." These include such delicacies as oysters, cockles, whelks, fish-and-chips, and "minerals." Barnet Fair also is noted for roundabouts † and palmists, pickpockets and pretty girls!

ST. GILES'S FAIR, OXFORD, OXFORDSHIRE

The Monday and Tuesday after the Sunday
following St. Giles's Day (September 1)

St. Giles's Fair, celebrated with scarcely a break for over eight hundred years, existed before Oxford University itself.

Thousands of visitors annually attend this pleasure fair, the only remaining one of five great fairs once held in Oxford. The grounds usually extend along St. Giles's Street to Martyrs' Monument, occupying the lands near Balliol and St. John's Colleges.

The fair features many kinds of sports and popular amusements. Dodgem cars, gaily painted roundabouts, swing-boats, all sorts of holiday foods and interesting merchandise characterize this famous old fair, which attracts visitors from throughout Oxfordshire and the surrounding counties.

* This couplet is a humorous reference to the traditional eating of roast goose on Michaelmas Day (September 29). See p 136.
† *See* "Glossary of English Festival Terms." p267.

THE HORN DANCE,* ABBOTS BROMLEY, STAFFORDSHIRE

*The first Monday following the first
Sunday after September 4*

At Abbots Bromley, a small Norman village close to Needwood Forest, the ancient Horn Dance is annually performed. The dance with its elements suggesting both forest and chase is the traditional feature of the hamlet's Wakes Monday celebration. Wakes Monday, the day after Wakes Sunday (always the first Sunday following September 4) is all that remains now of the original three-day Old St. Barthelmy Fair.

The Horn Dance is so old that its beginning is little more than a matter of conjecture. There are many popular theories about it. One local legend is that the dance originated in Norman times and commemorates the granting of certain hunting rights in Needwood Forest. Another speculation is that the stag horns the dancers carry indicate success in the chase.

Regardless of its past, the modern Horn Dance starts about eight o'clock on Wakes Monday morning when the performers meet at the parish church of St. Nicholas. The vicar, under whose supervision the dance properties are kept, greets the men in Hurst Chapel, where the reindeer horns which give the dance its name are hung throughout the year.

The men, who range in age from twelve to past fifty, include local farmers, laborers and artisans. There are a dozen characters in the team, six who carry the reindeer horns, a hobby horse, a man-woman who takes charge of collections and is known as Maid Marian, a Fool with an inflated bladder on a stick, a diminutive archer with a bow, a musician with a concertina, and a boy with a triangle suspended from his neck. These instruments were substituted at the turn of the century, the vicar told me, for the pipe and tabor originally used. At that time the character of some of the performers also was altered.

* The ceremony is described as I saw it in 1950. Variations in costume and performance are likely to occur from one year to another.

120

When everything is in readiness, the vicar blesses the troop. Trimly dressed in new sixteenth-century-style green and brown foresters' costumes and new hand-knitted green stockings (the costumes were made in London "professionally" and the men are paying for them gradually) the men perform a brief dance outside the church door, and then start toward Bagot Park on their rounds of the parish boundaries. The men stop to receive refreshment at the various farms. By late afternoon they will return to dance in the market square.

It is cold and drizzling now as our little knot of spectators gathers on the green near the Goat's Head to watch for the men's return. At last we glimpse them, coming down the lane. They are tired and footweary as they trudge along and finally set down the horns for a few minutes' rest.

Already the men have gone fourteen miles and danced at many farms, Hobby Horse tells me. He is past fifty. *His* family has participated in the Horn Dance for four hundred and thirty years, he tells me gravely. He wears a flat brown tam o' shanter, green leggings and a voluminous green-trimmed brown cape, which drapes over the heavy iron hobby horse frame. The animal's head emerges —maneless, earless, with sagging jaws that no longer snap when the string is pulled. The horse is old and decrepit, but for all that, greatly beloved. Little children pat him affectionately and stuff the aged mouth with grass, which his rider, even when capering, miraculously manages to keep from spilling to the ground.

Now the musicians take up their places at the roadside. The dancers lift the heavy horns. Although the peeling paint reveals traces of many colors, three pairs of horns are now white, three black. The men with the white horns have green stockings and jerkins; the black have green stockings and brown jerkins. Both groups have red and gold vests and green brocade breeches which someone told me were made from the vicarage curtains.

The antlers are of great antiquity. Local legend says they are petrified, having come from a breed of domesticated reindeer—now extinct in England—which the Norsemen imported centuries ago!

Each antler set is mounted on a short wooden stick. As the dance begins, the men hold the sticks high against chests, easing one side of the horns against their shoulders. The burden is heavy, since the lightest set weighs over sixteen pounds, the heaviest over twenty-five.

The dancers step out in single file, Horn Men first, Hobby Horse, Maid Marian and the Fool following; last of all, the little archer. He is neat and dapper in green shirt, breeches and stockings, red jerkin and brown tam. The Fool swings his stick and bounces the bladder toward the spectators.

The men's faces are immobile as the procession heads up the village street in a serpentine line. Suddenly the leader turns inward and describes a loop by passing between the second and third man. The others follow. Then the six deermen face each other in sets of three, white antlers on one side, black on the other. The other performers go to the sidelines. Raising the horns close to their faces, the white stags surge forward, charging the black stags. The little archer snaps his bow in time with the accordion accompaniment of such tunes as *Yankee Doodle,** *John Peel,* and *Capri.* The boy with the triangle stresses the music by lustily striking his instrument with a piece of metal. Perhaps traditional tunes once accompanied the dance and vanished long ago, along with the original tabor and pipe. The dance is repeated several times.

Throughout the performance, 'Obby 'Oss cavorts and prances. Maid Marian, in blue tunic and yellow shirt, moves in and out among the appreciative watchers, lined up along the market place. He carries a long-handled broken collection ladle, nowadays but a symbol of the jingling box suspended from his neck.

* *Yankee Doodle,* the well-known folk song, which many Americans claim as their own and which played such an important role during the American Revolution, is believed to have originated in England. The tune, familiarly known in connection with the old nursery rhyme, "Lucy Locket lost her pocket, Kitty Fisher found it," is said to have been first used as an accompaniment to a Cavalier jingle in ridicule of Cromwell. The words went, "Nankie Doodle came to town." A similar tune is found in Holland, Spain and Hungary.

During Revolutionary Days, English soldiers sang this song in derision of the Yankees; the Yankees, on the other hand, adopted the catchy tune and used it as an accompaniment to the surrender of Cornwallis at Yorktown.

SEPTEMBER

The dance ended, the men gather quickly under shelter of the ancient oak-beamed butter market, where their womenfolk pass out thick mugs of steaming tea. In a few minutes, despite cold and drizzle, the dance will continue. The fun goes on until about eight o'clock in the evening, when the men return horns * and regalia to the Parish Church, and then repair to the Goat's Head, to count their collections and receive well deserved refreshment and rest.

Abbots Bromley is by no means dull tonight, even when the performers go indoors. In the village hall there is folk dancing, and down the dark lane a pleasure fair, with roundabouts, shooting galleries, and "fair rock,"—sticks of white candy coated with bright pink sugar, costing "ninepence and no points!" I win a prize at a coconut shy and have my pick of dolls, ashtrays and dusty knick-knacks.

In every rose-covered cottage there are special treats tonight of large round scalloped Wakes cakes and crisp brandy snaps, which generations of villagers have eaten when the deermen dance.

Next morning I stop by the local bakeshop to get some feast day cakes. The proprietor shakes his head, sadly. He made up thirty tins yesterday. He is quite sold out. "But come inside," he gently urges. "I will give you my recipe and tell you just how to make them."

We sit down in the small tidy room adjoining the shop. He brings out the work book of formulas, and I write down his directions for the traditional

Abbots Bromley Wakes Cakes

4 lbs. cake flour
½ oz. baking powder
½ oz. salt
1½ oz. ground mixed spice
2 lbs. butter

* A complete replica of the Horn Dance regalia—the work of a local craftsman —is on permanent exhibition at the London headquarters of the English Folk Dance and Song Society, Cecil Sharp House, 2 Regent's Park Road, London N.W. 1.

123

Rub all together to form a paste. Then mix together:

1½ lbs. sugar
7½ oz. eggs

Combine thoroughly the first and second mixtures. Roll out on lightly floured board. Cut out with a 3½" scalloped cutter. Bake in a hot oven (400°-425° F.) until golden brown and dust with sugar.

Abbots Bromley Brandy Snaps

2 lbs. all-purpose flour
1 lb. butter

Rub these ingredients together until they are like meal. Then mix together:

2 lbs. molasses
3½ lbs. sugar
1 oz. ground ginger
5 oz. water

Combine first the butter and flour, then the molasses, sugar, ginger and water. Combine the two mixtures. Wet the hands and knead the dough into a cylinder. Pinch off pieces of dough the size of a walnut and place 4 to 5 inches apart on heavily greased tins. Bake at 380°-400° F. until tinted brown, but not too hard. Remove from oven. When the snaps *begin* to cool, loop over a wooden stick, or a cornucopia mold. When cold, store in tightly closed tins. Before serving, fill with whipped cream.

Before leaving Abbots Bromley at noon, a village woman invited me to her cottage. She served "elevenses"—hot coffee and ginger snaps—and pressed a small brown paper parcel into my hand. Mystified, I opened the paper. Inside were three sugar-topped, scalloped Wakes cakes!

"They are all we have left," my hostess explained shyly. "Just before leaving the confectioner's shop this morning, I heard you ask for Wakes cakes. Please take these. Perhaps you'll eat them when you get on the train!"

WIDECOMBE FAIR, WIDECOMBE-IN-THE-MOOR, DARTMOOR, DEVON-
SHIRE

First Tuesday in September

Widecombe (or Widdecombe) Fair is so old that nobody knows when it started. It still provides a flourishing opportunity for buying and selling of sheep, cows and horses, including the famous Dartmoor ponies.

Long ago, this song was well known. It tells about Thomas Pearce, who was asked to lend his old gray mare to go to the Fair, and how the ghost of the unfortunate mare, "gashly white," still appears "all along, down along, out along lee":

Widdecombe Fair

Tom Pearce, Tom Pearce, lend me your grey mare
   All along, down along, out along lee,
For I want for to go to Widdecombe Fair,
   (*Chorus*) Wi' Bill Brewer, Jan Stewer, Peter Gurney
     Peter Davy, Dan'l Whiddon, Harry Hawk,
     Old Uncle Tom Cobleigh and all.
     Old Uncle Tom Cobleigh and all.

And when shall I see again my grey mare?
   All along, down along, out along lee,
By Friday soon or Saturday noon,
     Wi' Bill Brewer, Jan Stewer, etc.

Then Friday came and Saturday noon,
   All along, down along, out along lee,
Tom Pearce's old mare hath not trotted home,
     Wi' Bill Brewer, Jan Stewer, etc.

So Tom Pearce he got to the top of the hill,
   All along, down along, out along lee,
And he seed his old mare a-making her will,
     Wi' Bill Brewer, Jan Stewer, etc.

125

So Tom Pearce's old mare, her took sick and died,
 All along, down along, out along lee,
And Tom he sat down on a stone and he cried,
  Wi' Bill Brewer, Jan Stewer, etc.

But this isn't the end of this shocking affair,
 All along, down along, out along lee,
Nor though they be dead, of the horrid career
  Of Bill Brewer, Jan Stewer, etc.

When the wind whistles cold on the moor of a night,
 All along, down along, out along lee,
Tom Pearce's old mare doth appear gashly white,
  Wi' Bill Brewer, Jan Stewer, etc.

And all the long night be heard skirling and groans,
 All along, down along, out along lee,
From Tom Pearce's old mare, in her rattling bones,
  And from Bill Brewer, Jan Stewer, Peter
   Gurney
  Peter Davy, Dan'l Whiddon, Harry Hawk,
  Old Uncle Tom Cobleigh and all
  Old Uncle Tom Cobleigh and all.

THE SHERIFF'S RIDE, LICHFIELD, STAFFORDSHIRE

*Feast of the Nativity of the Blessed
Virgin Mary, September 8*

The ceremony known as the Sheriff's Ride has been carried out for centuries, in accordance with terms of Queen Mary's Charter of 1553, which created Lichfield a city and county separate and distinct from Staffordshire. This charter (one of Lichfield's six charters of incorporation) ordered that a sheriff be elected annually. The citizen so chosen must accept the office, on pain of fine, imprisonment, and exclusion from city privileges. He must, moreover, perambulate Lichfield's boundaries each year, on the Feast of the Nativity of the Blessed Virgin, to see that they are intact, and that none of the city's boundary stones have been improperly moved.

126

Some time during August preparations for the annual ceremony begin. The under-sheriff inserts an advertisement in the local papers, inviting citizens to accompany the sheriff on his annual rounds. At ten o'clock on the morning of September 8, the sheriff, his lady and party are honored at the guildhall, where refreshments are served and toasts drunk to the sovereign and the royal family.

At about eleven o'clock the sheriff and his party start out on horseback, proceeding to ride about the twenty-four miles of the boundaries of the City and County of Lichfield. The cavalcade rides through the old narrow streets, down winding country lanes, along flower-bordered bridle paths, across broad flat pastures, rough stubble fields and golden corn lands. Now and then a pause for refreshment is made at certain public houses which for generations have cherished the honor of welcoming the horsemen on their annual rounds.

Horse racing is a feature of the afternoon entertainment. Toward evening the sheriff and his party return to Lichfield. They are met by the city sword bearer and mace bearers, who ceremoniously escort them back to the guildhall. There the waiting townsfolk greet their sheriff with three rousing cheers.

HOLY-CROSS, OR HOLY-ROOD DAY

September 14

Holy-Cross, or Holy-Rood Day, commemorates Constantine's miraculous vision of the Cross, in 312 A.D., when he was about to fight Maxentius. The day is important in rural weather lore, and popular for village feasts, wakes and revels. Most communities observe the day on the Old Style date of September 25.

"The Devil goes a-nutting on Holy-Rood Day," is an old proverb, for this holy day once was the accepted time for young people

127

to gather nuts. An early seventeenth century play refers to the custom in the following lines:

> This day, they say, is called Holy-rood day,
> And all the youth a-nutting gone.

PIG'S FACE FEAST, AVENING, NEAR STROUD, GLOUCESTERSHIRE

The Sunday following Holy-Cross Day
(September 14)

People say that Avening's Pig's Face Feast originated on Holy Cross Day, September 14, 1080, when Queen Matilda, wife of William the Conqueror, held a great feast at the consecration of the parish Church of Holy Cross.

There are many legends concerning the origin of Pig's Face Feast. The one current in the village centers about the Norman capital on one of two twisted pillars at the main church doorway. A tale of love and hate, violence and remorse, is told in the curious carving which shows two lion cubs facing each other, with bodies uniting in a single head.

The legend goes that before Avening Manor came into the possession of William the Conqueror, it belonged to Brictric, Lord of Gloucester, whose ancestors were kings of Mercia. Edward the Confessor sent this young man to the court of Flanders. There he met Matilda, who later became the wife of William the Conqueror.

Matilda fell madly in love with Brictric, we are told, but her passion never was returned. Scorned, humiliated, and seething with black revenge, she finally wed William. The Queen's hatred toward Brictric knew no bounds. First she had him dispossessed of his ancestral lands. Then she caused him to be thrown into Worcester prison. Finally she ordered his death.

At last, Avening folk claim, remorse succeeded revenge. Queen Matilda built their church as an act of penance, in the very place where Brictric had once ruled as lord of the manor. As if to remind herself of her love and passion, the Queen had carved in stone above the twisted column two young lions. The sculpture represented Matilda's pets. Brictric had seen them often thus, lying with overlapping heads and looking as if the two creatures had only one head. Matilda, in her determination to win Brictric's affection, once had this same motif carved on a gold ring. She cast a spell on it "to bind Brictric's love," and then dispatched it to the young ambassador, who, nevertheless, remained untouched.

Avening's church was completed on September 14, Holy Cross Day. In celebration, the Queen is said to have proclaimed a boar's head dedication feast, to which she invited the Archbishop of Canterbury, prelates, nuns, and distinguished Norman clergy. She also had masses said for the soul of the murdered Brictric.

The wild boars for the feast were slain in Avening Forest. The animals were so delicious, roasted, that generations of Avening folk have celebrated their church dedication by eating the same succulent meat.

Today the legend of the wicked queen is kept alive by re-enacting episodes from the first Pig's Face Feast. Following a seven o'clock evening anniversary service in the church, villagers go to Memorial Hall, where a two-shilling ticket admits them to a scene reminiscent of an eleventh century banquet. Trestle tables down the length of the hall are decorated with fruits and lighted candles. A stately procession, headed by a beautiful young girl as Queen Matilda, a Cardinal, Archbishop and visiting churchmen—all in period costume—slowly makes its way to the high table. On the table, which is spread with a scarlet cloth decorated with the golden fleur-de-lis of France, stand tall silver candlesticks, loaned by Avening Manor.

At last the villeins bring in the boar's head on a large charger. The feast begins—a simple one in these days, but nevertheless a feast—consisting of fruit and pig's face sandwiches. The meal is followed by a concert, an entertainment, or perhaps a play, to commemorate the founding of Avening's church nearly nine hundred years ago.

Nor is Pig's Face Feast forgotten at village public houses. Among them, Cross Inn reported, in 1951, that "six persons worked seven hours on Feast Sunday," to cut sixteen hundred pig's face sandwiches for patrons, including some three hundred customers and elderly folk too infirm to come to the inn. Bell Inn, on the other hand, which proudly displays a mounted boar's head in the bar, claims the proprietor and his wife "cut thirty loaves into feast day sandwiches" for customers, both present and absent.

Thus, the ancient Feast Day custom, interrupted by World War II and revived in 1948, still lives in the charming village of Avening, which lies in the heart of the Cotswold hills.

WORCESTER GREAT FAIR, WORCESTERSHIRE

Nativity of the Virgin, September 19 (Old Style)

Worcester Great Fair, coming as it does after harvest, is popular among farmers from many of Worcester's outlying districts. Once an important pleasure fair, but now chiefly concerned with business, Worcester Great Fair is mainly significant nowadays for its trade in farm stock, hops and cheeses.

CLIPPING THE CHURCH, PAINSWICK, GLOUCESTERSHIRE

First Sunday after the Nativity of the Virgin, September 19 (Old Style)

Painswick celebrates the patronal feast of St. Mary's, its fifteenth century parish church, with a "clipping" ceremony which, some think, originated in pre-Christian pastoral ceremonies to protect the lambs from wolves. The Church of St. Mary's, which stands on the site of an earlier Norman sanctuary, is famed throughout England for its aged clipped yews, traditionally numbering ninety-and-nine, but being about a hundred and five by actual count. The word "clipping" has nothing to do with cutting the trees, however, but derives its origin from the old English meaning, to "embrace." For on the annual Feast Sunday, local children express reverence and affection for their church by *embracing* it in this charming manner:

A procession of Sunday School children wearing posies and chaplets of flowers forms at the church to the "ting-tonging" of the bells. Vicar, churchwardens, choir, village band and congregation all join the children who march around the churchyard and finally assemble at the belfry tower. There everyone steps back except the boys and girls, who "clip" hands about their church and, facing it, sing the hymn which ends:

> O, that I had wings of Angels
> Here to spread and heavenward fly;
> I would seek the gates of Sion
> Far beyond the starry sky.

As the children sing, "they step backward, spreading out their arms like wings," proudly explained Brother Michael, who trains the boys and girls. Then they sweep forward, standing close together and still holding hands tightly clasped. "Clipping" is thus used in the Shakespearean sense of "embracing," for the young people, by surrounding the church with joined hands, are expressing their love for the house of God.

Hundreds of years ago, according to village lore, this feast, of heathen origin, was celebrated by eating "puppy dog pies."

"What were they?" I inquired.

"Well, in *our* family they were *hare* pies!" an elderly woman declared. A small china puppy always was baked in the crust, she went on; but her puppy—a prized possession of the last fifty-five years—she broke just the other day and threw out all the pieces!

Nowadays people continue to get china puppy dogs* for Feast Sunday, but they come, just a few each year, from the potteries in Stoke-on-Trent. The old ones are hard to come by in modern times.

* China dogs are still baked in Painswick's Feast Sunday pies. Although all sorts of stories, like the one described, are invented to explain the custom, some scholars suggest the china dogs may represent *real* animals, which once were sacrificed at the early pagan pastoral feast from which the modern ceremony developed.

131

There are many stories about the origin of "puppy dog pies." One old man, well versed in local tradition, said his great-great-uncle had often told him the story which had, as a matter of fact, started at this uncle's pub, in the days when Painswick was a great town and Stroud just an insignificant village. Great rivalry exists between the two places. Stroud, the center of West England's cloth industry, is a bustling little industrial center, while Painswick is a small, picturesque Cotswold town. The men of Painswick, my informant said, forgot for once their differences with the men of Stroud, and invited them to meet at the pub on Feast Sunday for a meat pie celebration. The Stroud men liked the pic mightily, and when not a crumb remained, inquired what kind of meat was in it.

"Remember that old dog that was 'round 'ere last week?" asked one of the Painswick men.

Yes, they all remembered.

"Well," said the Painswick man, "that pie's 'im!"

From that day to this, said the old man, Painswick's men have been called "Bow-wows," and Stroud's "Donkeys," and everyone eats "puppy dog pies" for Feast Sunday!

HARVEST FEAST SUNDAY, CHARLTON-ON-OTMOOR, OXFORDSHIRE

First Sunday after September 19

On Feast Sunday, people of Charlton-on-Otmoor renew the box on the large green boxwood cross* which always is fastened above the fifteenth century Rood Screen. Then they decorate the cross with pink dahlias, or other autumn flowers. Crimson woodbine adorns screen and altar, while fruits, vegetables and flowers, placed along window ledges and steps, add to the dim old church the rich splendor of harvest fields.

Feast Monday, following Feast Sunday, is a village holiday.

* *See p59-60.*

SEPTEMBER

Barnstable Fair, Devonshire

The Wednesday, Thursday and Friday
preceding September 20

People say that Barnstable Fair, sometimes called the "Saturnalia of North Devon," received its charter over a thousand years ago from King Athelstan. Be this as it may, the three-day fair is the county's largest and most famous. Traditionally, the first day is devoted to the sale of sheep and cattle; the second to that of horses; and the third to amusements. So significant is Barnstable Fair to Devonshire folk that many important dates are reckoned from it.

Like Exeter's Lammas Fair, Barnstable Fair is proclaimed by hoisting a gigantic flower-decorated glove to the top of the guildhall.

Typical Barnstable Fair refreshments are served at a state luncheon in the guildhall. The menu includes cheese and toast, and the potent spiced ale brewed from a secret formula said to have originated in Athelstan's day. A senior alderman always prepares the ale from a recipe which has been jealously guarded by a long line of Corporation officials. While the male guests quaff the famous drink, women guests receive the no less famous Barnstable Gingerbread,* made from a recipe which has been handed down from mother to daughter for many generations.

Wakes Week, Sandbach, Cheshire

The third week in September

A Fair in Scotch Commons celebrates Wakes Week for Sandbach, the cobbled Cheshire town which possesses two of England's most beautiful Saxon crosses. The Fair combines buying and selling with all kinds of amusements. Typical Wakes Week fairings are the traditional brandy snaps, or thin ginger wafers, which are curled into cornucopias over a stick or a wooden mold.

* For recipe, see Dorothy Gladys Spicer. *From an English Oven.* p52-53.

133

St. Matthew's Day

September 21

St. Matthew's Day is chiefly significant in rural weather lore. Early English almanacs abound in weather warnings, advice and predictions of the foul days St. Matthew brings.

> St. Mathee shut up the Bee;
> St. Mattho, take thy hopper and sow;
> St. Matthy all the year goes by;
> St. Matthie sends sap into the tree

is one ancient verse concerning the day, while another declared that,

> St. Matthew
> Brings the cold rain and dew.

Sussex people call St. Matthew's "the Devil's nutting day," while Midland millers say that at this season people may count on three consecutively windy days, known as the "windy days of the barley harvest."

Sturbridge Fair, Cambridgeshire

Old Holy-Cross Eve, September 24; or September 25, if the former falls on Sunday

Sturbridge (or Stourbridge) Fair usually continues for three days, following official proclamation by the Mayor of Cambridge, the town crier, four bailiffs, the sergeant-at-arms and the town clerk.

Once Sturbridge Fair claimed the distinction of being the most important event of its kind in all England. In the eighteenth century, Daniel Defoe wrote that this fair was "not only the greatest in the whole nation, but in the world." This was true, for the fair's commodities, including woolens, hops, horses, goldsmiths' trinkets, toys and food stuffs, once attracted traders from throughout Europe, as well as from all parts of the British Isles.

Now, the ancient fair's glory has passed into obscurity, and little remains to recall the once famous event, which King John founded in 1211 for the endowment of St. Mary Magdalen's Hospital for lepers.

PENNY LOAF SUNDAY, NEWARK, NOTTINGHAMSHIRE

Usually the last Sunday in September

Hercules Clay, who lived in the Market Place during Newark's siege of March 1643 dreamed the same dream on three different nights. His house was on fire! After the third dream, Hercules Clay roused his family and vacated his house. Shortly after, an explosion set the place on fire. Hercules Clay was so grateful for his deliverance that he bequeathed a sum to the Corporation of Newark to provide annually a commemorative sermon and a penny loaf for each poor person applying for it on what was to be known as Penny Loaf Sunday.

At first the loaves were dispensed at the church, later at the town hall, although why March 11, the original date of distribution, was changed to the last Sunday in September is a matter of conjecture. Over a thousand loaves of bread still are given to the parish poor, in memory of Hercules Clay's remarkable dreams.

BRIDGEWATER FAIR, SOMERSET

The last Wednesday in September

Bridgewater's modern three-day fair received its charter from King John, together with the promise that, "Bridgewater shall be a free borough, and that there shall be a market there, and a fair every year that shall last during eight days." The trading once carried on at Bridgewater now has diminished, and the pleasure features of the event overshadow business transactions.

This fragment of an old Bridgewater Fair Song expresses the spirit of the occasion:

> Come, lads and lassies, pray attend
> Unto these lines that's just been penned.
> From miles around, both far and near,
> They come to see the rigs o' the Fair:
> So, Master John, do you beware, and
> Don't go kissing the girls o' Bridgewater Fair.

MICHAELMAS DAY

September 29

For centuries, tenants customarily included a goose in their Michaelmas rent payments to the lord of the manor. Probably this is why the eating of roast goose is associated with the season.

> If t'geese-breest at Michaelmas be dour and dull,
> We's hev a sair winter te t'sure an' te t'full

says the old Yorkshireman, meaning that if the Michaelmas goose, when held up to the light, looks dark and dull, the coming winter is certain to be severe from beginning to end.

"If you eat goose on Michaelmas Day, you will not want for money all the year," is a popular Nottinghamshire saying. Norfolk people, on the contrary, reverse the proverb by laying the responsibility for family fortunes on the housewife! "If you do not baste the goose on Michaelmas Day, you will want money all the year."

Michaelmas is a popular term or quarter day. In many places, Michaelmas was the time for "hiring fairs," or for engaging farm laborers, maids and servants to enter into a twelve-month service agreement. In Gloucestershire, Buckinghamshire, Oxfordshire, and many other counties, Michaelmas still is the proper time for hiring workers, while the election of town officers and the celebration of village feasts often come at this season.

136

SEPTEMBER

PAYMENT OF QUIT RENT, ROYAL COURTS OF JUSTICE, LONDON

Michaelmas Day, September 29

The annual payment of the Quit Rent, made on Michaelmas Day* at the Royal Courts of Justice, is open to the public and probably is one of London's oldest and most unusual customs. People think the ceremony originally was performed at the Eleanor Cross,† in the Strand.

The ancient Quit Rent rites symbolize the Corporation of the City's payment to the Crown for two parcels of land: the first parcel by presentation of horseshoes and nails, the second by the cutting of faggots with bill-hook and hatchet.

The first piece of land featured in the Quit Rent ceremony has to do with "The Forge," which possibly was located at the northwest corner of modern Chancery Lane. It is thought that this smithy's site was the old tournament ground of the Knights Templars, which was rented in the year 1235, for an annual payment of horseshoes and nails. The history of the transaction is obscure and involved, and nobody seems able to explain just how the forge property came into the City's possession. For better than seven hundred years, however, the Corporation, which claims possession of the freehold land upon which the law courts now stand, has paid the sovereign an annual feudal Quit Rent, consisting of six gigantic horseshoes from Flemish war horses and "sixty and one more" large nails. At the ceremony the Crown is represented by the King's (or Queen's) Remembrancer, the Corporation by the City Solicitor.

The warrants, read out in Court, are followed by the summons: "Tenants and occupiers of a certain tenement called 'The Forge,' in the parish of St. Clement Danes in the County of Middlesex, come forth and do your services."

* The date for the observance of the ceremony sometimes varies and should be checked.

† The original Cross was destroyed in 1647. It occupied the site where the equestrian statue of Charles I now stands.

The City Solicitor then steps forward, counts out the centuries-old horseshoes and nails and hands them to the King's Remembrancer, who keeps them in his office until the following year.

The second Quit Rent ceremony, almost as ancient as the first, concerns a piece of Shropshire land called "The Moors," which came into the City's possession during Henry VIII's reign. The land, thought to have been in the neighborhood of Alveley, is rented from the Crown upon annual payment of a bill-hook and a hatchet.

In the course of the ceremony the City Solicitor takes a bundle of faggots. These he chops to bits with bill-hook and hatchet, to prove the keenness of the blades. He then presents the bill-hook and the hatchet to the King's Remembrancer, who accepts them in behalf of the sovereign.

Both customs are performed with the solemnity befitting ancient rites. The King's Remembrancer wears official robes and full-bottomed wig, while the other dignitaries are ceremoniously garbed, in accordance with their respective ranks.

OCTOBER

If ducks do slide at Hollantide,
At Christmas they will swim;
If ducks do swim at Hollantide,
At Christmas they will slide,
    —*Old Buckinghamshire Rhyme.*

OPENING THE PUDDING SEASON, "THE CHESHIRE CHEESE,"
LONDON

The first Monday in October

England's pudding season, which opens officially on the first Monday in October, has been observed for many years with the ceremony of Carrying in the Pudding, at Ye Olde Cheshire Cheese, Ltd., 145 Fleet Street.

Although this time-honored practice, originating in 1775, was discontinued in 1940, because of drastic meat rationing and the inability to procure necessary ingredients, the custom of making the traditional puddings has recently been revived. Whether or not the accompanying singing ceremony can be revived is a matter of conjecture, according to the proprietor. Now that ingredients are no longer rationed, he finds that singers are!

The Cheshire Cheese, with its low smoke-stained ceiling and high-backed wooden settles, probably looks much the same as when London notables of bygone days gathered there for lively discussions on literature and politics. The favorite arm chair of Dr. Johnson (which originally came from the Mitre Tavern) holds place of honor in what is called Dr. Johnson's nook. In modern times this chair is reserved for the distinguished guest who presides at the opening of the pudding season ceremony.

139

An enormous pastry-covered pudding, or pie, traditionally weighing between fifty and eighty pounds, is carried into the room with fitting honors. Beefsteaks, larks, spices, mushrooms and gravies constituted the contents of the original pie, which was made according to a secret formula. The pudding must be boiled from sixteen to twenty hours. On windy days, people say that the mouth-watering aroma reaches the nostrils of workers on the Stock Exchange!

"Be it known to all good citizens of thys antient citye of London that ye* famous pudding will be served for ye first time thys season on ye seventeenth day of October at 7 of ye clock," reads an announcement of "ye 160th pudding season" (1935) which continues with this colorful description of the ceremony:

"Many Days hath ye hirelings scoured ye country side for ye Plover Bird and tasty mushroom to mix with Ye Steak, Kidney and Succulent Oyster.

"Then with Spices from ye far West Indies Ye Pudding hath been built up to prodigious size and plunged into ye boiling cauldron to be tended day and night by Ye Chief Custodian.

"Perchance its fragrant aroma hath already been wafted from Ye Upper Chamber.

"Ye candles having been lighted, Ye Mighty Pudding borne aloft by Ye Chief Custodian and followed by his trusty henchmen enters Ye Dining Hall.

"Then shall ye guests with one accord rise in salutation and Ye Gresham Singers blend their voices to give praise.

"And a guest having been appointed to make the first cut, the savoury Pudding shall be served to ye assembled guests so that not a trace shall remain.

"Peradventure, before proceeding to Ye Pancakes and Toasted Cheese, Ye Gresham Singers will again delight Ye Company with Merry Madrigal.

* An old method of printing the article *the*, "*y*" being used for the Old English sound of *th*.

OCTOBER

"And Ye toast of His Most Gracious Majesty King George the Fifth having been honoured with Musick, a welcome shall be accorded to our distinguished guest His Excellency Dr. Ruy Ennes Ulrich, Ambassador from Portugal, ye oldest ally of Britain.

"And His Excellency having survived ye trying ordeals of cutting and also eating Ye Pudding shall not flinch from a suitable response to Ye Toast.

"It shall come to pass that with ye aid of old Ale (or other selected beverage) tongues shall be loosened and the Guests will vie one with another as to who has eaten Ye Pudding for ye greatest number of years.

"And it being so proven to the satisfaction of ye assembled Company such guest shall be proclaimed Father of Ye House and accorded ye special Toast from Ye Ladies present.

"And now, after perchance another toast and a further glee from Ye Singers, each guest shall depart, taking care as they leave Ye Portal of Ye Olde Tavern to 'MIND YE STEPPE.' "

The Cheshire Cheese, aside from its traditional reputation for lark pie,* or *pudden,* is noted also for its extensive wine vaults and for a unique collection of churchwarden pipes, which have been smoked by many visiting dignitaries. In spite of serious war damage, the Cheshire Cheese continues as one of London's celebrated landmarks. Just when the house originated nobody seems to know; but since records show it was rebuilt after the Great Fire of 1666, the tavern must have flourished well before that time.

GOOSE FAIR, NOTTINGHAM, NOTTINGHAMSHIRE

The first Thursday, Friday and Saturday in October

In 1954, Nottingham celebrates its 659th Goose Fair since Edward I granted the Royal Charter of 1284. As far as known, the only interruption in holding the event occurred during the Plague

---

* Galsworthy introduces the eating of lark pie at the Cheshire Cheese in *The Forsyte Saga,* while many other authors have referred to "the famous pudden" in their works.

of 1646, the year of the calendar revision of 1752, and several years during World Wars I and II. The Fair, which starts when Nottingham's Lord Mayor reads the original charter at the ceremonial civic opening, now lasts for only three days. Originally, however, the Goose Fair opened on St. Matthew's Day (September 21) and continued for eight days. The name "Goose Fair," which is not recorded officially until 1541, probably refers to the great number of geese brought in for trading from Norfolk and the Lincolnshire Fens.

In olden times, gooseherds on foot drove from county farms enormous flocks of geese and guided them through Nottingham's Goose Gate with the help of their crooks. Since the journey often took several weeks, gooseherds "shoed" the birds by dipping their feet first in tar, then in sand. In those days, as now, old and young poured into the fair from neighboring counties, for at this time fat geese were selected for Michaelmas and Christmas eating. But trading was by no means the only object of the fair. There was plenty of fun for everyone. Itinerant showmen exhibited curiosities. Hawkers tempted passers-by with fascinating and often useless wares. There were rich foods and ample amusements for all who wished to combine pleasure with serious business.

Today the business and pleasure parts of the Goose Fair are separate. The first day is important to farmers from throughout the Midlands, who do a brisk business in the cattle market, which is near the city's southern boundary. Here, thousands of breeding sheep, dairy cattle and other animals (but few geese) annually exchange hands.

In 1928, the Goose Fair was moved from the market place in the City Center to a ten-acre site, which forms part of the Nottingham Forest Recreation Ground. The fair now claims the distinction of being one of the best-planned and largest pleasure fairs in all England. As in ancient times, the Lord Mayor still presides at the ceremonial opening of the fair. An official tour of inspection follows, led by the Lord Mayor and the city officials.

Brandy snaps and nougat are two "fairings" everyone associates with Goose Fair. The demand far exceeds the supply of these traditional commodities, fame of which has persisted through the centuries. Other fairs, in other parts of England, also sell curled brandy snaps, filled with clotted cream; but Nottingham's dainties hold especially nostalgic memories for all who have ever tasted them.

Mr. T. J. Owen, Town Clerk of Nottingham, has very kindly given me directions for making the brandy snaps of which his townsmen are justly proud.

Nottingham Goose Fair Brandy Snaps *

4 cups flour

2 cups butter

3 cups brown sugar (firmly packed)

1¼ cups corn syrup (approximately)

2 tbsp. ground ginger

1 tbsp. lemon juice

Combine in a saucepan the butter, sugar, and corn syrup and melt over low heat. Add lemon juice and flour sifted together with ginger. Combine thoroughly.

Place teaspoonfuls of the mixture on well-greased baking sheet, allowing ample space around each spoonful.

Bake for 15 minutes in a slow oven (300°F). Allow to stand for 2 minutes before lifting with a knife and "roll them up quickly (one fold only) while warm. When cold, fill the hollow roll with clotted cream † and serve."

* The author has adapted the traditional recipe to popular use, by giving ingredients and measurements in terms that are familar to the average American housewife.

† Whipped cream is a good substitute for the clotted cream which is considered a great delicacy in many parts of England, especially in Devonshire and Cornwall. Clotted cream is the fresh cream which forms on the top of new whole milk when it is heated slowly in shallow pans on top of the stove. The cream is left undisturbed until settled and then skimmed off.

HARVEST FESTIVAL, ST. GILES'S CHURCH, STOKE POGES, BUCKING-
HAMSHIRE

Usually the first Sunday in October

The Harvest Festival of St. Giles's Church, in Stoke Poges. is
described in detail, since the service typifies the thanksgiving ceremonies of towns and villages throughout England. The festival time
varies from August to mid-October, according to local harvest condi-
tions.

Usually various women's church organizations are responsible
for harvest decorations. One group does the baptismal font, another
the altar, a third the window ledges, and so on. Since much friendly
rivalry exists between individual groups, the composite result is as
brilliant as the autumn fields, as gay as a cottage garden.

In St. Giles's Church, the yellows, greens and russets of pumpkins,
carrots, apples and potatoes, arranged in deeply recessed window
ledges and along the chancel steps present pleasing contrast to the
weathered gray of ancient walls and pillars. A small basket of
precious eggs and a long loaf of wheat bread braided down the
center hold place of honor on the altar. The Easter Sepulchre in the
chancel's north wall is piled high with polished apples, in strange
contrast to the Host and crucifix which, in medieval times reposed in
Christ's symbolic tomb.

The carved screen of the old Penn pew is festooned with crimson
Virginia creeper, while the long shelf below is thickly massed with
pink and mauve Michaelmas daisies, long sprays of goldenrod, and
clusters of Chinese lanterns. Wheat sheaves, piles of red and yellow
apples, and orange pumpkins are effectively arranged against the
background of flowers and vines.

The baptismal font glows with a wreath of late garden flowers.
Most pleasing of all the decorations, however, are four spirally-
woven straw cones, hanging from the pulpit stand. Each cornucopia

is tassled with ears of wheat. "Those are horns of plenty," the old vicar explains. "Each year they are loaned as harvest decorations."

They are more than harvest decorations, I thought, as I inquired for their owner. Two old farm hands had fashioned the cornucopias many years before, I learned. Once, I was told, the straw cones were slipped over the horns of oxen competing in local ploughing meets, suggesting that these "horns of plenty" may have been associated originally with fertility rites. Perhaps the old countrymen unconsciously paid honor to the Corn* Spirit by plaiting symbols from the last sheaf bound at the end of the harvest.

St. Giles's holds morning thanksgiving services for the entire parish. The church is packed with worshippers. In the afternoon the children have their special festival. Whole families come, from babies in arms, to parents and grandparents. "Prams" are parked beneath the ancient yew, made famous by Thomas Gray, who according to tradition wrote his *Elegy* under its spreading branches. The children gather in excited knots at the church porch. A choir boy staggers under a heavy sack of onions; a tiny fair-haired girl clutches a slippery vegetable marrow, almost as big as herself; a little lad proudly fondles a large bunch of well-scrubbed carrots. Each child brings his gift, large or small, and later carries it in procession to the altar, to be received and blessed by the vicar.

"Thankfulness," he says, "is the rent we pay God for living in this wonderful earth."

Childish voices recite prayers of thanksgiving and shrilly chant old harvest hymns in many different keys. Tomorrow, gifts of fruits and flowers will be distributed among the parish poor and ailing, and taken to the Girls' Moral Welfare Home in Slough. Today, young and old express deep gratitude for the rich gifts God has bestowed, in return for their labor in His fields.

* In British usage the word *corn* describes the chief cereal crop of a country. In England the word refers to wheat.

145

BLESSING THE FISHING SMACKS, BRIXHAM, DEVONSHIRE

About the first Sunday in October

Before launching the fishing smacks for the first big catch of the season, the vicar at Brixham and neighboring hamlets always blesses the boats and prays God for their safe return. For just as the farmer asks blessing on his plough, on Plough Monday, and later gives thanks for the earth's harvest, so the miner asks God to bless the pithead before opening a new mine and prays for an abundant seam, and the fisherman invokes divine blessing on his smacks and nets and offers thanks for the harvest of the sea. Most coastal towns hold services on the first Sunday in October, although some communities observe ceremonies on a Sunday earlier, or later, in the season.

BLESSING THE NETS, CHURCH OF ST. NICHOLAS, GREAT YARMOUTH, NORFOLK

The first Sunday in October

Great Yarmouth consecrates the fishermen's nets at the altar of the Church of St. Nicholas, while the congregation sings an old fishing hymn, which has been set to modern music.

WEYHILL STOCK FAIR, HAMPSHIRE

*Old Michaelmas Day, October 10,
and six days following*

Weyhill Fair is so old that people have forgotten when it began. Some say it originated in the eleventh century, and the ground it occupies today is the same as then. Sheep, horses, cheeses and hops still are among the principal commodities of the fair, which once represented England's largest sheep market.

Weyhill Fair is famed for literary allusion and ancient custom. In 1362, William Langland mentioned it in *Piers Plowman*: "To Wy and to Winchestre ich wente to the fair." Thomas Hardy, in writing *The Mayor of Casterbridge,* uses Weyhill Fair—Weydon-Priors in the story—as the scene for Michael Henchard's sale of his wife in the refreshment tent with the sign, "Good Furmity Sold Here."

A traditional ceremony, called "Horning the Colt," once was performed at this fair. A "colt" was a greenhorn, a person who attended for the first time. People seated the colt in a chair at one of the local public houses, and crowned him with a cap, trimmed with two horns, and a cup set between. Crowding about the colt, the leader of the ceremony sang this old song, bystanders joining in the chorus:

> So swift runs the hare and so cunning runs the fox,
> Why shouldn't this young heifer grew up to be an ox,
> And drink with his daddy with a large pair of horns?
> *Chorus:* With a large pair of horns.

It was customary for the colt to remove the cup from his hat, take a deep draught and then stand treat for his comrades.

PACK MONDAY FAIR, SHERBORNE, DORSETSHIRE

The Monday following Old Michaelmas Day (October 10)

For generations, bands of young people have opened Pack Monday Fair by locking arms and surging through Sherborne's streets. The throng blows horns, bugles or whistles, beats on pans and tea trays, and raises a racket that rivals Times Square on New Year's Eve! This extraordinary din begins at midnight on Sunday as the noisy parade perambulates the town. The next day is a holiday for everyone, including students of Sherborne's famous schools, who enjoy to the full this festival of noise.

According to one current tradition, the fair (formerly called "St. Michell's Fair," because it is held on the Monday after Old Michaelmas) originated in 1490, when Abbot Peter Ramsam* and his

* The abbot's rebus, consisting of a ram, combined with the letters SAM, is carved in the nave.

147

masons had finished restoring the Abbey Church of Saint Mary the Virgin, with its magnificent fan-vaulted Perpendicular nave. The abbot, pleased with the work, ordered the workmen to pack up their tools and make holiday. Pack Monday Fair is said to have derived its name from this event, when the men, under the leadership of Teddy Roe, the chief mason, packed up their tools and, joyfully blowing cow horns, marched about the town or, according to some sources, the churchyard.

Mr. A. L. Harris, verger of Sherborne Abbey, says the abbey records do not date back as far as 1490. Although we may naturally assume that a great celebration followed the completion of the work, according to Mr. Harris, "Teddy Roe had no connection whatsoever with the abbey or the rebuilding." It is thought that many years later, a Mr. Teddy Roe came to Sherborne and revived the ancient tradition of Pack Monday Fair, which evidently had lapsed, or was in danger of doing so.

Modern Pack Monday festivities start in the upper end of town, taking the form of a pleasure fair rather than the cattle, sheep, and horse fair of former times. The name "Teddy Roe's Band" is given to the noise makers who parade up and down Sherborne's streets, banging on pots and pans.

MOP FAIR, STRATFORD-ON-AVON, WARWICKSHIRE

St. Wilfred's Day, October 12

Stratford's Mop, once a Hiring Fair, now a pleasure carnival, takes place in Rother Market and the town's main street. The mayor, assisted by visiting mayors and dignitaries, opens the event from a platform in the square.

Originally, the Mop Fair's main attraction was an ox-roasting which was done in a great brick fireplace, erected in the middle of town. The roasting was presided over by persons skilled in the art. The mayor always cut off the first slice with great ceremony, and later slices were sold to bystanders. Since 1938, the traditional ox-roasting has given way to other events.

In olden times a "mop" was a statute fair, at which farm workers and others were hired. The term of service usually extended from Michaelmas to Michaelmas. Now the hiring no longer takes place, but as a pleasure event, Stratford's Mop annually attracts thousands of visitors.

Nine days after the Mop, the "Runaway" Mop is held. Originally, servants who had already hired themselves out and were dissatisfied (i.e., had run away) returned to this fair to get a second chance of employment.

PILGRIMAGE TO EDWARD THE CONFESSOR'S TOMB, WESTMINSTER ABBEY, LONDON

October 13

Westminster Abbey holds an impressive annual service to commemorate the translation of Edward the Confessor's remains, in 1163, by Thomas à Becket.

The clergy's magnificent brocade copes; the acolytes in gold and white robes, carrying tall white lighted candles; the rich ecclesiastical banners—all give the atmosphere of a medieval pageant to the processional which moves slowly through the Abbey's dimly lighted nave and finally approaches the altar.

Westminster choir boys, clad in white and scarlet, include among their hymns the Latin *Sequence for St. Edward's Day*: *

> From a kingly line descending,
> On a King of Kings depending,
> Edward, from his childhood years,
> Strove to live that, death surmounted,
> He thereafter might be counted
> Heir with Christ in heavenly spheres.

* The *Sequence* is from the Missal of Abbot Litlynton; the English translation is by H. F. Westlake (1879-1925).

Following the ceremony, worshippers kneel at the mutilated shrine of St. Edward the Confessor, in the chapel which once constituted the Abbey's most magnificent part and still is its most sacred. Originally, the shrine was gold, encrusted with gems and decorated with golden images of the saints. Now the upper part of the monument, which was destroyed at the Dissolution, is of wood, and is covered with a cloth-of-gold pall. But at the monument's base one still sees the worn niches where infirm pilgrims once knelt the night through in the hope that their prayers for restoration to health might be answered.

BLESSING THE FISH HARVEST, FLAMBOROUGH HEAD, YORKSHIRE

About mid-October

Flamborough Head observes one of England's most interesting fishermen's harvest festivals.

Fishermen decorate the village church with lobster pots, nets and lines, and with fish from the previous day's catch. At a special service, the vicar offers thanks for the sea's rich harvest, just as, earlier in the season, he expresses gratitude to God for earth's abundant harvest.

Flamborough Head perches high above the North Sea on a four-hundred-foot cliff. Formerly, it was customary at low tide to let the women down over the cliffs by ropes to get the fishermen's mussel bait. Nowadays, villagers obtain their bait from Boston, in Lincolnshire.

THE LION SERMON, ST. KATHERINE CREE, LONDON

October 16 (except when this date falls on a Saturday or Sunday)

The church of St. Katherine Cree in Leadenhall Street has a Lion Sermon preached annually, at 1:05 P.M. in accordance with the will of Sir John Gayer, Sheriff of London in 1635, and Lord Mayor in

1647. The bequest commemorates two important deliverances in Sir John's life, the first, from a lion in the Arabian desert in 1630, the second, from the Tower, where the Commonwealth Parliament imprisoned him for two years for his loyalty to Charles I. Because of these events, the sermon always centers about the biblical lessons of Daniel's deliverance from the lion's den, and St. Peter's from prison.

Sir John Gayer, a member of the Turkey and Levant Company, journeyed to many remote countries of the Near East in search of spices, rugs and other merchandise to bring back to England.

The story goes that when on one of his trading expeditions in Arabia, Sir John became separated at dusk from his caravan. After wandering about for some time, vainly trying to find his companions, he was suddenly confronted by a lion. The pious merchant fell to his knees, praying for deliverance, even as Daniel * was delivered from the lion's den. The lion, instead of devouring the kneeling man, turned and left him in peace.

Gratitude for his rescue prompted the rich merchant to bequeath two hundred pounds to the parish of St. Katherine Cree, part of the sum to provide for the Lion Sermon, and part to go to the parish poor. Nowadays the charity amounts to eight pounds annually, the vicar tells me. Of this amount (which is sustained by the Gayer family) the preacher receives one pound for delivering the sermon, the clerk two shillings and the sexton one shilling and eightpence. The residue is divided among the poor, in amounts of not less than three, or more than five, shillings for each person.

Sir John Gayer's request that the Lion Sermon be preached each year on the anniversary of his encounter with the beast has been complied with every year since the merchant's death on July 20, 1649. The service of October 16, 1954, marks the sermon's three hundred

* Daniel 6:10-23.

and fifth anniversary. A favorite hymn of the commemorative service is the one which begins:

> The Hosts of God encamp around
> The dwellings of the just;
> Deliverance He affords to all
> Who in His succour trust."

ST. LUKE'S DAY

October 18

"St. Luke's is a lucky day on which to choose a husband," is an old saying, for St. Luke's once figured extensively in the divinations and charms young girls practiced in order to evoke visions of their future husbands. Today St. Luke's Day figures in weather lore.

ST. SIMON AND ST. JUDE

October 28

According to an old saying, "There will be rain on the day of St. Simon and St. Jude." That the belief dates back to early times is attested by writings of Raphael Holinshed, sixteenth century chronicler: a battle was planned on October 28, 1536, between the King's forces and rebel Yorkshire troops, but so much rain fell on the eve of St. Simon and St. Jude, that combat was impossible!

The saints' day is famous not only for rain, but also for the baked warden pears Bedford boys once sold in the streets. Their traditional cry has come down through the years:

> Who knows what I have got?
> In a hot pot?
> Baked *wardens*—all hot?
> Who knows what I have got?

OCTOBER

Punkie Night, Hinton St. George, Somerset

The last Thursday in October

On the last Thursday in October, Hinton St. George children parade the village streets with "punkies," or lanterns, made from large hollowed-out mangolds, which are lighted from within by a bit of candle.

The custom of carrying punkies is very old. People say it originated in times when parish women made crude scooped-out vegetable lanterns, so they could guide their menfolk back across the fields after too prolonged celebration at the village pub.

All Hallows' Eve

October 31

All Hallows' Eve or All Hallow E'en, with its tradition of witches, ghosts, hobgoblins and sprites, its games and incantations, still is a gay time for pranks and parties in many North Country homes. Fun-loving Americans have borrowed from their British ancestors many Hallow E'en games, such as apple-bobbing, nut roasting and tossing of apple parings. Transplanted to New World soil, the old practices have become revitalized and currently are observed with more enthusiasm than in the country of their birth.

To ancient Druids the end of October commemorated the festival of the waning year, when the sun began his downward course and ripened grain was garnered from the fields. *Samhain*, or "Summer's End," as this feast to the dying sun was called, was celebrated with human sacrifice, augury and prayer; for at this season spirits walked and evil had power over souls of men.

Not until the fourth century did the pagan vigil for the god of light give way to All Hallows, the mass for Christian saints; and not until the tenth, did the Druids' death feast become All Souls', the day of prayer for souls that had entered rest. Cakes for the dead were substituted for human sacrifice, fortune-telling for heathen augury, lighted candles for the old Baal fires.

Gradually, the last night of October—first a Druid feast, then a Christian holy day—emerged as a night of gaiety, when young people played games and read fortunes from simple objects, such as apples, cabbages, or nuts.

Indeed, nuts became such a favorite means of divination, that All Hallow E'en was known as "Nutcrack Night." Girls and boys placed nuts side by side in the dying embers. If the nuts flew apart, quarrels and disaster were sure to follow. But if they burned brightly side by side, a peaceful married life was foretold.

Next to nuts, apples feature in All Hallow E'en divinations. Apple-bobbing still is as popular in the North Country as in rural America. Even pips and parings come in for their share of attention. This old rhyme accompanies the swinging of a paring, to learn the loved one's initials:

> I pare this pippin round and round again,
> My sweetheart's name to flourish on the plain:
> I fling the unbroken paring o'er my head,
> My sweetheart's letter on the ground to read.

Though many old All Hallow E'en customs have disappeared survivals of All Souls' (November 2), as will be seen, still exist in many communities. Soulers, not very unlike American Halloween mummers, still make village rounds and beg for "soul cakes," instead of "something for Halloween."

NOVEMBER

Remember, remember, the fifth of November,
Gunpowder treason and plot;
I see no reason why Gunpowder Treason
Should ever be forgot.
A stick and a stake
For King George's sake
Holla, boys, Holla, make the town ring;
Holla, boys, holla, boys, God save the King.
    —*Old Sussex song for Guy Fawkes's Day.*

ALL SAINTS' AND ALL SOULS'

November 1 and 2

The early English Church called All Saints', the feast to commemorate *all the saints,* All Hallows. Hallow E'en, All Saints' and
All Souls' (October 31, November 1 and 2, respectively) share a
common tradition. The three festivals concern remembrance of departed souls. Hallow E'en, as already noted, is celebrated with games
and divination rites, since people once believed spirits of the dead
walked abroad on this night. All Saints' and All Souls', on the
other hand, are popularly observed with "souling" customs and
plays. Originally, these demonstrations were intended to honor the
faithful departed and to ease the pain of the bereaved.

"Souling," or "Soul-caking," is the custom descended from pre-
Reformation times, of going about on All Saints' or All Souls' and
begging for cakes, in remembrance of the dead. The Soulers, singing verses inherited from a remote past, are rewarded with "soul
cakes." Originally these were buns, rich with eggs and milk, spices
and saffron. Although the cakes varied a good deal from county
to county, they were generally oval or round in shape, and rather flat.

155

Cheshire and Shropshire always have been souling strongholds. Many small towns and hamlets of these counties, and also of Staffordshire, Derbyshire and Lancashire, continue observance of the old custom.

Soul cakes, in their modern meaning, are any sort of offering, cakes, coins, apples or ale, which the singers receive. As already noted, English souling and American Halloween mumming are similar. This song, which I found current in Sandbach and towns of Cheshire's Wirral peninsula, corresponds to the demand of American youth for "something for Halloween":

> Soul! Soul! for an apple or two!
> If you have no apples,
> Pears will do.
> If you have no pears,
> Money will do.
> If you have no money,
> God bless you!

In West Felton, Llynclys, and neighboring northwestern Shropshire villages, souling ditties may be long or short, simple or elaborate, according to locality. The general meaning is the same, however:

> Soul! Soul! for a souling-cake!
> I pray you, good missus, a souling-cake.
> Apple, or pear, plum, or cherry,
> Anything good to make us merry,
> Up with your apple, and down with your pan,
> Give us an answer, and we'll be gone.

Sometimes, in olden times, soulers added a blessing for the family dispensing bounty:

> God bless the master of this house, and the mistress also,
> And all the little children that round the table go;
> Likewise your men and maidens, your cattle and your store,
> And all that lies within your gates we wish you ten times more.
> We wish you ten times more with your apples and strong beer,
> And we'll come no more a-souling until another year.

Once soulers of certain villages began their rounds with services in the parish church. The cakes householders gave were in exchange for prayers for the dead, a "charity" for the departed. In other words, soul cakes were intended as a bread dole to the community poor. Bonfires, "to light souls out of purgatory," and the ringing of church bells, also characterized old-time observances.

SOULCAKERS' PLAY, COMBERBACH, FRODSHAM AND VICINITY, CHESHIRE

All Souls' Day, November 2

Cheshire Soulcakers perform the traditional play of King George and the Dragon, which is really just another version of the Christmas Mummers' St. George's Play. Children generally sing the souling ditties, while young men act in the play.

There are many variations of the Soulcakers' performance, but the general pattern is this:

The Old Woman introduces King George, who challenges anyone to oppose him. The Turk (sometimes the Black Prince) finally presents himself, declaring he will kill George, then return him to Turkey to be made into mince pies! A conflict follows, in which George is victorious, the Turk killed. King George then sends for the Quack Doctor, who resuscitates the Turk. Endless antics and buffoonery follow, with the appearance, in some cases, of Beelzebub, or of the Hobby Horse.

The theme, obviously, represents death and resurrection, as in the Christmas Mummers' plays.

FISH HARVEST FESTIVAL, ST. DUNSTAN'S-IN-THE-EAST, LONDON

The Sunday nearest All Souls'
(November 2)

St. Dunstan's-in-the-East, on London's Lower Thames Street, holds its annual Fish Harvest Festival with strict regard to ancient tradition.

Thirty-nine different kinds of fish, representing the thirty-nine articles of religion, are offered for blessing. People also bring offerings of game and groceries for distribution, after the service, among the parish poor. The fish go to Guy's Hospital.

Formerly the service took place at St. Magnus the Martyr, now closed because of war damage. In this church the powerful Fishmongers' Company, which claims to antedate Henry II's reign, held the annual ceremony.

GUY FAWKES'S DAY

November 5

The failure of Guy Fawkes's plot to blow up the Houses of Parliament on November 5, 1605, is celebrated all over England, by lighting bonfires and "burning the guy" in effigy.

The Gunpowder Plot originated when James I refused religious freedom to Roman Catholics. Guy Fawkes, Robert Catesby, Thomas Percy, Thomas Winter and others, buried some thirty-six barrels of gunpowder under piles of wood and coal in the House of Lords cellar. Guy Fawkes, selected to set off the pile at an appointed hour, was discovered in hiding and he, together with other conspirators, was captured and executed. Consequently, November 5, was popularly acclaimed as Guy Fawkes's Day. The House of Commons instituted it as ". . . a holiday for ever, in thankfulness to God for our deliverance."

Today Yeomen of the Guard still follow the traditional ceremony of inspecting the House of Parliament vaults, before that body convenes. The Guards light their lanterns and, beginning with the cellars, search the entire building. Then the King is notified that the search has been made and the Houses can meet in safety.

Bonfires, parkin and treacle toffee are the three essentials which make Guy Fawkes's Day an event to most boys and girls. Parkin, a traditional cake made from oatmeal, treacle, butter and ginger, differs from county to county, although Yorkshire claims the delicacy rightfully belongs to it alone. In Leeds and many other Yorkshire towns, indeed, the eating of parkin is so important a feature that November 5, is known as Parkin Day.

The "guy," or effigy of the traitor, is prominent everywhere. In some places bands of boys and girls go about from house to house, begging pennies for the "guy" and singing ditties descriptive of the occasion. A typical Nottingham verse begins:

> Gunpowder Plot shall never be forgot
> While Nottingham Castle stands upon a rock.

London urchins differ little from their country cousins in begging passers-by for "a penny for the guy," as they roam the streets at night, shaking homemade tin can collection boxes and soliciting funds for the celebration.

English colonists brought the Guy Fawkes tradition with them to the New World. In 1665, according to New York State laws, every minister had to preach a sermon to commemorate deliverance from the Gunpowder Plot. And in the United States, as in England, November 5 was once observed with bonfires, mummery and anti-Popish ditties. Although the custom has died out now, some vestiges of it may continue, here and there, in the election bonfires and in the traditional 'Lection Day cake, which old-fashioned New England housewives still bake. Some British experts even maintain that the ragamuffin habit of begging for "something for Thanksgiving," and the mummers' parades of Philadelphia and New York originated in Guy Fawkes's Day. It was natural, they reason, for the early settlers to perpetuate the customs of November 5 in their own new November holiday!

GUY FAWKES'S DAY, LEWES, SUSSEX

November 5

For over two hundred years, Lewes has claimed the most elaborate Guy Fawkes's Day celebration of any English town. The Bonfire Boys' torchlight processions, the elaborate fireworks, the revels in costume about immense bonfires, all make the Lewes event famous. People from all over Sussex and surrounding counties pour in by bus, train and car, to witness the spectacle.

Lewes is divided into four "Bonfire Societies," or districts, each competing for costume prizes. Each of the groups, known as the Cliffe, Commercial Square, Borough and South Street Bonfire Societies, is responsible for supplying torches, bonfires and processions for its own district and for maintaining order.

Festivities, starting in early evening with individual society processions and floats, end at midnight with an all-participating grand procession.

The most spectacular procession of all probably is that of the Cliffe Society, which leads off with two local bands. Then come the "Archbishop" of the Cliffe and various members in fancy dress costume, who carry waving banners and lighted torches. Men stationed all along the line of march replenish the torches as the procession impressively advances toward the Cliffe, a settlement across the River Ouse, on the outskirts of town.

A truck transports a huge tableau with over life-sized effigies of Guy Fawkes, complete with high hat and lantern, and Pope Pius IV, who is popularly regarded as instigator of the plot. Both effigies are loaded with gunpowder.

Upon arrival at the Cliffe, there are an immense bonfire and an elaborate program of speeches, readings on the Gunpowder Plot and a recital of the eighteenth century Bonfire Prayer. At length the "Archbishop" sings out loudly, "What shall we do?" "Burn him!" the crowd roars in response, as stalwart men throw the effigies on the blazing bonfire.

A deafening explosion follows. When the fire finally subsides, refreshments are served. A grand procession forms and awards are made for the best costumes. The celebration breaks up in the small hours of the morning, following votes of thanks and the singing of *Auld Lang Syne* and *God Save the Queen*.

NOVEMBER

Gunpowder Plot Sermon, St. Mary-le-Bow, London

November 5, or the Sunday nearest

A Gunpowder Plot Sermon has been preached each year for almost three centuries, in the old Cheapside church of St. Mary-le-Bow.

The sermon (which nowadays is not always preached on November 5, but on or about the nearest Sunday) originated under the will, dated February 12, 1655, of Theophilus Royley, a London citizen and draper. The document directed that the sum of twenty shillings be ". . . paid to the Ministers of the parish of St. Mary-le-Bow for the time being, to preach a sermon yearly in the evening of the fifth of November"; also, the sum of ten shillings to the ". . . clerk or Sexton for his pains and for candles to be spent every time."

Swearing in the Lord Mayor-Elect, London

Usually on November 9

Usually on November 9, the Lord Mayor-Elect of London, who is chosen on Michaelmas Day (September 29), goes in state from the Mansion House to the Guildhall, to be presented to the Chief Justice for final swearing in. This ceremony takes place on the day preceding the Lord Mayor's Day.

The Lord Mayor's Show, London

November 10

On November 10 the Lord Mayor rides through the City* in his magnificent glass and gilt coach,† which is sumptuously adorned

* The City is that part of London which comprises the district within the ancient boundaries; it extends from Temple Bar to Aldgate, and from Southwark to City Road. Under the special jurisdiction of the Lord Mayor and Corporation, it is the commercial center of Greater London, and, to the British, the most important square mile in the world.

† Used only for the Lord Mayor's Show.

with griffins, the City's arms, figures of Commerce and Plenty, and other symbolic emblems. The fabulous coach (a replica of the original vehicle, built in 1757) is drawn by six bay horses, and looks as if it originated in a fairy tale.

The colorful procession, said to have begun in 1215 with King John, symbolizes the tradition of privilege and duty attached to one of the world's most important civic offices. The Lord Mayor, as Chief Magistrate of the City, holds absolute authority. He has his own police* to enforce the law. Troops may not pass through his territory without permission. Traditionally, processions of even the monarch must halt at Temple Bar, to ask leave to enter the Lord Mayor's square-mile realm. The ceremony of meeting royalty at Temple Bar, where the City's pearl-handled sword is offered to the ruler and returned, probably originated with Queen Elizabeth I, who visited the City in 1588, when going to St. Paul's to give thanks for the Spanish Armada's defeat.

Of course, the character of the Lord Mayor's Show has altered greatly since the fifteenth century, when the river Thames was the thoroughfare used for the triumphal procession. Then a hundred-odd barges were featured in the pageant. In the mid-nineteenth century, however, a street procession was substituted for the water pageant of earlier times.

Today, the Lord Mayor's Show, although shorn of much of its medieval splendor, is still highly impressive. For the pageant combines ancient and historical tableaux with modern Army, Navy and Air Force displays, and floats of recent achievement in industry, commerce and manufacturing.

MARTINMAS

November 11

For hundreds of years the Feast of St. Martin, or Martinmas, has been an important term or quarter day for rent settlements and

* City police are distinguished from those of the rest of London by a red-and-white wristlet.

162

land payments. In olden times, Martinmas was considered a period for hearty feasting and drinking. Roast goose is as traditional to Martinmas as turkey to Thanksgiving.

Once, hiring of farm servants was so common on November 11, that St. Martin's was popularly called Pack-rag Day; for on this day farm servants customarily bundled up their belongings, slung them over their shoulders and went out to seek new employment.

WROTH SILVER CEREMONY, KNIGHTLOW CROSS, RYTON-ON-DUNSMORE, WARWICKSHIRE

St. Martin's Day, November 11

For over a thousand years, St. Martin's Day has been the time to pay tribute, known as Wroth Silver, to the Duke of Buccleuch, lord of the manor, at Knightlow Cross.

Representatives of the tributaries (who are notified previously through local press) assemble on Knightlow Hill at seven in the morning. They gather about the "Cross," as people still call the huge square hollow stone, which once was the base of a wayside shrine. The "Wroth Silver," or monies exacted, range from a penny to two shillings and threepence halfpenny.

As the representatives from eighteen parishes meet and the Duke's steward reads off the names of communities which must pay tribute, each delegate drops his Wroth Silver into the hollow of the stone.

According to the original terms of the tribute, defaulters are liable to a twenty shilling fine for every unpaid penny, and also "a white bull with red ears and a red nose."

This ancient manorial custom, thought by some to have originated in Anglo-Saxon times, was really a toll, exacted in return for granting cattle owners valuable rights of way.

After the ceremony, tributaries drink to the health of the lord of the manor in the hot rum and milk he traditionally provides.

FIRING THE FENNY POPPERS, FENNY STRATFORD, NEAR BLETCHLEY, BUCKINGHAMSHIRE

St. Martin's Day, November 11

On November 11, patronal festival of the church of St. Martin, the vicar sets off the first of six small cannons, called "Fenny Poppers," in the churchyard. The cannon are fired at three different times during the day, at twelve o'clock, two o'clock and six o'clock, to remind people of the dedication of the church by Dr. Browne Willis, in 1730.

Soon after the death of Dr. Willis the custom was initiated of celebrating the feast by a special service, "firing the poppers," and a special dinner.

ST. CECILIA'S DAY, CHURCH OF ST. SEPULCHRE, LONDON

November 22

The Church of St. Sepulchre, in Giltspur Street, holds an annual service in honor of St. Cecilia, patroness of music. The event is attended by London's Lord Mayor and other officials, as well as by persons prominent in the musical world. Among other observances are an official luncheon, and Philharmonic and Symphony concerts of modern music composed for the occasion, as well as of English traditional music.

According to Chaucer's *Seconde Nonnes Tale*, Cecilia was a Christian of noble Roman birth. Although secretly sworn to virginity, the maiden was betrothed to the pagan Valerian. On their wedding night, Cecilia revealed her vow to her husband, adding that her guardian angel would destroy him, should Valerian disregard her wishes. Valerian, prompted by his love, went out and was baptized. Upon returning to his wife, the story goes, Valerian found her in company of the angel, who crowned the young couple with lilies and roses.

The legend goes on to tell of the conversion of Valerian's brother, the martyrdom of the two men, and finally of Cecilia's decapitation, after the executioner had failed in his effort to suffocate her in a bath.

In the Middle Ages, musicians' Guilds adopted St. Cecilia as their patroness. During the Reformation, however, when stiff-necked Puritans forbade all forms of musical expression, the saint's patronage was largely discontinued. By 1683, however, when the "Musical Society" was organized, St. Cecilia's Day was observed in London's Church of St. Bride.

During the next two decades people continued to honor the saint's day fairly regularly with religious ceremonies followed by musical programs. Dryden's "Song for St. Cecilia's Day" was written, and presented in musical form with many variations. In 1708, Pope wrote another famous work dedicated to the saint, the "Ode for Music on St. Cecilia's Day."

Although the festival's observance as a musical event was sporadic for a time, the custom of celebrating the day was again revived in 1942.

ST. CLEMENT'S EVE

November 22

In 1950, the Hatters' Information Service revived the Festival of St. Clement, patron saint of hatters. The hatters claim that Clement "invented" felt. For, tradition says, the good saint, when on a long pilgrimage, tried to relieve his aching feet by stuffing wool between them and the soles of his sandals. The constant pressure caused by walking, combined with the moisture from his feet, matted the wool down until it became felt!

ST. CATHERINE'S DAY

November 25

St. Catherine of Alexandria, who traditionally was tortured on the wheel and beheaded in the year 307, is patroness of spinners, lace makers, rope makers, spinsters, and many others. Young girls and unmarried women in many industries, especially lace making, once observed their patron's festival as a holiday and an occasion for special merrymaking.

When machinery superseded hand work at the turn of the century, St. Catherine's Day observances died out officially. For all that, Bedfordshire people still call November 25 the "Feast Day of the Lace Makers," and eat "Cattern's (or Kattern) Cakes" and "Wigs," which for generations have been the lace makers' holiday fare.

The Kattern Cake is made from bread dough, into which butter, caraway seeds, sugar and eggs are kneaded. The cake, baked round and cut into wedges, is an excellent tea accompaniment.

Wigs, the day's other specialty, always were served at the lace makers' annual tea. This event was called "washing the candle-block," since the girls all sat around the block, which held their water flasks. Through these flasks the light of a candle shone, providing workers with light for their lace making. *Wigs* are so-called, according to Bedfordshire people, because the batter (which is poured into round muffin pans) curls over the sides when baked, and looks like the curls of a wig. Wigs are still made. The ingredients consist of flour, butter and sour milk, flavored with ginger and mixed spices.

"Catherning," or "Cattening," is the name given to the custom of children going about from farm to farm and singing ditties that mention Catherine. The children ask for apples, pennies or other gifts, in memory of her day.

The following rhyme, well known especially in Staffordshire, Leicestershire and Derbyshire, refers to both Catherine and to Clement:

> Catherine and Clement, be here, be here,
> Some of your apples and some of your beer,
> Some for Peter and some for Paul,
> And some for Him that made us all.

NOVEMBER

In Dorsetshire folk references to Saint Catherine are numerous and chapels dedicated to her still stand on high hilltops at both Abbotsbury and Milton Abbas. Legend says that, in bygone days, a secret passage led from Cerne Abbas to Cat-and-Chapel Hill (thought to have been a colloquial form of Saint Catherine's Chapel), where there was another chapel honoring the saint of spinsters. According to tradition, angels buried Saint Catherine on top of Mount Sinai, and this is said to account for the erection of her sanctuaries on high points. In ancient times unmarried girls made pilgrimages to these shrines to implore their patron saint for husbands. To judge from the old folk prayer one frequently hears in Dorset, spinsters were not too discriminating, since any husband was deemed preferable to *none at all!* This is the jingle* which has come down through the centuries in slightly varying form in Dorset communities:

> Sweet Saint Catherine, send me a husband,
> A good one, I pray:
> But arn a one better than narn a one,
> Oh Saint Catherine, lend me thine aid,
> And grant that I never may
> Die an old maid.

STIR-UP SUNDAY

The Sunday before Advent Sunday†

Stir-up Sunday is so-named after the words of the *Collect*:

> Stir up, we beseech Thee, O Lord, the wills of thy faithful people; that they, plenteously bringing forth the fruit of good works, may of Thee be plenteously rewarded.

Stir-up Sunday is the traditional time for housewives to go home from church and begin stirring up the currants, raisins, fruit peels, and other good things for the Christmas plum puddings.

---

* Margaret R. Dacombe, ed. *Dorset Up Along and Down Along.* p 119.
† The Sunday nearest to St. Andrew's Day (November 30).

> Stir up, we beseech thee,
> The pudding in the pot,
> And when we get home,
> Well eat it all hot

is a favorite schoolboy rhyme.

"Well do I remember, as a child, walking home from church with Grandmother," reminisced an English woman in the United States, who still makes her puddings at the traditional season, "and hearing her remark, 'Well, Stir-up Sunday! Now we've got to get at the mincemeat and plum puddings!'"

St. Andrew's Day

November 30

St. Andrew, like St. Catherine, was the lace makers' patron. His was the occasion for special rejoicing among lace makers of Bedfordshire, Buckinghamshire, Hertfordshire and Northamptonshire, in times when these counties were famous for their handmade needle-point and pillow laces. Feasting, drinking elderberry wine, and sports all characterized the holiday, sometimes known as "Tander."

A survival of the Tander is the Tandra Cake, a special holiday treat. Although the festival is almost forgotten now, Bedfordshire people still make the delicacy. It has a bread dough base, to which lard, sugar, currants, lemon peel and eggs are added.

Many weather predictions and folk sayings are associated with St. Andrew's Day. In Suffolk, people say:

> St. Andrew the King,
> Three weeks and three days
> Before Christmas comes in

while many affirm that wherever lilies-of-the-valley grow wild, there you will find a parish church dedicated to St. Andrew.

NOVEMBER

ETON COLLEGE WALL GAME, ETON, BUCKINGHAMSHIRE

St. Andrew's Day (November 30)

Annually on St. Andrew's Day, Eton College plays the famous and highly technical Eton Wall Game, between Collegers and Oppidans. The renowned match gets its name from the fact that the game is held against the wall bordering the college athletic field.

Come all you faithful Christians
That dwell here on earth,
Come celebrate the morning
Of our dear Saviour's birth.
This is the happy morning,
This is the blessèd morn:
To save our souls from ruin,
The Son of God was born.
—*Old Carol from Herefordshire*

ADVENT

The four-week period preceding Christmas

Advent, meaning "the coming of the Savior," is the name of the four-week period which precedes the anniversary of Christ's birth. Advent, starting on the Sunday nearest St. Andrew's Day (November 30), begins the cycle which the Christian Church regards as a spiritual preparation for Christmas, just as Lent is for Easter. Advent Sunday marks the beginning of the ecclesiastical year.

Once many popular customs were connected with the season; now comparatively few remain. In Staffordshire and elsewhere, as already seen, housewives start mixing ingredients for the Christmas plum puddings during the first week in Advent. Each member of the family takes a turn at the stirring, "for luck."

In the northern counties until recently, and possibly even now in some communities, poor parish women make neighborhood rounds at this season. The women carry two dolls, called the Advent Images. As they exhibit the figures, which represent the Virgin and Christ-Child, they sing the ancient carol, "The first joy that Mary

170

had, it was the joy of one." Each person viewing the dolls customarily contributes a coin.

St. Thomas's Day

December 21

> The day of St. Thomas, the blessed divine,
> Is good for brewing, baking and killing fat swine

is one of many old sayings associated with St. Thomas's or "Gooding" Day, when, from time immemorial, poor people have gone from house to house in the neighborhood, begging gifts for their Christmas goodies. This custom, which continues in rural areas, is called variously, "Thomasing," "Going a-gooding," "a-corning," or "goodening." In Cheshire and some other places, donors receive sprigs of mistletoe or holly, in return for their gifts.

The Christmas Season

Christmas Eve (December 24) to New Year's Eve (December 31)

Christmas is the traditional time for feasting and hearty good cheer. Throughout England Yuletide is characterized by picturesque customs, carol singing, blazing logs, mummers' plays and old-time games. Even in places where old ways are dying out and restrictions in both materials and means prevent the traditional preparation of holiday foods, the English housewife manages, somehow, her plum puddings and mince pies, and gaiety prevails in even the humblest homes.

"He has more to do than the ovens in England at Christmas," is an Italian proverb, descriptive of the thoroughness with which the festival is prepared. Each locality boasts its special foods. In the Midlands, there are pikelets, or glorified pancakes, featured at the five-o'clock Christmas tea. Yorkshire has her rich Yule spice cake, bursting with candied peels and spices, currants and sultanas. The

171

cake cannot be cut before Christmas Eve, if luck is to stay with the household! Cornwall's pride are individual saffron and currant cakes, which each member of the family receives, but everyone nibbles, in token of good will. Durham and Northumberland have Yule Doos, or Hyul-doos, quaint pastry images, rolled out in human shape, with hands neatly crossed over stomachs and currant buttons down the front.

Nor may one forget the hot mulled elderberry wine,* sloe gin, ale posset, or spiced cider, which are such good accompaniments to the traditional cakes, and add much to the cheer of family reunions.

Even farm beasts are remembered at the season of good will. Cows and horses, pigs and sheep all receive a bit of extra food, for country folk claim that humble animals, having witnessed the Divine Birth, are blessed with special gifts on Christmas Eve.

The Norsemen introduced into England the custom of providing a wheat sheaf for the wild birds' Christmas feast. Some northeastern county hamlets, like Ackworth in Yorkshire, still observe this charming rite. Ackworth's parish church is dedicated to St. Cuthbert, whose image stands in a niche in the sanctuary porch. At the annual Christmas morning service, a small sheaf of grain is tied about the statue's neck, so all birds may have a special breakfast treat.

With beasts and birds well tended, the family turns to celebrating its own Christmas. Evergreens and holly, box, mistletoe, ivy and yew, all are popular decorations. Holly is said to discourage witches and tax collectors, ivy is associated with Bacchus. Superstition dictates that on no account may holly (or mistletoe, in some places) be brought indoors prior to Christmas, lest bad luck result. By Candlemas, according to old tradition, all greens must be removed and burned.

Nowadays the Christmas tree, introduced from Germany during the nineteenth century, has been widely adopted in England. Many churches and cathedrals are decorated with trees. Annually, two

* Black Country people (those living in mining areas) claim that mulled elderberry wine protects from power of demon, witch and evil spirit!

giant trees, sent from the royal Sandringham estate, are set up in St. Paul's Cathedral, one at the nave's west end, the other in the portico.

The Christmas tree has widely supplanted the indigenous English mistletoe bough, or "Kissing Bush," which once was an attractive decoration in every farm house and humble cottage. The mistletoe bough was popular in Worcestershire, Herefordshire, and other counties where the plant grows freely in orchards. The Kissing Bush, on the other hand, developed further north, in such areas as Cheshire, Northumberland, Derbyshire, Nottinghamshire and Lincolnshire, where mistletoe is scarce. Although the pretty device varied from place to place, its foundation usually consisted of wooden hoops, set up athwart each other so that they intersect at right angles. Ivy, holly, or evergreens completely concealed the framework, which was studded with a circle of lighted candles and hung with polished apples, glass or tin ornaments and small gifts for the family. Suspended from the center of the Kissing Bush was a spray of mistletoe, the sacred Druid plant.

The Kissing Bush, which was hung from a beam in the ceiling, was the focal point of all festivities. The candles were lighted on Christmas Eve, Christmas night, and each of the Twelve Days between Christmas and Epiphany. Generations of English boys and girls have kissed under the symbolic bush; for British people claim that the custom of kissing under the mistletoe originated with them. Tradition says the mistletoe was a regal forest tree, until men used it for the Cross. From then on, it was condemned to live upon other trees, a parasite forever.

The Kissing Bush's popularity has never entirely waned. In some remote Northumbrian farms the Bush still hangs from blackened kitchen rafters. In parts of Derbyshire, Cheshire and Staffordshire, as well as in Devon and Cornwall, vestiges of this old and charming decoration may still be found.

A most important feature of the Christmas celebration is lighting the Yule log or ashen faggot. Traditionally, the log, as large as the

173

fireplace can accommodate, is brought in ceremoniously and burned at least twelve hours, to ensure the family luck!

In many West Country homes people tie ash sticks together with bramble binds and burn the faggot bundles on Christmas night. This rite, like burning the Yule log, is thought to safeguard household fortunes throughout the coming year. Just when the custom began, nobody seems to know; but people say it is in memory of the Infant Jesus, who, on the night he was born, was bathed before an ash-faggot fire.

From time immemorial, the faggot binds have been popular in divination. As the sticks burn, old folk sit about the blazing fire, playing cards and drinking cider. The young people crowd closer to watch the burning of the binds. In Devonshire, each girl decides upon a particular bind before the faggots are lighted. The owner of the first bind to ignite will be the year's first bride!

Many other divinations and games liven Christmas Eve family parties, for the Holy Night figures extensively in augury and charm. A popular Oxfordshire fortune game is for a girl to silently mix up a dough cake. Picking it with her initials, she places it on the hearth. Then, leaving the door wide open, she awaits midnight, when the future husband appears, walks straight to the hearth, pricks his initials beside the maker's, and quickly withdraws!

North Country churches, particularly, celebrate Christmas Eve with carol singing and nativity plays. Shepherds and farm hands, wall builders and miners, are actors in the plays which commemorate the Manger Birth. Words are simple, performers are unlettered; but the plays are characterized by a sincerity and simplicity which have made them popular for hundreds of years.

Just at midnight, church bells peal forth their age-old message of peace on earth, good will to men. The ringers, like the actors, are humble men. The art of bell-ringing is an ancient one, which has been handed down from father to son for generations. Often teams of hand-bell ringers such as those of Appleton, in Berkshire, go about from village to village, playing the well-loved carols that proclaim the Christ Child's birth.

DECEMBER

CAROL SINGING, COVENTRY CATHEDRAL, WARWICKSHIRE

Christmas Eve, December 24

In war-damaged Coventry, choristers stand among the cathedral ruins and sing the traditional *Coventry Carol* on Christmas Eve. This carol has been sung ever since Henry VI's time, when it was part of the pageant of Shearmen and Tailors. In the old play, Bethlehem's women sing the following words, immediately before Herod's soldiers enter to slay the children:

> *Lully, lulla, thou little tiny child,*
> *By by, lully, lullay.*
>
> O sisters too,
> How may we do
> For to preserve this day
> This poor youngling,
> For whom we do sing,
> By by, lully lullay?
>
> Herod, the king,
> In his raging,
> Chargèd he hath this day
> His men of might
> In his sight
> All young children to slay.
>
> That woe is me,
> Poor child for thee!
> And ever morn and day,
> For thy parting
> Neither say or sing
> By by, lully, lullay!

TOLLING THE DEVIL'S KNELL, DEWSBURY, YORKSHIRE

Christmas Eve, December 24

The Parish Church of All Saints' in Dewsbury has "tolled the Devil's Knell" on Christmas Eve for the greater part of seven hun-

175

dred years. For some reason, the custom was interrupted in the early nineteenth century; and again in 1940, when all bell-ringing was banned except to signal enemy invasion. The ringing was revived on Christmas Eve, 1948, however, and as for centuries past, the great tenor bell tolls out once for each year of the Christian era.

"*Why* do you do it?" I once asked the man who had rung the bell one thousand nine hundred and forty-nine times the previous Christmas.

"I don't remember," he said. "We just *do* it!"

Like many traditional practices which have defied onslaughts of time, change and total war, the custom continues even when its origin has been forgotten.

Legend says the thirteenth century Sir Thomas Soothill gave All Saints' its tenor bell in penance for murdering a boy servant and then trying to hide his guilt by throwing the body into the dam. "Black Tom of Soothill," they call the bell, which the repentant baron ordered tolled each Christmas Eve, to remind him of his crime.

It takes approximately an hour for the bell ringers to toll the devil's knell. The final stroke must be timed exactly with the hour of midnight for, as anybody will tell you, "The Devil died when Christ was born." After the knell is sounded, Christmas morn is joyously ushered into Dewsbury by the ringing of the Grandsire Doubles.

Tolling Black Tom is more than a custom. It is a safeguard to keep the Devil from the parish for the next twelvemonth!

WASSAILING CUSTOMS, WAKEFIELD, YORKSHIRE

Christmas Eve, December 24

Bands of wassailers, singing traditional ditties, go about from house to house on Christmas Eve in the neighborhood of Wakefield, in Yorkshire's West Riding. Everybody invites the singers in and treats them to spiced Yule Cake and cheese, which are washed down by cider or wine. Although the Christmas song varies from place to place, I found this version to be widely popular:

> I wish you a merry Christmas
> And a happy New Year,
> A hole in ma stocking,
> A hole in ma shoe,
> Please, can you spare
> A copper or two?
> If ye haven't a penny
> A ha'penny will do;
> And if ye haven't a ha'penny,
> *God bless you!*

SWORD DANCERS, GRENOSIDE, YORKSHIRE

Christmas Eve, December 24

On Christmas Eve and the days following, the Sword Dance Team from the town of Grenoside, near Sheffield, comes out to perform traditional dances. The team boasts a long family history, since members of the present group claim kinship with the team for over seventy years. Many of the dances, which are characterized by clogging, as well as "stepping" or tap dancing, have been handed down from father to son for several generations. The custom of wearing clogs by team members is very old indeed, having survived from the Danish settlers of ten centuries ago.

In olden times, the Sword Dancers had a Christmas Day performance at the turnpike, in the center of Grenoside. When snow was on the ground, the villagers scooped out a ring, so the men could dance their steps on the bare ground.

Although much of the dramatic quality of the original sword dance has now been lost at Grenoside, the principal character—the Captain or Fool—still wears a close-fitting cloth cap, to which an animal skin is attached. The skin varies from time to time, according to the Captain. For years the late leader wore a rabbit's head on his cap. According to local tradition, any other man who tried to put it on while the Captain was in the pub had to pay a forfeit of a half a gallon of beer.

A hare skin, and, more recently, a fox's skin, have distinguished the headdress of the Captain, who struts up and down his line of dancers, introducing them with a "calling-on" song like actors in a play. The dancers "clog step" a spirited dramatic performance in which they knock off the leader's cap and pretend to cut off his head. This is but one of many parts in the presentation. Costumes of the performers also undergo considerable variation with the passing years.

A tradition which the team always observed in the past was to give each deceased dancer's widow the sum of two and six, as her rightful share of the Yuletide collections.

FESTIVAL OF NINE LESSONS AND CAROLS, KING'S COLLEGE, CAMBRIDGE, CAMRBIDGESHIRE

Christmas Eve, December 24

One of England's most celebrated carol services is held on Christmas Eve in King's College Chapel. The magnificent chapel is illuminated by candles only. The choir enters by the west door, each singer carrying a lighted taper. During the service, the reading of the Gospel story alternates with the singing of nine ancient carols.

BURNING THE ASHEN FAGGOT, DUNSTER, SOMERSET

Christmas Eve, December 24

Inhabitants of Dunster customarily burn the Ashen Faggot on Christmas Eve, "to bring luck" to their families. They say the custom originated in the local battles which were fought between Saxons and Danes over a thousand years ago. The Saxons, knowing that ash is the only green timber which will burn, built a great bonfire of ash branches at night and warmed themselves on the eves of battle. The Danes, on the contrary, unable to find any dry wood, shivered and shook through many a cold night. In commemoration

178

of this incident in Wessex battles of 878, Dunster's people rejoice in the ashen faggot fires of Christmas Eve.

THE VESSEL CUP, CARLTON, YORKSHIRE

During the Christmas season

In Carlton and certain other Yorkshire villages, wassailers carry about the Vessel Cup, a variation of the Gloucestershire Wassail Bowl.

The Vessel Cup is a cardboard box, containing a small doll (possibly representing the baby Jesus), which is decorated with flowers, bits of ribbon and muslin scraps. Neighborhood children take the cup from house to house, singing the seventeenth century *Vessel Song* (evidently a corruption of *Wassail Song*) and receiving small gifts in return. The song ends with the verse:

> Good Master and good Mistress,
> While you're sitting by the fire,
> Pray think of us poor children
> Who are wandering in the mire.

CALLING THE WAITS, PICKERING, YORKSHIRE

During the Christmas season

The "callers," accompanied by a shouter and musician, divide Pickering into two halves. The men visit all the houses in one half the first night; those in the other, the second. This system of alternate visits continues throughout the holiday season.

The usual procedure is for the waits to gather between midnight and two o'clock in the morning, under the windows of a house. The shouter calls by name the householder, who then comes to the window. The shouter tells the time of night and remarks on the weather. Then the waits, led by the musician, sing old Christmas songs.

On Christmas morning the waits visit *every* house in Pickering and receive rewards of coins and good things to eat.

179

CHRISTMASTIDE WASSAILING, LITTLE WITTENHAM, BERKSHIRE

During the Christmas season

At Christmas time boys and girls go about the picturesque village of Little Wittenham, chanting from house to house this old sing-song rhyme which ends similarly to the Wakefield* Wassailing song:

> Christmas is coming,
> The goose is getting fat;
> Please put a penny
> In the old man's hat.
> If you haven't got a penny
> A ha'penny will do;
> And if you haven't got a ha'penny
> God bless *you!*

BRINGING IN THE BOAR'S HEAD, QUEEN'S COLLEGE, OXFORD

Christmas Day, December 25

Ringing blasts on a hunting horn summon the diners, led by the provost, fellows and officials of Queen's College to Oxford's Christmas feast in the Great Hall. After the company is seated and grace has been said, musicians sound their trumpets. Then a herald enters, followed by four bearers who carry the ceremonial boar's head on a great silver basin. The company rises as the procession moves slowly up the long hall.

The boar's head, an orange in its jaws, is surrounded by small banners and wreathed with sprays of gilded rosemary, holly, laurel and bay. The procession pauses three times as the herald chants the "Carol Bryngyne in the Boar's Head," † and diners join in the Latin refrain:

> *Caput apri defero*
> *Reddens laudes Domino.*

* *See* p 176.

† This famous song, found among Wynkyn de Worde's *Christmasse Carolles,* was considered old even in 1521, when that collection was published.

DECEMBER

The bore's head in hande bring I
With garlandes gay and rosemary,
I pray you all synge merely,
Qui estis in convivio.

As the carol ends, the bearers set the boar's head before the provost, who gives the orange to the herald and the greens to choir, townspeople and guests. Then the hall s cleared and the feast begins.

St. Stephen's, or Boxing Day

December 26

St. Stephen's, or Boxing Day, is celebrated widely by visits among friends and relatives, giving and receiving gifts, eating, drinking, and generally continuing Christmas holiday festivities. Formerly, all sorts of rough sports characterized the day, which commemorates the stoning of St. Stephen, the first Christian martyr.

"Boxing Day" probably gets its name from the "Christmas box," or container, which people once used as a receptacle for money gifts. These boxes generally were made of pottery and had a hole in the lid. Coins were dropped into this slit. Like the proverbial piggy bank, the boxes had to be broken, eventually, to remove the coins. As time went on, the term "Christmas box" was applied to any sort of Christmas gift.

Just as, in olden times, masters gave money gifts to servants, journeymen and apprentices on Boxing Day, so it is customary today to give Christmas boxes to the milkman, postman, dustman, the butcher's boy, and others who have rendered service during the past year.

The Paper Boys, Marshfield, Gloucestershire

Boxing Day, December 26

The Marshfield Paper Boys' play, like that of all other mummers, is traditional and has been handed down from father to son for

181

many generations. Nobody knows just when it started, but people claim the drama originated some eight hundred years ago.

On Boxing Day the Town Crier leads the Paper Boys through the village streets and introduces them to the bystanders. First, there is Father Christmas, who praises the day and then bids Little Man John to present himself. Little Man John steps up and invites King William to do likewise. The King not only comes forward, but proceeds to kill Little Man John! Later Little Man John is resuscitated by a dose of the Doctor's pills.

Other characters in the play are Father Beelzebub, Saucy Jack and Tenpenny Nit, all of whom make speeches. The performance ends with the "Mummers' Song" by the troupe.

The killing of Little Man John may be remotely connected with the death of Jesus Christ and the ancient passion plays; or, as is suggested by some, it may represent the symbolic theme of Winter's death and Spring's rebirth.

The Paper Boys get their name from the long paper streamers which are sewed to high headdresses and hang down, concealing the men's faces and giving them the appearance of fantastic birds.

Formerly, mummers and mummers' plays were seen at Yuletide in almost every English village. Nowadays, the original actors have died, have arthritis or other ailments, and the younger men have never learned the traditional words which usually have been transmitted from father to son by oral tradition only. The once-famous mummers of Overton and Longparish, in Hampshire, as of Alderley Edge, in Cheshire, have disbanded in recent years. Uffington, in Berkshire, revived its traditional play in 1949, but it soon lapsed, since most of the actors, as the leader explained, "performed in my father's day, but now are very old men." In some Cotswold villages, notably Chipping Campden, in Gloucestershire, mummers still perform. In Avening, according to the Reverend Canon C. W. Cooper, at least one of the old mummers still lives and knows the words of the play. The vicar hopes he may be persuaded to revive the traditional performances in the village.

DECEMBER

Plays are still given at Uttoxetor, in Staffordshire; in the Yorkshire dales and in various Cornish parishes. One of the oldest mumming plays to continue to modern times is the Evershot, Dorsetshire,
play of St. George and the Turkish Knight; but ever since World
War II, even this performance has been sporadic. Generally speaking, mummers' plays, which date from the Crusades, follow the
theme of the battle between King George (later St. George) and his
enemies, their subsequnt slaying and restoration to life.

BOAR'S HEAD SUPPER, ST. JOHN'S COLLEGE, CAMBRIDGE, CAMBRIDGE-
SHIRE
Day of St. John the Evangelist, December 27

The Boar's Head Supper of St. John's College, corresponds in
general character to Oxford's ceremony of Bringing in the Boar's
Head.

The custom of eating boar's head at Yuletide is thought to have
originated in pagan times, when a boar was killed at the winter
solstice and the head offered to Freya, goddess of plenty and peace.

Since Freya traditionally rode a gold-bristled boar, a lemon or
orange often is placed in the jaws, while the greens which decorate
the platter are gilded.

HOLY INNOCENTS' DAY
December 28

The Cross Day of the year is the name popularly given to Holy
Innocents' or Childermas, the time that commemorates Herod's
massacre of the Innocents. Sometimes, church bells are half or entirely muffled, in symbol of mourning, while for the same reason,
church altars used to be draped in black or violet. In popular tradition, fasting, inaction and special indulgence to children characterize
this day of ill omen when anything that is begun "is likely to turn
out badly."

183

Even Edward IV, whose coronation was set for Childermas, is said to have postponed the ceremony, because he thought the day was inauspicious for beginning his reign.

"It must have been begun on Cross Day," Shropshire people say about any unlucky enterprise. The proverb finds a counterpart in half a dozen counties from north to south, east to west. Among Cornish women, scrubbing, washing and cleaning are strictly taboo, while Northumbrian miners declare that to enter the mines on Childermas is to expose themselves to fatal accident.

NEW YEAR'S EVE

December 31

New Year's Eve is celebrated with watch services in chapels and churches, convivial home gatherings of friends and relatives, and the joyous pealing of church bells. In many northern communities, as already seen, a "first foot" lets in the New Year, bringing symbolic gifts to ensure the household's luck.

New Year's Eve is the accepted time for parties and merry-making. Young and old delight in divination games and fortune-telling rites, to disclose coming events. In Cornwall, one favorite device is to open the Bible at random, place the finger on a verse and from the sacred words interpret the "luck" of the next twelve months.

Girls try to learn the professions of their mates through the shapes that are made by dropping egg white or melted lead into a glass of water. An old North Country device is for girls to wash their chemises on New Year's Eve and hang them over a chair. During the night, the future husband appears in a vision and turns the garment!

New Year's Eve is no less significant in predicting the weather for the entire year than in foretelling affairs of the heart; for the way the wind blows, according to the old jingle, indicates the vagaries of the English climate for the next twelvemonth:

> If New Year's Eve night wind blows south,
> It betokeneth warmth and growth;
> If west, much milk, and fish in the sea;
> If north, much cold and storms there'll be;
> If east, the trees will bear much fruit;
> If north-east, flee it, man and brute!

NEW YEAR'S EVE WASSAILERS, WESTBURY-ON-SEVERN, GLOU-CESTERSHIRE

New Year's Eve

Wassailers used to go about the Gloucestershire communities of Michinhampton, Randwick, Avening, Stowe-on-the-wold, Stroud, and Westbury all through the holidays with a bowl decorated with greens and colored paper. Stopping from house to house, the wassailers would sing some such traditional carol as:

> Wassail, wassail, all over the town!
> Our toast is white, and our ale is brown,
> Our bowl is made of the white maple tree;
> With the wassailing bowl we'll drink to thee.

The wassailers' song continued with verses in praise of the master's horses, Cherry and Dobbin, and of his cows, Broad May, Fillpail and Colly, and ended with lines exhorting the master to fill up their bowl. The maid, too, "in the lily white smock," was enjoined to "let these jolly wassailers in."

Today Westbury-on-Severn is about the only place in Gloucestershire where the "jolly wassailers" still pass around the wassail, or health bowl, on New Year's Eve. According to one account of their singing, the men ". . . make no attempt to harmonize the song, but confine themselves to the simple melody, which they sing in stentorian tones, in a somewhat drawling fashion."

185

Formerly the Gloucestershire wassailers carried a maple wood bowl, adorned with greens and little dolls. This bowl, which was kept throughout the year at Michinhampton, later was replaced by a modern vessel. Wassailers, in olden times, as today, customarily receive coins and holiday cheer at each house visited.

PART II

THE EASTER CYCLE

THE EASTER CYCLE

Awake thou wintry earth,
Fling off thy sadness!
Fair vernal flowers, laugh forth
Your ancient gladness!
Christ is risen.
—THOMAS BLACKBURN, *An Easter Hymn.*

Easter is a movable feast. Therefore all other festivals in the Easter cycle—beginning with Septuagesima, or the Lost Sunday, nine weeks before Easter, and ending with Trinity, eight weeks after—depend upon Easter for their dates.

Easter always is reckoned as the first Sunday following the paschal full moon of the vernal equinox (March 21). Should the paschal full moon occur on a Sunday, Easter is observed on the Sunday following. Easter never comes *before* March 22, or *after* April 23.

In the pages that follow, movable days of the Easter cycle are arranged together in proper sequence and treated as a single unit, to avoid the confusion that always results when attempting to combine fixed and movable holiday dates.

Part III contains a "Table of Easter Dates and Movable Days of the Easter Cycle to 1984" (p254-55), which provides an accurate and usable chart. The summary of chronologically arranged "Movable Days of the Easter Cycle" found on pages 251-52 gives supplemental information concerning important days within this group.

189

THE EASTER CYCLE

SHROVE TUESDAY, OR PANCAKE DAY

But hark, I hear the pancake bell,
And fritters make a gallant smell,
The cooks are baking, frying, boyling,
Stewing, mincing, cutting, broyling,
Carving, gormandizing, roasting,
Carbonating, cracking, slashing, toasting.

This verse, written in *Poor Robin's Almanack* for 1684, gives a vivid picture of seventeenth century England's Shrove Tuesday preparations.

As the last day before Ash Wednesday and the beginning of Lent, Shrove Tuesday has for centuries been a day of pancake* feasting and indulgence in time-honored amusements, such as pancake-tossing contests, hurling and football games. In olden times cock-fighting and throwing,† rope-pulling, egg-throwing (egg-rolling) and many other sports characterized the day. London apprentices were given such complete freedom on Shrove Tuesday that at one time the day degenerated into a period of unbridled license.

Shrove Tuesday derives its popular name of Pancake Day from the great bell which, in pre-Reformation times, summoned villagers to confession and shriving by the parish priest. Later, when the bell which once called people to church became the signal for making pancakes, the day was designated Pancake Day and the bell, the Pancake Bell.

School children, apprentices, journeymen and shop workers joyously welcomed the bell's ringing, because it was the signal for

* Since no meat is eaten during Lent, it has been customary, from early times, to use up all the fat in the house for pancake-making.

† Tradition says the custom of cock-fighting and throwing originated in the idea of punishing *all* cocks for the crowing bird once associated with Peter's denial of Jesus! Another superstition is that cocks were punishable because they once betrayed the Saxons, at the time when the Danes had invaded Britain. The Saxons resolved to murder their oppressors Shrove Tuesday morning. The early crowing of cocks awoke the Danes, however, and gave them advance warning of the plan.

dropping work and rushing out to participate in the day's festivities, which in gaiety and variety were a close second to Christmas.

In some places it is still customary for bands of children to go about the villages, singing ditties and asking (or rather, *demanding*) something for Shrovetide!

> Nicky, Nicky, Nan,
> Give me some pancakes and then I'll be gone,
> But if you give me none,
> I'll throw a great stone
> And down your house will come

is the threat generations of Polperro lads have sung, to persuade housewives to give them a gift. In olden times the youngsters emphasized the words, at appropriate intervals, with smart blows of the club.

Although many of the day's old customs are forgotten, England universally celebrates Shrove Tuesday by eating pancakes made according to the cherished recipes mothers have handed down to daughters for many generations.

PANCAKE GREAZE, WESTMINSTER SCHOOL, LONDON

Shrove Tuesday

Annually on Shrove Tuesday Westminster School students enthusiastically perform their Lent Term Pancake Greaze, or ceremony of "Tossing the Pancake." According to time-honored tradition, the school cook carries the pancake in a procession headed by the college beadle, bearing the silver mace. The cook, attired in tall white cap, apron and jacket and carrying the pancake in a frying pan, is followed by the dean's verger, the dean and the head master. The arrival of the college cook is ceremoniously announced to the students assembled in the great hall, where a high bar running from wall to wall divides the upper from the lower schools. Formerly, a curtain hanging from this bar separated the two schools. The

Greaze competitors, consisting of one student chosen from each form, are lined up under the bar.

At a signal from the head master the college cook throws the pancake over the bar. Pandemonium breaks loose. Amid wild shouts and cheers, the contestants dive for the pancake. A terrible scrimmage ensues. At one time the entire school competed but the resulting scuffle became so ferocious that the representative system now prevails.

After two minutes of wild tussling, the head master calls time. Now one can hear a pin drop as the torn shreds of pancake are carefully examined. The lad retrieving the largest piece is announced the winner. He receives a guinea from the dean and cheers from the students, while the college cook gets ten shillings for the successful completion of his part in the proceedings.

Should the school cook make an unsuccessful throw, however, he may be "booked" by the indignant students, that is, receive a barrage of books for his clumsiness. This happened once in the annals of Westminster history, and the angry cook is said to have returned the blows by crowning a lad with his frying pan and cutting open his head. The feat of tossing a pancake over the high bar is a difficult task, but one in which school cooks are highly proficient.

The origin of the Pancake Greaze is unknown. Although Jeremy Bentham, a student from 1755 to 1760, writes that "the higher school was divided from the lower by a bar, and it was one of our pastimes to get the cook to throw a pancake over it," there is every reason to suppose that the school's traditional Shrovetide sport originated earlier than eighteenth century, or so, at least, Westminster boys like to think!

PANCAKE RACE, OLNEY, BUCKINGHAMSHIRE

Shrove Tuesday

On Shrove Tuesday Olney's parish church of Saints Peter and Paul rings the pancake bell which summons housewives to the traditional Pancake Race from Market Square to the church porch. The old custom was revived in 1948, after a war-time lapse.

People say that the pancake bell first rang in 1445, when it called parishioners to church for confession. Today, Olney's bell sounds at 11:30, and again at 11:45, to warn housewives to prepare their pancakes and be ready for the race. Sometimes the sounding of the church bell is supplemented by handbells because, as the inhabitants say, "If the wind doesn't blow right, you can't hear the pancake bell."

Promptly at 11:55 the contestants, who assemble by the pump in the market square, start the unique 415-yard course to the church. Each woman holds a frying pan containing a sizzling-hot pancake. A set of four rules is strictly enforced:

1. No competitor may be under eighteen, and she must have lived in Olney Parish (or Warrington) for at least six months previous to the race.
2. Each woman must wear an apron and cover her head with hat or scarf.
3. Slacks or trousers are strictly forbidden.
4. Contestants must toss their pancakes at least three times during the race, once at the start, once during the final spurt up the church path, and once at some other point during the race.

Following the race, there is a short church service, obligatory for all contestants. The vicar gives his blessing to the winner, and the verger the traditional kiss. According to old custom, all pancakes surviving the race should go to the bell-ringers for their Shrove Tuesday feast.

In recent years the idea of celebrating Shrove Tuesday's Pancake Race spread to America, and now housewives of Liberal, Kansas, compete with housewives of Olney, England, for the coveted skillet trophy awarded to the winner of this exciting international contest.

The custom of ringing the Pancake or "Fritter" Bell continues in several parishes besides Olney: notably, Pontefract, in Yorkshire;

194

Shrewsbury, in Shropshire; Claybrook and Belgrave, in Leicestershire; Ilmington, in Warwickshire; and in some other communities.

GOING A-SHROVING, DURWESTON, DORSETSHIRE

Shrove Tuesday

In Durweston, a picturesque Dorset hamlet where horses wear gaily tasseled ear muffs in winter, and a carving of St. Ledger, patron of blacksmiths, is over the parish church door, village children still "go a-shroving" as they probably did in pre-Reformation days. Small groups of boys and girls visit the neighborhood cottages singing the following ditty and receiving gifts of "biscuits, fruit, cakes and money," according to an old man who has witnessed the custom many years. Here is the traditional shroving song, as given by my informant, with the exception of the truckle cheese, which he insisted upon calling *knuckle* cheese.

> Here we come a-shroving
> For a little piece of pancake
> For a little truckle cheese
> Of your own making.
>
> Blow the fire and het the pan,
> For we come a-shroving.

On July 3, 1925, Valentine Rickman died, leaving a fifty-pound bequest, to be administered by Durweston's rector and churchwardens. The will specified that interest from the sum, now amounting to an annual one pound, fourteen and six, should be divided among children who perpetuate the old custom by going a-shroving to at least three village houses.

"Contributions are added to the interest money and the sum divided equally among the children," said the old man, who went on to explain that once the boys and girls went about in groups from door to door. Now, because the teacher is afraid of accidents, "she lines 'em up in funeral procession style!"

195

In Piddlehinton and some other Dorsetshire villages, as well as in Durweston, boys and girls also go a-shroving on the last day before Lent, but sometimes they take shards or broken crockery along to bombard the doors where they stop and sing for pancakes.

HURLING MATCH, ST. COLOMB MAJOR, CORNWALL

Shrove Tuesday

Parishioners of St. Colomb Major and their rural neighbors hold a Shrove Tuesday Hurling Match between town and country. Because the number of contestants is unlimited, the game often includes eight hundred or a thousand players.

Since hurling is a rough sport, St. Colomb protects its shop and house windows with wooden screens and shutters. As the crowd gathers in the afternoon and waits for the contest to begin, the old battered ball is passed reverently from hand to hand. In olden times, perhaps, people may have believed that some of the ball's virtue was transferred to those who touched it.

The ball is thrown up in the center of town. The goals are two old stone troughs (possibly ancient cross bases), each located a mile distant, at opposite sides of the starting point. The game consists of a series of rushes, runs and tacklings before the ball finally is carried to the goal. Each of the two teams tries to take the ball to its respective goal; or, failing this, to get it beyond the parish boundary.

The hurling ends in the evening, when everyone gathers in the market place to hear the winner announced, to cheer for the "town" or the "country" ball, as the case may be, and to carry the victor shoulder high through the crowd.

Then comes the ceremony of "drinking the silver ball." The ball is washed, then dropped into a beer receptacle. The beer is offered to bystanders, amid cheers, huzzas, toasts and wishes for good luck.

The nearby town of St. Colomb Minor, like its better known neighbor St. Colomb Major, also holds an annual hurling match. Once hurling was a widespread sport among Cornish men; but now it survives in only three parishes, St. Ives,* St. Colomb Major, and St. Colomb Minor.

Although nobody really knows the origin of Shrovetide hurling matches and football contests, some people think that these games, like the morris dancers' leapings, originated in primitive ceremonies symbolizing the conflict between winter and spring. Just as the sun ascends in early spring, according to this explanation, so balls are thrown high into the air.

FOOTBALL MATCH, ASHBOURNE, DERBYSHIRE

Shrove Tuesday

The little town of Ashbourne celebrates Shrove Tuesday by closing shops, drawing shutters, and giving itself over to complete enjoyment of the day's events. Shrove Tuesday football games in Ashbourne and many other English communities doubtless are an outgrowth of medieval practice, when apprentices celebrated the last day before Lent with feasting, drinking and rough sports.

Ashbourne still observes the two-day festival with much of her old-time gusto on the part of more than five thousand townsfolk and spectators. Housewives have a busy day, watching the sport and at the same time preparing quantities of pancakes for the menfolk, who come home hungry, tired and soaked to the skin after the day's activities. The pancakes are made after a traditional recipe.

The players divide into two teams, according to whether they live on the north or the south side of the Henmore, which flows serenely through the center of town. The goals (located three miles apart) are water wheels. In order to reach them, contestants must go through streets, alleys, fields and deep water—everywhere, in fact, except the graveyard.

*See p34.

197

To start the game, a great cork-filled multicolored football is tossed up in the center of town about two o'clock. "One year, the Prince of Wales kicked it off," an eighty-three-year-old man proudly confided. The team catching the ball tries to get it over to the opposite side of town. The game rages furiously for hours. "It's a rough sport," chuckled the old man, "what with leaping after the ball and wading through the stream, which is cold at that time of year." The winner, after depositing the ball in the goal, celebrates by visiting Ashbourne's public-houses, which treat him to as much free beer as he wants.

But the rest of Ashbourne's inhabitants go home to dry clothes and cozy fires and as many hot Shrovetide pancakes as their stomachs can hold. These traditional cakes are made from a half pound of flour, two eggs, a pinch of salt, and milk to make a thin batter, according to the old man's daughter, who read me the family recipe, neatly hand-written in a long, ledger-like book. "You put four table-spoons of batter into a teacup," she said, "and then pour it onto a greased griddle, baking till golden brown." The pancakes are dinner-plate size, proper for appetites of hungry men.

"Nobody knows how Ashbourne's Shrovetide festival started," smiled the old man in answer to my query as to when it all began. "Like our Wakes Week, it all started years and years and years before I was born."

OTHER SHROVETIDE FOOTBALL MATCHES

Shrove Tuesday

Among some of many places which, like Ashbourne, are especially noted for their Shrove Tuesday football matches are Alnwick and Rothbury, in Northumberland; Corfe Castle, in Dorset; Atherstone and Nuneaton, in Warwickshire; Dorking, in Surrey; Sedgefield and Chester-le-Street, in Durham, and Derby, county town of Derbyshire.

Each town celebrates the sport in local fashion. At Alnwick, for example, the game was played, until 1813, between the married and the unmarried men. Today the contest is between the parishes of St. Michael's and St. Peter's. The player finally capturing the ball is entitled to keep it.

At Corfe Castle, center of the Purbeck stone quarries, the Court of Marblers and Stone Cutters is held, and then the football is kicked through the village and along the old road to Poole. This custom is to commemorate preservation of ancient rights of way to the nearest harbor from which stone could be shipped.

Atherstone citizens start their game at three in the afternoon, end it at five, and proclaim as winner the man able to escape his pursuing comrades and get away with the ball.

Dorking, on the other hand, applies the old name of "camping" to the game. Dorking plays football between goals set up in the north and the south ends of town, and makes the village clerk and church sexton responsible for furnishing the ball. In olden times, the ball was carried in procession through the streets by men who exhibited the motto:

> Kick away, both Whig and Tory;
> Wind and Water, Dorking's Glory.

In 1930, town authorities tried unsuccessfully to suppress Shrovetide football in Chester-le-Street, where people have indulged in the sport for over six hundred years.

This old rhyme refers to Derby's famous football match, in which parishioners of All Saints' and St. Peter's compete. Similar football jingles exist in many parts of England:

> Pancakes and fritters
> Say All Saints' and St. Peter's.
> When will the ball come?
> Say the bells of St. Alkumen (Alkmund).
> Says St. Werabo (Werburgh)
> O very well,
> Says little Michael.

ENGLISH FESTIVALS

ASH WEDNESDAY

Ash Wednesday, the first day of Lent, is called *Dies cinerum,* after the Western Church's ancient custom of strewing ashes on the heads of parishioners as a sign of penitence. Gregory the Great is thought to have originated the custom.

Traditionally the ashes are made from palms blessed and used on the previous Palm Sunday. As the priest consecrates the ashes at the altar, he dips his thumb and strews ashes on the heads of worshippers, or marks a cross on the forehead, saying, *Memento quod cines es, et in cinerem reverteris* (Remember man that thou art dust, and unto dust thou shalt return.)

The forty-day Lenten fast, beginning on Ash Wednesday, commemorates Jesus Christ's forty-day fast in the wilderness.

In England, as in European countries, many popular superstitions are associated with Ash Wednesday. In Norfolk and Suffolk people say the direction of Ash Wednesday's wind foretells its direction throughout Lent, while Worcestershire housewives declare bad luck dogs the footsteps of any woman who leaves soap suds in her tubs over Ash Wednesday!

In Ditchling, Sussex, and possibly elsewhere, children carry pointed ash wood sticks to school on Ash Wednesday. The boys and girls dip the sticks into ink and run about trying to mark each other's foreheads. If any child escapes and goes about "unblacked," the others tread on his toes! This sport, like April Fool errands,* stops promptly at noon.

Nobody could tell me the origin of the game, although it was suggested that possibly the children use ash for their sticks because of its identification in native gipsy lore with the tree upon which Christ was crucified.

"Marble Day" was the popular name Sussex people used to give Ash Wednesday, because from early times marble playing was a favorite sport on the first day of Lent. The official marble season

---

* *See* April Fool's Day, p44.

opens on Ash Wednesday and continues until twelve noon Good Friday, after which, according to the old rules, anyone found playing can have his marbles destroyed. Sussex marble matches always excite as much attention as cricket matches elsewhere, and championship in this game is a deeply coveted honor.

Ash Wednesday is associated with special foods, which vary from county to county. In Herefordshire, Worcestershire, and Cheshire, hasty pudding (quickly stirred up from flour, milk and sweet syrup) is a favorite dish, while Leicestershire goes in for fritters and fish, peas and frumenty; Worcestershire has its simnels, which in other parts of England are associated with Mid-Lent, or Mothering Sunday, rather than with Lent's beginning.

STATIONERS' COMPANY SERVICE, CHURCH OF ST. FAITH, LONDON

Ash Wednesday

The Stationers' Company, which was incorporated by Royal Charter in 1557 and once held sole right of printing in England, observes an annual Ash Wednesday service in the Church of St. Faith, in the crypt of St. Paul's Cathedral, at about 2:40 in the afternoon.

On May 21, 1612, Alderman John Norton left a will which provided for buns and ale, to be given every Ash Wednesday to members of this ancient company. Following the annual service, the terms of the will are carried out at Stationers' Hall, which is located in the narrow Stationers' Hall Court, off the north side of Ludgate Hill.

MID-LENT, OR MOTHERING SUNDAY

Mothering Sunday, which falls on the fourth Sunday in Lent, started as a purely religious occasion. In medieval times faithful worshippers presented gifts to the Mother Church on this day. The old and still widely observed custom of "going a-mothering" at Mid-Lent is an outgrowth of this earlier ceremony.

Mothering Sunday is the traditional occasion for English sons and daughters, wherever they may be, to return home bringing their mothers gifts of flowers and cakes; sometimes of comfits,* or "lambs' tails"; or of white sugar candies, flavored with caraway and spice. The custom is very ancient. Long before the Christian Church, the Greeks held festival for Cybele, mother of the gods, and the Romans celebrated rites in honor of divine motherhood. Although America's custom of dedicating the second Sunday in May to the mothers of the land originated less than fifty years ago, the idea came from England, and before that, from pagan ceremonies to honor motherhood.

English Mothering Day customs vary pleasantly from county to county. In northern England, for example, the "mothering" cakes are *simnels*. In pre-war days these creations resembled rich fruit cakes, with delightful decorations of glacéd fruits, or almond paste flowers, birds and intertwining garlands. In olden times parents and children usually attended morning services at the parish church, and then participated in a family dinner of such traditional foods as roast lamb or veal, rice pudding, frumenty, and home-brewed wine, in addition to the simnel cake.

Herrick wrote of the Gloucestershire custom of "going a-mothering" in the lines:

> I'le to thee a Simnell bring,
> 'Gainst thou go'st a *mothering,*
> So that, when she blesseth thee,
> Half that blessing thou'lt give me.†

Bury, in Lancashire, is famous for its simnels which have been shipped in tins to British subjects all over the world, so that, wherever they may be, they can celebrate Mothering Sunday in traditional fashion. In Bury, boys and girls take their mothers small bunches of primroses (once of violets), and the *mothers* (not the children) furnish the simnel, which holds place of honor at a large family tea.

* Sugar balls with seeds in the center, or some other kind of sweet.
† Robert Herrick. *Hesperides.* "To Dianeme. A Ceremonie in Gloscester."

In London's East End, as in the little church of Stoke Poges, Buckinghamshire, and many communities throughout England, special Mothering Sunday services are held for the parish children. Boys and girls bring nosegays of violets and primroses, to be blessed at the altar and presented to their mothers.

Shrewsbury, in Shropshire, is no less famed for simnels than Bury. Both Shrewsbury and Devizes, in Wiltshire, claim first honors as makers of the renowned cake. Be this as it may, Shrewsbury simnels differ greatly from those of Lancashire, Wiltshire, and other counties. Her simnels are rather heavy, *boiled*, black cakes, made within a saffron-colored crust. The Devizes simnel is star-shaped and crustless, while Bury's variety is baked, crustless, and often decorated with preserved fruits or sugar trimmings.

In southern England, on the other hand, the simnel is supplanted by wafers, or thin waffles. They are baked in elaborately designed tongs or irons,* cherished heirlooms in many families, which hand them down from one generation to another. These little round wafers are eaten in such quantity that Mothering Day often is called "Waffering Sunday."

Although the celebration of the fourth Sunday in Lent differs from county to county and strong rivalry exists regarding recipes and methods of simnel making, the old custom of observing Mothering Sunday remains an enduring symbol of the loyalty and affection which unite British families of every class, both in England and her colonies.

* Many English museums have rare examples of these irons. One of the finest collections is in London's Victoria and Albert Museum. Salisbury Museum has an excellent small group of irons, while Winchester Museum possesses some three-hundred-year-old irons, which are loaned annually to the Baverstock family of Chilbolton, in Hampshire, which for at least two centuries has been famous for making stamped Mid-Lent wafers.

Wafer irons or tongs have been used in England since the sixteenth century. The old method is to heat the irons in the fire and grease them with butter. A spoonful of thin batter, made of flour, sugar and water, is placed on one side of the plate. The iron is closed and the wafer baked. Doubtless the wafers, like Mothering Sunday itself, originally had religious significance, and the irons probably once made the holy Church wafers.

ENGLISH FESTIVALS

CARLING,* OR PASSION SUNDAY

Since early times the fifth Sunday in Lent has been called Carling Sunday, and it is the custom to eat *carlings,* or peas, which are soaked in water overnight, fried in butter, and seasoned with pepper and salt. Sometimes, as in Northumberland, sugar and rum are added for greater tastiness. The practice of eating carlings is particularly popular in northern England, and Scotland. Although the custom is not so universal as in olden times, Rothbury, Belford, and other Northumbrian towns, as well as various Yorkshire communities, still eat carlings on the fifth Sunday in Lent.

In Nottinghamshire there is a folk rhyme:

> Care Sunday, Care away,
> Palm Sunday and Easter Day

which means, of course, that Care Sunday is just two weeks before Easter.

From time immemorial boys and girls have used carlings in fortune-telling games; for, according to tradition, the person getting the last pea in the dish will be first to marry!

DISTRIBUTION OF PAX CAKES, HENTLAND, KING'S CAPLE AND SELLACK, HEREFORDSHIRE

Palm Sunday

Three hundred years ago someone left the sum of five shillings, tenpence, to provide Pax cakes on Palm Sunday in each of the three charming Wye valley hamlets of Hentland, King's Caple and Sellack. The giver of the symbolic peace cakes has long since been forgotten,

---

* Carling Sunday goes by many different names, which vary from place to place, according to local dialect and custom. *Carline, Carlin, Carl,* and *Care,* probably meaning the period of care or sorrow connected with the Lord's Passion, are other forms applied to the day. In early Worcestershire records the day is referred to as *Patient* Sunday, which some think is a colloquial form of *Passion,* and others an indication that patience still is needed to get through the rest of Lent! In parts of Cambridgeshire *Whirlin' Sunday* was the name once applied to the day because of a special delicacy known as "Whirlin' Cakes." Burnley, in Lancashire, on the contrary, eats fig, or fag, pies on this Sunday.

but the custom he instituted, said to be one of Herefordshire's oldest folk practices, still is observed with scrupulous care. In the three villages the cakes are distributed with the vicar's admonition to accept them in spiritual preparation for Easter, with the solemn resolve to forgive all jealousies and quarrels.

The Pax Cakes (for which buns sometimes are substituted) are round and hard, and about four-and-a-half inches in diameter by a quarter-inch thick. The surface of the cakes is stamped with the conventional figure of the Lamb of God enclosed in a circle.

Following the morning service, members of the congregation often receive the Pax Cakes from the churchwardens, who give out the charity from white linen-covered baskets. At one time a cup of beer was added. Later, when funds for this portion of the bequest gave out, neighborhood farmers brewed their own beer so the original custom might be perpetuated.

In Hentland, the vicar usually breaks a cake with two or three parishioners as he says, "Peace and good will," or "Peace and good neighborhood." His example is followed by others in the group. In Sellack, where the custom varies slightly, the women often leave church holding the Pax Cakes on top of their prayer books, while the men usually slip the cakes into their pockets.

HOLY WEEK, EASTER AND THE EASTER HOLIDAYS

Old folk say that on Easter the sun dances on the horizon for joy. People used to rise at dawn and walk out into the fields to see this miracle. Until the late nineteenth century, it was customary in Shropshire to ascend the Wrekin to see the sun dance. In Sussex, on the contrary, nobody ever actually saw the occurrence, because the Devil always put something between the sun and the observer's eyes!

The Venerable Bede says that the name Easter comes from *Eostre*, goddess of dawn and spring, whom the Anglo-Saxons worshipped in April, or *Eastermonath*.

The Christian Resurrection festival reflects many elements of earlier vernal solstice rites, to which it bears symbolic parallel; for just as the pagan Saxons in early spring welcomed the sun's rising and the death of winter, so Christians rejoice in the rise of the Sun of Righteousness and His triumph over death.

Many folk sayings and weather predictions center about Easter which, to country people everywhere, was important in sowing and reaping. In Hertfordshire, Worcestershire and Wiltshire, for example, there is the familiar saying that

> A good deal of rain on Easter Day
> Gives a crop of good grass, but little good hay.

Easter sunshine, on the other hand, predicts fair Whitsun weather, an added reason for wishing to see the sun shine on Easter morning.

Since early times England's Easter holidays have been the occasion for participating in popular sports and pastimes, and eating traditional foods.

Among the customary Eastertide amusements, observed in ancient times but now discontinued, were "holly-bussing," or going into the woods with music and laughter, to gather holly to decorate the village cross; "heaving," or "lifting," the custom tradition says originated with Edward I, in 1290, who gave money to his householders to heave or lift him out of bed, in commemoration of Christ's resurrection. Then there was "playing at handball for a tansy cake," which refers to the bitter herbs used to flavor the Easter cakes. Although the tansy reminded people of Christ's sufferings, the cakes, which were made with butter, eggs and sugar, could not have been too unpalatable rewards for winners of the Easter ball games!

> At stool-ball, *Lucia,* let us play,
> For Sugar-cakes and Wine;
> Or for a Tansie let us pay,
> The losse, or thine, or mine,

wrote Herrick,* in reference to this custom, which was popular in his day.

Cheese cakes in Hertfordshire, pudding-pies in Kent, baked custards in Yorkshire, roast lamb in Sussex, roast veal in the Midlands—

* Robert Herrick. *Hesperides.*

206

these are some of England's traditional Easter foods; and even though food restrictions still prohibit many of them, the fragrant memory lingers on from a more prosperous era, when people said, "Each different county boasts a different taste."

The Easter festival, with its rough sports, robust foods and picturesque customs originated, as already noted, in primitive agricultural beliefs connected with growth of crops and increase of flocks. Largely because of its roots in remote antiquity, Easter forges pagan and Christian elements into a chain of lasting faith.

DISTRIBUTION OF THE ROYAL MAUNDY, WESTMINSTER ABBEY, LONDON

Maundy Thursday

On Maundy Thursday Westminster Abbey holds a special service,* when the Lord High Almoner, representing the sovereign, and attendant officials perform an ancient ceremony to commemorate Jesus Christ's washing of His disciples' feet at the Last Supper. On this occasion the Royal Maundy money is dispensed to as many poor men and as many poor women as the years of the sovereign's age.

The Maundy Money, consisting of silver pennies minted for the occasion and equaling in value the number of the monarch's years, are placed in white leather purses with long leather drawstrings. Red purses, containing additional money gifts, are also prepared, as a substitute for the food British sovereigns once bestowed on the poor. The purses—both white and red—are piled on the great golden Maundy vessel which, throughout the year, is exhibited in the London Tower Jewel Room. The red and white drawstrings, hanging over the edge of the alms plate, recall olden days when purses were fastned to the girdles by long leather thongs.

The Yeomen of the Guard in full dress uniform carry the Maundy gifts through the Abbey nave as part of an impressive and picturesque procession. The Lord High Almoner and officiating clergy wear

* Although the Abbey is open to the public for the ceremony, tickets for reserved sections should be obtained in advance at the Royal Almonry Office, 7 Queen Anne's Gate, London.

towels about their waists, in memory of days of actual foot-washing. White flowers are also carried, reminders of the time when a preliminary foot-washing with sweet herbs was considered necessary before a sovereign could perform the ceremony.

Following the service, traditionally opened with the Latin words, *Mandatum novum do vobis* ("A new commandment I give unto you"), the Lord High Almoner, in the sovereign's name, distributes the Royal Maundy to each of the men and women who have been selected as alms recipients.

The history of this ceremonial is filled with picturesque detail. Although nobody knows just when the custom began in England, it has certainly grown in impressiveness with the passage of years.

Foot-washing in Westminster Abbey was said to have originated with the medieval monks, who annually bathed the feet of thirteen poor men, seated in the East Cloister. Following the rite, the abbot dried the men's feet with a towel, kissed them, and then gave the paupers alms, food and drink. It was not until later that this simple ceremony, dictated by Christ's mandate "to love one another," began to be performed by British sovereigns.

Edward II, in 1326, at the age of forty, seems to have been the first ruler to observe Maundy Thursday by washing the feet of fifty poor men. Edward III, when fifty, provided gifts of slippers for each of a like number of men at his Maundy, in 1361. In all probability he thus established the modern custom of distributing gifts equal to the years of the sovereign's age.

Queen Mary, in 1556, celebrated her Maundy by giving her magnificent fur-lined coat to the oldest and neediest of the women recipients of her gifts. It was Queen Elizabeth I, however, who finally substituted money for the gowns she had previously bestowed, thus inaugurating the present practice of Royal Maundy alms.

Queen Elizabeth I, when thirty-nine, in the year 1572, presided over a magnificent Maundy for thirty-nine poor women. The Queen knelt upon cushions, and, assisted by her ladies-in-waiting, successively washed one foot of each person (following a preliminary foot-washing by her sub-almoner, almoner and others). For each woman, the Queen used a silver basin, filled with warm water, upon which pungent flowers floated. After the ceremony, Queen Elizabeth distributed lavish gifts including, in addition to food and clothing, small purses each holding thirty-nine pence, and other leather purses containing twenty shillings each.

Early in the eighteenth century, actual foot-washings by English sovereigns ceased, and today's symbolic ceremony of the Royal Maundy was substituted for the older rite.

GOOD FRIDAY

Good Friday, anniversary of Christ's crucifixion, is a day of mourning and solemnity in the Christian Church. Places of worship are draped in black. In the village of Ayot St. Peter, in Herefordshire, the church bells begin tolling at three in the afternoon—the reputed hour of Christ's death—and continue for thirty-three times, in commemoration of the years of the Savior's life. Corresponding customs are observed in some other villages.

According to folk belief, Durham blacksmiths consider it unlucky to drive a nail on Good Friday; Derbyshire and Northumbrian lead miners refuse to enter the mines; and housewives everywhere agree that if you wash on Good Friday, the suds will turn to blood, but should you, on the contrary, break a dish, you will have good luck, since the sharp edges pierce Judas Iscariot's body!

In contrast to the gloomy conviction that to wash on Good Friday is unlucky, is the widespread belief that to bake is good. This goes back to the legend that when on the way to Golgotha, Christ stopped to rest at the cottage of a woman who was washing. Not wishing to be seen with a common malefactor, the woman threw suds at Jesus and ordered him to leave.

He shouldered his cross again and started on his way. He soon came to a cottage where a woman was baking. She offered him a bench to sit on, bread to eat and water to drink. From then on, people have said that women who wash on Good Friday are cursed, but those who bake are blessed.

209

Perhaps this folk belief accounts for the superstition that Good Friday cross buns possess rare virtues. They will keep all year without growing moldy, and a bit of the loaf, grated and mixed with water, brandy or milk, cures diarrhea and other ailments! In some humble Devonshire and Worcestershire cottages a Good Friday bun hangs from the smoke-stained rafters, since people think the holy bread protects sailors from shipwreck, clothes from moths and corn from mice!

In olden days London streets were filled with the cries of the Good Friday bun vendors, who lured the last penny from pockets of the unwary, with reminders, such as:

> One a penny, two a penny,
> Hot cross buns.
> If you have no daughters,
> Give them to your sons;
> But if you have none of these merry little elves,
> Then you may keep them all for yourselves.

Bees should be shifted on Good Friday and no other day, according to farmers of Devonshire, Herefordshire and Cornwall; while in Dorsetshire, Worcestershire, Norfolk and some other places, peas, potatoes and beans planted on Good Friday will prosper. West Riding Yorkshire farmers hotly disagree, however, claiming that soil should never be touched on this day!

Good Friday is important in rural weather lore, for,

> If it rain on Good Friday *or* Easter Day,
> Twill be a good year of grass but a sorry year of hay.

GIVING THE WIDOWS' SIXPENCES, ST. BARTHOLOMEW THE GREAT, LONDON

Good Friday

Every Good Friday the old Norman Church of St. Bartholomew the Great, in London's Smithfield area, gives a curious dole of twenty-one sixpences to twenty-one parish widows. Following the usual morning service, the congregation, led by rector, churchwardens and verger, go out to the churchyard, to a certain mossy, table-topped tombstone. Here, for several centuries, twenty-one sixpences have been placed. The poor widows come forward to receive their gifts. Each woman, in turn, kneels before picking up her coin, then walks across the low tombstone to receive a hot cross bun and a share in the morning's offering. Should any of the widows be too infirm to attend the service in person, someone carries her present to her house.

The donor of the Good Friday charity is unknown. Some say his name was lost when the Great Fire of 1666 swept away the parish records. Others claim the custom was first mentioned in a bequest of 1686. Regardless of the originator of the charity, however, it continues to modern times as one of London's many delightful old customs.

Hanging up the Hot Cross Bun, "The Widow's Son," London

Good Friday

Every Good Friday morning, a sailor suspends a fresh, dated, hot cross bun to a bunch of dusty buns hanging from the rafters of "The Widow's Son," a public house at 75 Devons Road, in London.

After performing the curious ceremony, the sailor is treated to beer "on the house."

"The custom started on Good Friday, back in 1823," the proprietor told me. "A poor widow and her son were tenants in a cottage which stood right here. The boy went to sea, and the mother was so upset that the sailor, trying to comfort her, wrote a letter saying he would be back by Good Friday and to save him a hot cross bun.

"The boy was lost at sea, but his mother expected him home and kept him a cross bun," the man continued. "Even when he never returned, the widow refused to believe him dead. She saved a bun for her missing son and hung it up from the cottage ceiling. There they are!" said the proprietor, pointing to a bunch of dusty, discolored buns suspended above the bar. "Another year, another Good Friday, another bun!"

The custom of bun-hanging has been going on now for over a hundred and thirty years. When the original cottage was torn down, the public house called "The Widow's Son" was erected on the site. The annual bun ceremony is required, according to the terms of the property's lease. During World War I and II, when enemy bombs fell throughout the neighborhood, some of the original buns were lost. The main bunch remains, however. In addition to supplying the bun for the annual ceremony, the proprietor tells me, he furnishes four trays of hot cross buns for his Good Friday patrons.

PACE-EGGING, NORTHWESTERN COUNTIES

Easter Eve

The old customs of Pace-Egging,* or going about on Easter Eve in fantastic garb and performing plays from house to house in the neighborhood, is still observed by bands of school boys at Far and Near Sawrey, in Ambleside, and at Grasmere, in Westmorland, and some parts of Cheshire, West Yorkshire and Lancashire.

Once pace-egging, or "jolly boying," as it sometimes is called, was a popular custom throughout the Lake country and elsewhere. The performers were men and boys who went about, the week before Easter, singing and reciting amusing lines and enacting a folk drama something like the mummers' play of St. George and the Dragon. Like the mummers, the players blackened faces, dressed grotesquely and presented a traditional set of personages, including Lord Nelson (with a star on his bosom and a blue garter on his knee), Old Mister Brown Bags, Toss-pot, a man-woman who had charge of the finances, and other stock characters.

Nowadays pace-egging is fast dying out, but here and there, well-known bands, such as the school boys of Midgeley, in Yorkshire, who wear wonderful beflowered and beribboned headdresses,

* Pace is a dialect form of *Pasch,* meaning Easter. Hence a *pace* egg (sometimes called a *paste egg*) is an Easter egg, and Pace-egging is "Easter-egging."

continue the custom with old-time enthusiasm. In the Sawreys a band of six boys and girls ranging in age from about ten or twelve to the early teens have learned the traditional pace-eggers' play from their elders and give it annually. The children maintain their own wardrobe and do everything without adult assistance. Coins, sweets or goodies of any sort are acceptable gifts to the pace-eggers, but originally eggs were their principal reward.

Pace eggs are hard-boiled, and then gilded, decorated or colored with vegetable or flower dyes. The Pasque-flower (*anemone pulsatilla*) used to be, and may still be used for green; gorse or furze blossoms for yellow; beet root for red. In the Sawreys, onion skins tied to the egg shells and then immersed in boiling water for fifteen minutes produce charming effects in yellow and brown. Later, the eggs are used for Easter sports, such as egg-hitting, throwing, or rolling contests. Once the shells were broken, the eggs were eaten.

In many parts of England the Pace-eggers consist of bands of children who go about singing ditties such as this rhyme from Wilmslow, in Cheshire:

> Please, Mr. ——
> Please give us an Easter egg;
> If you do not give us one,
> Your hen will lay an addled one,
> Your cock shall lay a stone.

DISTRIBUTION OF THE EASTER DOLE, ELLINGTON, HAMPSHIRE

Easter, or Easter Monday

The old Hampshire village of Ellington has an Easter dole which goes to a traveler having slept in the parish for at least one night.

Probably this gift, which is made in accordance with an early charity, dates back to times when poor and destitute wayfarers had to depend upon village bounty for sufficient meat and drink to sustain them on their journey.

213

PACE EGG-ROLLING, PRESTON, LANCASHIRE

Easter Monday

An annual pace egg-rolling contest is traditional to Preston, in Lancashire, as to Selby, in Yorkshire, Far and Near Sawrey, near Ambleside, in Westmorland, and other North Country places. Pace eggs, as already noted, are hard-boiled eggs, dyed every color of the rainbow. The eggs are rolled in lively competition down the grassy slopes of Avenham Park and used in games of many sorts.

Possibly America's custom of Easter Monday egg-rolling for children on the White House lawn originated in the Old World pace-egg games and sports, which doubtless were familiar to many of the early English settlers.

COCONUT DANCERS, BACUP, LANCASHIRE

Easter Monday

Bacup, in Lancashire, celebrates Easter Monday with one of England's most picturesque dance survivals.

Eight men, with blackened hands and faces and wooden clogs on their feet, parade through the streets in single file, then break up and dance in figure formation. The dancers wear fantastic costumes, recently consisting of frilled white headdresses, black jerseys and short red and white horizontally striped barrel skirts worn over black breeches. The most remarkable features of their attire, however, are the small wooden discs, or "nuts," which the dancers fasten to hands and knees. Larger nuts are attached at the waist. These nuts give the ceremony the name of the "Coconut," or "Coco-Nutters'" Dance, because, as the performers dance, they strike the wooden nuts together, making a tattoo accompaniment for the various steps.

Beside the "Coconut" Dance, the performers also give the "Garland Dance," which is also characterized by wooden clogs, but in which the men hold large artificial garlands.

214

THE EASTER CYCLE

Easter Monday

At ten o'clock on Easter Monday, the bells of Biddenden's Church of All Saints' ring, summoning the parish poor to the workhouse, to receive a charity established centuries ago. Trustees of the charity and the village schoolmaster dispense the dole, consisting nowadays of bread and cocoa, or some other obtainable food, in lieu of the bread and cheese stipulated in the original bequest. In addition to the foods, which are given to all local poor who apply, parishioners and visitors alike receive the gift of a "Biddenden Cake," to commemorate the two sisters who established the bequest.

Biddenden is very proud of the donors, Mary and Eliza Chulkhurst, known as the "Biddenden Twins." The tiny village green has a gaily painted sign in memory of the sisters whose legend has made the picturesque Kentish village famous for hundreds of years.

The two girls were born Siamese twins, joined together at shoulder and hips. Legend says the sisters lived in the eleventh century. At the age of thirty-four one of them died. Physicians urged the other to let them save her life by severing her from the dead twin. "No," she replied. "As we came together, we will go together."

About six hours later the second sister died. The "Biddenden Maids" bequeathed to their village a tract of twenty acres, to be known as "Bread and Cheese Lands." Income from the property was to provide an annual charity of bread and cheese for the parish poor and cakes for strangers. The "Biddenden Cakes" are not actually cakes, but hard inedible biscuits, measuring four-and-a-quarter by two-and-a-quarter inches. The biscuits are stamped with images of the twins, joined at shoulder and hips. At the top of the cake are engraved the names,

Eliza and Mary
Chulkhurst

and on one stiff apron is 34, the sisters' supposed age, and on the other "in 1100," the legendary birth date. "Biddenden" is written across the bottom.

The local baker makes the cakes in a special mold. Sometimes as many as a thousand are needed for the ceremony. In 1950, seven hundred were used. People keep the cakes from year to year, treasuring them as relics. A new baker had taken over the old bake shop when I was in Biddenden; but he had bought the original mold. He made up a half dozen cakes, specially for me, so I might take them back to America.

The local workhouse, where the annual ceremony is held, is built on a hill on the supposed Chulkhurst property, and looks out across the beautiful rolling meadows of the "Bread and Cheese Lands." The distribution of loaves generally takes from an hour to an hour and a half, says Mr. H. Gordon Jones, Hon. Secretary to the Trust. About seventy persons apply for the charity, each one bringing a clean white pillowcase to hold the two two-pound loaves and other foods which are given away. The administrator of the charity stands inside the workhouse, and passes out the dole from the open window.

Edward Hasted, historian of Kent, wrote in 1778, in his *History and Topographical Survey of Kent*, that the donors of the charity were named Preston, rather than Chulkhurst, and that the figures engraved on the cakes represent two poor widows—intended recipients of the dole—and not the celebrated twins. He reasoned that the "Biddenden myth" arose from the engraving on the cakes which he asserted could be no more than fifty years old. There is always someone who tries to disprove an old legend! But in this case, the great Hasted himself is thoroughly disproved. Biddenden still cherishes the original Churchwardens' accounts which I was permitted to study. These records show that, as far back as 1645, a hundred and thirty-three years before Hasted's work, the charity was being administered. A few years later, in Cromwell's time, a certain village rector laid claim to the Bread and Cheese Charity. The faded entries in the yellowed pages bear witness to the fact that even then the dole was continued. It took two trips to London and the expenditure of parish funds to settle the dispute, but settled it was. Although nobody really knows the origin of Biddenden's dole, it has been administered on down through the years, stopping only during World War II, when rationing forbade the distribution of foods.

Hare Pie Scramble and Bottle Kicking, Hallaton, Leicestershire

Easter Monday

The annual Easter Monday "Hare Pie Scramble and Bottle Kicking" of Hallaton, in Leicestershire, is another ancient custom which is carried out according to the terms of a curious bequest.

Legend says that long ago, when a parish woman crossed the fields she was attacked by a bull. The woman probably would have been gored to death had not a hare suddenly popped up from the meadow grasses and distracted the bull's attention. As a thanks offering for deliverance, the woman reputedly bequeathed a piece of land to the parish rector, on condition that he and his successors annually provide two hare pies, ale, and two dozen penny loaves, to be "scrambled for" on Easter Monday, on Hare-Pie Bank, a hill about a quarter mile south of Hallaton.

The story may be fanciful, but generations of Hallaton folk have participated in the scramble, which is a popular Easter Monday sport. Since hares are out of season at this time of year, beef, or other kinds of pies are substituted for the original ones.

Following a service in the parish church, a deputation of citizens calls at the rectory, where the vicar cuts up the pies. The pieces are thrown into sacks and carried by two men. Three others carry "bottles" or small wooden casks which are preserved from one year to another. Two are filled with beer, the other is a dummy. A procession, led by the village band, starts for Hare-Pie Bank. There the contents of the sacks are thrown out and scrambled for by the assembled villagers and spectators. Then comes the famous "Hallaton Bottle-Kicking," actually a relic of an old type of football game.

One of the "bottles" is thrown into a hollow of the hill and fiercely contended for by Hallaton's men and their rivals from Melbourne and neighboring parishes. Then the dummy is thrown out. Hallaton inhabitants boast that never have its rivals from other villages gained possession of this symbol of village prowess. The goals are two streams, located a mile apart.

The contents of the remaining bottle are reserved for the final celebration in the market place, after the day's sport is over. The bottles usually are preserved from one year to the next.

HOCKTIDE FESTIVAL, HUNGERFORD, BERKSHIRE

The Tuesday after Easter Tuesday

Hungerford, which proudly claims John of Gaunt, Duke of Lancaster, as its patron, celebrates the Hocktide festival in memory of his charter to the town, 1360, which gave fishing rights in the River Kennet, as well as shooting and land rights to ninety-nine commoners.

Once Hocktide was observed throughout England. Now Hungerford alone retains the ancient customs connected with the one-time popular feast. Originally Hocktide was the occasion for "tripping up and binding," in order to force persons of the opposite sex into payment of dues for charity. The men, on Monday, and the women, on Tuesday, used to bar passage by stretching ropes or chains across the roads and demanding money of all passers-by. In Dorset, and possibly other counties, women bound up the men as prisoners when payment of monies was denied. The men, on the other hand, allowed free passage to the women, if they would substitute payment of coin for a kiss! This old custom still holds in Hungerford where tithing men make Hocktide rounds and demand a coin or a kiss from each woman they meet.

Hungerford boasts no mayor or alderman. Authority for civic administration is vested in the high constable, the "keeper of the town," a bailiff, port reeve, tithing men and minor officials. The high constable, also known as lord of the manor, is elected annually at Hocktide from the ranks of former office holders.

The town crier (who has held his office for the last twenty-eight years and is son of a town crier of forty-three years' standing) officially opens the Hocktide festivities. Stepping out on the Town Hall balcony at eight o'clock in the morning, he lets go a series of blasts from "John o' Gaunt's horn." At intervals between eight and nine, the town crier, nattily uniformed in crimson-faced gray, brass buttons agleam and top hat on head, continues to arouse Hungerford's citizenry and remind them of their debt to John o' Gaunt.

The horn that is sounded so lustily is a replica of a very ancient one, reputedly presented to the town by the great John himself. Now the old horn is carefully preserved in the bank vault. The "new" one, dating from the seventeenth century and copied, inscription and all from the original, is called the "Lucas horn," after John Lucas, Constable. In 1640, after the old horn had seen some three hundred years of hard service, Lucas gave this horn to Hungerford. Ever since, it has been regarded as the constable's traditional badge of service. The inscription on its side tells Hungerford's proud story:

> John a Gavn did give and grant the riall of
> Fishing to Hungerford tovn from Eldred
> Stub to Irish Still excepting som several mil pound.
> Jehosophat Lvas was Constable.

Following his early blasting from the balcony, the town crier proceeds through the community summoning the appearance of all commoners at the nine o'clock Hocktide Court. Swinging a large hand bell, he repeats the age-old summons:

> O-yez, O-yez, O-yez,
> All ye commoners of the Borough and Manor of Hungerford
> Are requested to attend your Court House

At nine o'clock this morning
To answer your names, on penalty of being fined.
God save the King!

Hungerford still has ninety-nine commoners. Any one of them unable to attend Court pays the bellman a penny fine in passing, so their ancient rights as commoners shall not be forfeited when their names are called.

The Hocktide Court, one of the few feudal courts still held in England, convenes with traditional solemnity. The newly appointed high constable sits in the seventeenth century ebony chair. The town clerk reads the ancient rights and privileges John o' Gaunt granted to Hungerford's citizens. Commoners are granted permission to fish three days weekly in the River Kennet without payment of the usual three-guinea fee, and are also given common pasturage and shooting rights as specified by their patron over five hundred years ago.

A high point of the court session is the election of the various officials. Among them are two tithing men, or "tuttimen" (so-called from the West Country word "tutty," meaning flower or nosegay), to whom the high constable presents tall tutti poles or staves. These unique emblems of office are decorated on top with blue ribbons and nosegays of long-stemmed spring flowers, such as arum lilies, daffodils and anemones. Accompanied by the orange man, the tuttimen, wearing tall hats trimmed with cock-feathers, set out on their rounds. They stop at each of the ninety-nine commoners' houses, demanding payment of a penny or a kiss from every woman, for services rendered during the past year. In return for these dues, each householder receives an orange from the orange man's sack. Deep draughts of punch in John o' Gaunt's memory are frequent during rounds, so, as the town crier says with magnificent understatement, the tuttimen "sometimes get a bit giddy" before returning to the one o'clock civic luncheon at the Three Swans.

At this affair the tuttimen sit in state to the right and left of the newly-elected high constable. After a repast of good food, lengthy speech making "to the immortal memory of John o' Gaunt," and

220

drinks of steaming punch* from the great silver bowl, the quaint initiation ceremony of the "Shoeing of the Colts" begins. The "smiths," complete with aprons and shoeing box, circulate among the company, choosing as their subjects newcomers among the guests. Playfully the men drive a smithy's nail into the heel of the victim's shoe. Only when the victim shouts "punch" is the nail knocked out. Then follows payment of the ten-shilling initiation fee, which is applied toward the luncheon expenses.

After all the fun, windows are opened and oranges and hot pennies showered down on the mob of children assembled in the courtyard below. Hungerford's children, indeed, play an important part in the annual festivities. In addition to all the excitement of a procession, the election of a queen of festivities and following the tuttimen about, they have a special Hocktide song:

> The ancient market-place has heard
> For half a thousand years,
> The summons of the mighty horn,
> Time-honored Lancaster's.
> The Tuttimen have trimmed the poles
> With blossoms fresh and gay,
> And kissed the merry, bashful maids,
> On Hock Day holiday.

THE SPITAL SERMON, CHURCH OF ST. MARY WOOLNOTH, LONDON

The second Wednesday after Easter

The Spital Sermon (which gets its name from the twelfth century Priory of St. Mary Spittle, or Hospital), is preached in St. Mary Woolnoth's on the second Wednesday after Easter. The congregation includes the lord mayor, representatives of the Corporation of London and the governor of the royal hospitals.

In early times the sermons were given at the Priory. Even when the Priory was dissolved under Henry VIII, the sermons continued. They were delivered on Easter Monday, Tuesday and Wednesday

---

* Made from a traditional local recipe known as "The Ancient Plantagenet Punch."

221

at Pulpit Cross, in the hospital churchyard, Spitalsfield. The lord mayor, alderman, sheriffs and other officials, listened to the sermon from a small two-storied building, opposite the pulpit. Many notables, including Queen Elizabeth I herself, attended the early services.

The Spital Sermons have been preached in various places. Until 1797, services were held at St. Bride's, in Fleet Street; and after that, at Christ Church, in Newgate. Since Christ Church was almost destroyed during World War II, the sermons are now preached at St. Mary Woolnoth's, the only City church to remain intact during the 1940-45 raids. The sermon is given in connection with the Royal Hospitals, Christ's Hospital, St. Bartholomew's and Bridewell.

ROGATIONTIDE AND ASCENSION

The Rogation Days are the Monday, Tuesday and Wednesday preceding Ascension Thursday, the fortieth day after Easter. For many English communities the season marks two important events: a religious procession to the fields, to ask God's blessing on all growing things, and Beating the Bounds, or visiting the village boundaries, in order to impress their location on parishioners' minds.

The two ceremonies originated in the Roman festivals of the *Ambarvalia* and the *Terminalia,* which later were adapted by the Christian Church.

The *Ambarvalia,* held toward the end of May, was a religious procession made about the fields in order to "drive out the winter." Prayers were said to Mars for the prosperity of the land. Animals were sacrificed and young maidens danced and sang.

The *Terminalia,* on the other hand, was a ceremony to honor Terminus, god of boundaries, whose shrine was the post or stone set up between two pieces of property. Each year the owners of the land met at the border to offer sacrifice and to adorn the stone with flowers.

222

These two pagan festivals have come down through the centuries and are celebrated widely in their Christianized form. During the Rogation Days the vicar of many rural communities holds a service in the parish church, then leads his congregation to the fields, meadows and gardens, to ask divine blessing. A churchwarden or other church official carries the cross. Halting at a field or pond, the group listens reverently as a young farmer reads an appropriate litany or rogation. At the village green a prayer is given for unity and brotherhood for all who dwell within the community; at wells and streams God is implored to prosper the waters and to protect all who go to sea; at corn fields, farmyards, allotments and gardens, prayers are said for growth of crops, prosperity of harvests and health for those who seek livelihood from the soil.

Rogation ceremonies are especially frequent in southern farming counties such as Sussex. Sussex is a county of ponds, streams and rivers. Farther north, as in Derbyshire and Staffordshire, where wells and springs refresh a stony land yielding a harvest of coal, lead and precious spar, people often ask blessings of the water on Ascension Day. In these counties the wells* are "dressed" with elaborate flower mosaic screens and thanksgiving services are held beside the waters.

The parish choir boys usually play an important role in the Ascension Day ceremonies of Beating the Bounds. Often the boys carry elm branches or willow wands, which they decorate with flowers and ribbons. As the procession consisting of clergy and parishioners visits the various boundaries, the youths strike the spot with their branches. Traditionally, at some point along the way, one of the choristers must be seized, held upside-down by the feet and have his head thumped on the ground, "so he will never forget the boundary!"

In olden times the ceremony often was rugged, since the lads had the boundaries impressed on them with floggings, duckings and bumpings. These indignities the boys were said to gladly endure,

* See p229, 231-4.

in view of the customary treats of cakes, buns, sweets and coins. In 1497, Worcestershire's boundary beatings evidently became really rough, for old records tell that people were ordered to go peacefully, carrying no weapons other than walking sticks.

In the course of parish perambulations it was customary in some places to stop and read the Gospel beneath a boundary tree, known as the "Gospel tree," or "Gospel oak," elm, or some other tree.

Herrick alludes to this custom in the lines:

> Dearest, bury me
> Under that *Holy-oke* or *Gospel-tree*:
> Where (though thou see'st not) thou may'st think upon
> Me, when thou yeerly go'st Procession.*

Nowadays, modern surveying has taken the place of perambulations to mark parish lines, and the custom of Beating the Bounds is largely a matter of keeping up a time-honored tradition. The Rogationtide ceremony of going out to bless the corn, however, happily is being revived in many communities.

PLANTING THE PENNY HEDGE, WHITBY, YORKSHIRE

Ascension Eve

"Planting the Penny Hedge" is the name given to the Ascension Eve penance which has been performed at Whitby for almost eight hundred years. The ceremony consists of cutting from the abbot's former wood enough stakes and branches to build a hedge at the harbor's edge. The hedge, which must be built at low tide, before nine in the morning, has to be sufficiently strong to withstand three incoming tides.

* Robert Herrick. To Althea. *Hesperides*. 1648.

Tradition says that the abbot of Whitby imposed this annual penance in 1159 upon three noblemen and their descendants, in punishment for murder of a Whitby monk. Now the ceremony is performed by the owners of lands that formerly belonged to the abbot. The service is held in the presence of the manor bailiff, who concludes the penance by blowing three sharp blasts to the lady of the manor upon an eight-hundred-year-old horn. She then responds with the ancient cry of, "Out on ye! Out-on ye! Out-on ye!"

The legend* of the Penny Hedge, taken from an ancient manuscript printed on vellum, recounts how, in the fifth year of King Henry II's reign, three noblemen, William de Bruce, Ralph de Piercie and Allatson, were hunting a wild boar in the abbot of Whitby's forest, on Eskdale-Side. The animal, wounded and pursued by the noblemen's hounds, took refuge in a hermitage where a Whitby Abbey monk lived. The monk gave sanctuary to the beast, shutting out the bloodthirsty hounds and refusing to release their prey to the angry noblemen.

The legend goes on to tell how the enraged huntsmen belabored the monk with their boar staves to the point of death. The Abbot of Whitby, upon learning of the deed, would have had the noblemen put to death; but the dying monk pled for their lives, ". . . if they be content to be enjoyned to this Penance, for the safeguard of their souls."

In the quaint wording of the ancient book, the penance, the terms of which have been carried out in modified form for almost eight centuries, reads as follows:

You and yours shall hold your Lands of the Abbot of Whitby, and his successors in this manner:

That upon Ascension Eve you, or some of you, shall come to the Wood of the Strayhead, which is in the Eskdale-Side, the same Day at Sun-rising, and there shall the Officer of the Abbot blow his horn, to the intent that you may know how to find him, and he shall deliver unto you, William de Bruce, ten Stakes, ten Stout-Stowers and ten Yedders, to be cut by you, or those that

* The author is indebted to Mr. Alexander C. Ross, D.P.A., barrister-at-law, and Clerk of the Whitby Urban District Council, for this version of the Penny Hedge legend.

come for you, with a knife of a Penny Price; and you, Ralph de Piercie, shall take one and twenty of each sort, to be cut in the same manner; and you, Allatson, shall take nine of each sort, to be cut as aforesaid; and to be taken on your backs, and carried to the town of Whitby; and so to be there before nine of the Clock (if it be full Sea, to cease Service), as long as it is low Water, at nine of the Clock, the same hour each of you shall set your Stakes at the Brim of the Water, each Stake a Yard from another, and so Yedder them, as with Yedders, and so Stake on each side with your Stout-Stowers that they stand three Tides without removing by the Force of the Water. Each of you shall make them in several Places at the Hour above-named (except it be full Sea at that hour, which, when it shall happen to pass, that Service shall cease), and you shall do this Service in remembrance that you did most cruelly slay me. And that you may the better call to God for Repentance, and find Mercy, and do good Works, the Officer of Eskdale-Side shall blow his Horn, Out on you, Out on you, for the heinous Crime of you. And if you, and your Successors do refuse this Service, so long as it shall not be full sea, at that Hour aforesaid, you and yours shall forfeit all your Lands to the Abbot, or his successors. Thus I do entreat the Abbot that you may have your Lives and Goods for this Service, and you to promise by your Parts in Heaven, that it shall be done by you and your successors, as it is aforesaid.

Today the story of the crime no longer is recited during the performance of the task, nor is the hedge still built by the murderers' descendants. Sometimes it is the harbor master himself who continues the old tradition by building the hedge.

The following lines from *Marmion** recall the penance of the three noblemen, William de Bruce, Ralph de Percy and Allatson. While hunting in Eskdale-Side, the Abbot of Whitby's forest, they slew the hermit who had given sanctuary to the wild boar they wounded in the hunt:

> Then Whitby's nuns exulting told,
> How to their house three Barons bold
> Must menial service do;
> While horns blow out a note of shame,
> And monks cry, "Fie upon your name!

* Walter Scott. *Marmion.*

226

In wrath for loss of sylvan game,
Saint Hilda's priest ye slew."
This, on Ascension-day, each year,
While laboring on our harbor-pier,
Must Herbert, Bruce and Percy hear.

BEATING THE BOUNDS, ST. CLEMENT DANES, LONDON

Ascension Day

On Ascension Day the clergymen and choristers of St. Clement Danes on the Strand—thought to be the original of the "Oranges and Lemons, say the bells of St. Clements" nursery rhyme—still beat the parish bounds. Starting at the church, a procession, following the beadle with his mace, sets out to inspect the boundaries, some twenty-five of which still remain. The choir boys carry willow wands, decorated with blue ribbons and nosegays. At one point in the ceremony, when boats are boarded on the Thames, the boys dabble the wands in the water, to indicate the southern parish boundaries.

The course of the perambulation includes many boundaries difficult of access, since some are located at warehouses and private dwellings. When the procession reaches the parish mark in Middle Temple Gardens, it is traditional to bump one of the lads on the head, so "he will never forget the boundary." The ceremony concludes about three in the afternoon, when each youth who has beaten the bounds is rewarded with a newly-minted shilling. Although the church of St. Clement Danes was badly bombed, the traditional ceremony continues.

Records of May 4, 1769, show that a hundred and thirty children participated in the annual ceremony of beating the bounds. Instead of a shilling for each participant, there was a meal of hot rolls, butter and radishes.*

* Considered an important delicacy in early spring.

227

BEATING THE BOUNDS, THE CATHEDRAL, LICHFIELD, STAFFORD-SHIRE

Ascension Day

Lichfield Cathedral, like St. Clement Danes, "Beats the Bounds" on Ascension Day. Following the morning service, choristers, accompanied by the dean, the Bishop of Stafford and other clergymen, go about the cathedral close with elm boughs in hand. At each of the eight places where wells once existed, the procession halts, while the Gospel of the day is read and a hymn sung. Then the boys beat the spot with their branches.

After the ceremony the procession returns to the cathedral, to lay down the elm boughs at the font, as a final prayer is offered and the benediction pronounced.

LOVE FEAST, WICKEN, BUCKINGHAMSHIRE

Ascension Day

Wicken, near Bletchley, in Buckinghamshire, still celebrates a love feast, which originated almost four hundred years ago.

The parish of Wicken today consists of two hamlets. Wyke Hamon and Wyke Dyke, which once were bitter rivals. In olden times so much jealousy existed between the villages that there were constant quarreling and bickering among the people. In 1586, however, the two communities decided to put aside their differences, and unite. A Love Feast was instituted in memory of the event and in the hope of future harmony.

The annual feast is celebrated under the "Gospel Elm," where parishioners gather for a short service. After singing the *Old Hundredth,* the congregation gathers before the rectory to eat cakes and drink to the spirit of peace and good-will which now exists among the people of Wicken.

THE EASTER CYCLE

WELL-DRESSING, TISSINGTON, DERBYSHIRE

Ascension Day

Tissington's ancient well-dressing ceremony, one of the most beautiful in all England, is thought by many villagers to date back to 1650, by others, to the thirteenth century. The rite, which was discontinued during World War II, was revived in 1950.

The most plausible explanation of the origin of Tissington's well-dressing is found in the current local story that, during the Black Death of 1348-49, Tissington alone, of the surrounding Derbyshire hamlets, had a plentiful supply of pure water for her five village springs, and that she alone was immune from the dreaded scourge.

In thankfulness for deliverance from the epidemic which wrought havoc throughout the area, Tissington folk instituted her famous well-dressings.

Each of the five village wells—the Hall, Yew Tree, Salt Cellar, Coffin and Town—are covered with flower mosaic screens, such as have been described elsewhere.* A picturesque processional and a religious service honor each well, as the villagers, joined by thousands of visitors from far and near, offer grateful thanks for the age-old gift of pure and abundant water.

WHITSUNTIDE

The festival of Whitsun or Pentecost, occurring on the seventh Sunday and the fiftieth day after Easter, commemorates the miraculous descent of the Holy Spirit upon the heads of three thousand apostles who were baptized into the Christian faith. Although the origin of word *whit* is somewhat obscure, many believe it means "white" in reference to the white albs, or robes, worn by those who were baptized.

* *See* Well-Dressings; Buxton, p87-9; Stoney Middleton, p 110-11.

A humorous fourteenth century verse suggests the word *whit* means not "white," but "wit" or "wisdom," in allusion to the Apostles' reception of the gift of knowledge and ability to speak many tongues on Pentecost.

> This day Whitsunday is cald,
> For wisdom and wit sevenfald
> Was goven to the Apostles on this day.

From early times, Whitsunday, Monday, Tuesday and Wednesday, were celebrated as a special time for games and sports, merrymaking and rejoicing in the early spring. Morris dances and mystery plays, Biblical dramas and Whitsun Church Ales all characterized English Whitsun festivities of the Middle Ages. Some of these ancient customs still exist in the modern celebration of the season.

In the twelfth century the clergy instituted the giving of mystery and miracle plays at Whitsuntide. Probably the most famous of all these plays were performed at Chester, between the fourteenth and eighteenth centuries. The Chester plays, given by the city's various guilds, often depicted the story of creation, or traced man's progress through harrowing Doomsday scenes.

One vastly popular play dealt with the story of Noah's wife, who preferred staying outside the ark with her cronies, to entering with her husband and children. The action, designed to illustrate the perversity of a stubborn woman, brought particular glee to the spectators, who rocked with laughter as Noah's wife, finally dragged into the Ark by her son Shem, grew angry and soundly boxed Noah's ears!

This play, which illustrates the boisterous gaiety of early Whitsun celebrations, may account for the robust zest with which today's clerk and cotton spinner, miner and shop worker enter into enjoyment of the Whit Monday holiday.

The ancient Whitsuntide custom of decorating churches with birch branches and strewing the stone floors with flowers and rushes unfortunately is falling into disuse; but here and there, when such ceremonials are found, they come as a pleasant reminder of the days when men sought the Vegetation Spirit's blessing in early spring.

Many quaint folk superstitions have arisen regarding the miraculous character of Whitsun. Some say "the sun skips, dances and turns about like a wheel" on the holy day, while others declare that "whatsoever one asks of God upon Whitsunday morning at the instant when the sun arises and plays, God will grant it him."

In some parts of England it is said one must wear new clothes on Whitsun, in order to have luck. According to others, bad luck dogs those who cut their nails on Whit Monday. But when it comes to weather, Huntingtonshire farmers say that Whit Sunday weather always is just the opposite of Holy Thursday's, and a fair Whit Sunday means a big harvest!

Whitsun, like most other high days of the Easter cycle, claims its own traditional foods. They differ from county to county, but each locality declares its own specialty is best. In Yorkshire and Durham there are cheese cakes; in Lancashire, muffin-shaped "top cakes," so-called because of the topping of egg white and sugar. Sussex housewives still pride themselves on fresh gooseberry pudding, though the traditional roast veal may be difficult to come by nowadays. The old-time Londoner who attended the Greenwich Whitsun Fair expected his plum cakes, cheese cakes, custards and bottled ale, but today settles for whatever sweets he can get.

But with or without the old foods and the old amusements, Whitsun is modern England's favorite Bank Holiday. Whoever *can* go away, does so. North Country folk stream southward, South Country folk travel north. Savings are set aside, months in advance, to spend on Whitsuntide fun.

WELL-DRESSING, ENDON, STAFFORDSHIRE

Whit Saturday, Sunday and Monday

The tiny Staffordshire hamlet of Endon proudly displays a well in its coat of arms. The emblem is singularly appropriate, for life in the entire village revolves about the mossy, spring-fed well, picturesquely located by the roadside, under the branches of a spreading wych elm. Each Whitsuntide Endon's inhabitants express gratitude for the bubbling waters by dressing the well with elaborate flower mosaics, holding a special thanksgiving ceremony and choosing a Festival Queen.

It all began back in 1845, when Thomas Heaton presented Endon, which never had enjoyed an adequate water supply, with a well having an inexhaustible source in hillside springs. The villagers were so happy that, with characteristic Midland heartiness, they prepared a well-dressing for Royal Oak Day. It was a real "do,"—a never-to-be-forgotten rural feast, attended by the shoemaker, carpenter, tailor, blacksmith, and all other substantial citizens. The shoemaker decorated the well with oak boughs, while housewives set about preparing Staffordshire food delicacies, such as pikelets, well soaked in butter, home-cured ham, home-baked bread and, of course, tea with thick cream for the more conservative, and rum "for those who thought fit." This initial celebration was a far cry from the elaborate flower pictures which have since developed under the skillful direction of village craftsmen.

The original deed for the right to dress the well is carefully preserved in St. Luke's parish church, which is perched high on the hill above the peaceful valley. The deed, dated May 29, 1868, states that the parishioners must wait for profits from the well-dressing before determining how much to apportion, on December 21, for annual bread distribution to the very poor! The poor must have fared meagerly for some time, since records show that for a period of twenty-seven years profits averaged only five pounds a year. Nowadays, the festival nets approximately a hundred pounds.

The deed, which further warns against "all excessive drinking and immorality in connection with the well-dressing," is signed and sealed under the names of Thomas Heaton and eleven trustees. From the beginning, Endon's well-dressing has been a matter of civic interest and pride.

The real core of Endon's modern well-dressing is the children's May festival, held in the adjoining fair grounds, known as Jaw Bone* field. Here the May Queen holds traditional court with her ladies-in-waiting, pages, and dancing troupes. Here are roundabouts and swings, sweet stalls, ice stands, and all sorts of other delights, calculated to lure pennies from the pockets of country children. A shilling admits a person to this paradise of fun and laughter, where Endon's retiring May Queen crowns her successor, and youngsters in white frocks and fluttering bows thread the Maypole, according to ancient tradition.

All these festivities accompany the well-dressing. Percy Williamson, like his father before him, is the local artist who designs the elaborately executed flower mosaic panels, which decorate the village. A farmer by profession, Mr. Williamson is typical of the fine Midland craftsmen who have perpetuated the art of making these unique pictures. Sometimes he chooses biblical subjects or scenes of current interest. Recently, his panels have featured such topics as the royal South African tour, the marriage of the former Princess Elizabeth to Prince Philip, and Anglo-American unity.

As is usual in all well-dressings, Endon's flower panels represent a real community effort, which is guided by a single craftsman. Each villager contributes time, skill and effort toward making the flower mosaics the most perfect of their kind. Against a background of thin wooden boards, which are first soaked overnight, then covered with salt-dampened native clay and well leveled off, Mr. Williamson (as he himself explained) traces the designs he has first made on paper. "Everyone joins in filling in the design," he told me. "First of all the frame is made from alder cones or beech nuts, filled in with wall moss and tiny flowers. Colored oyster grit is used for sky; pussy willow catkins, variegated box, bits of golden yew and sycamore blossoms, for trees and shrubs; wall mosses make shaded buildings; bluebells, lilac blossoms, rock roses and other flowers,

---

* The name is derived from the entrance arch, which is made from a whale's jaw bone. A part of the bone still remains. At one time many Midland communities prided themselves on having whale bone arches, which are rather rare in modern times.

233

the skin, drapery and hair. The damp wood and wet clay keep the pictures fresh for days."

The well-dressing festival starts with a service in the parish church. The Queen and her followers, preceded by the local band, go from there to the well, where the vicar pronounces his blessing. He draws a glass of sparkling fresh water, touches it with his lips, then hands it to the Queen. Thus does Endon's well-dressing begin.

RUSH SUNDAY, ST. MARY REDCLIFFE CHURCH, BRISTOL, GLOUCES-
TERSHIRE

Whit Sunday

Whit Sunday is Rush Sunday at Bristol's Church of St. Mary Redcliffe, which has observed its annual rush-strewing with great regularity. The center aisle of the church is covered with green rushes; pews are decorated with bunches of flowers. The Lord Mayor and Corporation officials attend the service, walking in procession to the sanctuary door. There they are met by the Bishop of Bristol. Trumpets greet the procession as it enters the doors and slowly proceeds down the nave.

MORRIS DANCE FESTIVAL, THAXTED, ESSEX

Whit Monday

At Whitsuntide the morris men appear on Thaxted's streets to perform traditional dances. Members of the morris dance clubs and folk dance societies meet annually at this tiny Essex town, once a Saxon village, to revive the tradition of medieval days. The morris men, indeed, have more than passing interest in Thaxted. In 1948-1949, when several church bells were recast and rehung by voluntary subscription, the Morris Ring, together with The Friends of Thaxted, donated the fourth, or "Fellowship" bell.

This bell, etched with a frieze of dancing morris men and the legend,

THE EASTER CYCLE

I RING

FOR THE GENERAL DANCE

Praise Him in the cymbals and dances
Praise Him upon the strings and pipe

is inspired by an ancient Cornish carol which relates episodes in the life of Jesus and invites all mankind to come into the "general dance." The final verse of the carol is:

Then up to Heaven I did ascend,
Where now I dwell in sure substance,
On the right hand of God, that man
May come unto the general dance.

Sing, oh my love, O my love, my love, my love;
This have I done for my true love.

Annually, on Whitsunday, the morris men, attired in white suits, ribbons and flowers, go about the churchyard in procession and down the church nave as in olden times. For now, as then, Thaxted's church, dedicated to Saint John the Baptist, Our Lady, and Saint Lawrence, is a joyous place, belonging to the people in the true medieval sense.

The day before the festival, spring flowers are massed in jars along the uneven pavement of this lovely fourteenth century sanctuary, with its wide aisles, whitewashed walls and colorful hanging banners of Our Lady and the saints. The air is filled with the scent of syringa, rose and lilac. Young girls hurry about, adding extra rubs to already gleaming brasses. The church has a *lived in* feeling. Young children scuttle out of the soft spring rain and continue their play in the spacious porch. Gentle laughter and orderliness are as related to this House of God as solemn prayer and ceremonial chant.

On Whit Monday the morris men gather early to dance in the square—really a triangle—in front of the church. The vicar is there, in white suit and traditional beflowered "high-low" hat, vigorously squeezing an accordion; he is assisted by the school mistress, who

235

also plays an accordion, and the handsome bearded weaver, who alternately beats the drum and dances. On the walls of his shop across the street I read this verse:*

> God loveth sinners,
> Dyers and spinners;
> Weavers, even
> May hope for Heaven.
> When naught is left
> Of warp and weft,
> With spindle and loom
> They meet their Doom.
> The Lamb's white fleece
> Has bought their peace.

I am certain "God loveth morris men," also, as I watch them dance and swing in Thaxted's streets. Occasionally townsfolk, closely gathered along the curb and churchyard wall, step into the center of the square and join the dancing. The Fool, meanwhile, goes up and down the line of bystanders, flourishing from one hand a long switch with inflated bladder tied to the end of a string; from the other a cow's tail. Following close behind is a man with a collection box, into which pennies are freely dropped. The coins jingle merrily as the morris men dance on. Now and then a gentle rain falls, umbrellas go up along the line of spectators. An automobile horn honks. The dancers step aside to give the vehicle right of way. None of us minds weather or interruption, for this is Thaxted's gala day.

The morris has long been associated with Whitsun festivities in England. Originally the dance was introduced from the continent where it flourished in fifteenth century Italy and France. The name *morris*, a corruption of *morisco* or *moresca*, is thought to have come from the Moors. Even today certain groups of English dancers, like Bacup's Coconut team† still blacken their faces like Moors.

* Source unknown.
† *See* p214.

The morris bears a certain resemblance to the sword dance, although the former is generally characterized by bells worn on the knees or legs. Sword dancers seldom wear bells. Instead of swords, the morris men carry staves, or even handkerchiefs. Just as the sword dance is thought to have originated as a ritualistic mid-winter dance, so the morris may have developed as a ritualistic spring or summer dance in which the men leapt high so grain would grow, flocks increase and health come to the community.

From the sixteenth century on, the morris was popular in England, both as a court and folk dance. English literature seldom mentions the morris before the time of Henry VIII. By then, however, it had become essential to parish festivals especially at Easter and Whitsun.

> How they become the morris, with whose bells
> They ring all in to Whitsun ales

wrote Randle Cotgrove, in 1665. He refers to the dancers who, with bells jingling on legs, furnished entertainment at England's famous sixteenth and seventeenth century Whitsun Ales, just as Thaxted's morris men entertain modern Whitsun crowds on the village streets.

MORRIS DANCE FESTIVAL, BAMPTON-IN-THE-BUSH, OXFORDSHIRE

Whit Monday

Bampton's Morris Dancers, England's oldest troupe, holds annual Whit Monday festival in the little town of Bampton, set like a jewel among Oxfordshire's pasture lands. Bampton's celebration is the only Cotswold Morris festival to have survived the Second World War.

For over thirty years William Wells, affectionately known as Billy, or "Jingle" Wells, directed the Bampton team and acted as their "Squire" and fiddler. Recently, the honor has passed to other hands. The Fool carries a stick to which an inflated bladder is attached by a string. The six dancers wear white costumes and bowler hats, adorned with bright nosegays and long ribbon streamers. Colored leather bell pads are strapped to the legs below the knees.

As at Thaxted, the Morris Dance Festival is a gala occasion for the sleepy old village, whose citizens turn out in holiday attire. Little girls and boys, dressed in Sunday best, carry about May garlands, and both young and old gather about to watch. But the crowd dares not press too close, for fear of a smart reminder from the Fool's stick!

Bampton's dancers claim a continuous history of over five centuries. The men demonstrate with skill and precision such traditional features as the *Rose Tree, Handkerchief,* and *Pipe and Bean* dances, in addition to numbers which include both set pieces and processionals. As the dancers stamp and kick, the bells on their legs jingle in gay accompaniment.

The festival ends in the market place. Sometimes there is a joint performance by the Bampton Morris Team and the Morris Dancers of Ilmington, in Warwickshire.

The Ilmington Morris Dancers, unlike the Bampton Team, have not had an uninterrupted history of performance. This group, originally organized in the fourteenth century, lapsed and was revived some years ago. Sam Bennett and his Hobby Horse are this team's leading attractions.

CHEESE-ROLLING, COOPER'S HILL, NEAR BROCKWORTH, GLOU-
CESTERSHIRE

Whit Monday

Whit Monday Cheese-Rolling contests from Cooper's Hill, near Brockworth, have been famous for at least five hundred years. And even though the fine Gloucestershire cheeses of olden times are imitated nowadays by three or four large wooden discs, both the traditional ceremony and the traditional fun are well kept up. Cheese-rolling, like wrestling, cudgeling, and climbing a greased pole for a leg o' mutton prize, has been a popular Whit Monday sport since early days.

Cooper's Hill, which is a thousand feet above the level of the Painswick-Cheltenham Road, provides excellent grazing lands. People say that the old custom of annually rolling cheeses downhill is so the villagers may preserve free grazing rights on Cooper's Hill Common.

On top of the steep grassy slope stands a tall flagstaff. Once it was a Maypole, around which village girls from both Brockworth and Whitcombe used to hold dancing competitions for ribbon awards. Today the pole is ceremoniously lowered, then raised, before the crowds of people from several parishes.

Competitors in the Cheese-Rolling are boys from surrounding hamlets. At a given signal, the impressive master of ceremonies, who is dressed in top hat and white smock, sets the discs spinning down the green hillside from the flagstaff. The boys chase after, each trying to capture a "cheese." The task is more difficult than it sounds, for Cooper's Hill is very steep and youths sometimes roll down its slippery slopes faster than the wooden "cheese"! The first contestant to successfully grab a rolling disc wins, and receives a prize of seven-and-six.

WALKING DAYS, MANCHESTER AND SALFORD, LANCASHIRE

Whit Monday

Manchester and Salford have annual "Walking Days" when thousands of Sunday School children parade through the streets. The children carry colorful banners and wear white suits, or frocks and veils, adorned with garlands and ribbons. The procession follows given routes through the cities. Traffic is stopped and streets jammed with thousands of spectators, who come from far and near to watch the boys and girls in the annual parade. The Sunday following Whit Monday, each community celebrates its own Walking Day.

Throughout Lancashire and Yorkshire, "Walking Days" are an important feature of community life. Usually each small town or village has its own procession. Often traditional foods, originally made for other events, now are eaten on these days. Eccles' famous currant-filled cakes, for example, once a specialty of the town's Wakes Week,* now are made for the local Sunday Schools' annual Walking Day.

Possibly the Walking Days are modern versions of old-time Club Walks. These ceremonial walks to church, with their banners and colored insignia, were made by various groups, which were bound together for sociability and mutual benefit. The Whitsun Church Ales, which once gave parishioners opportunity to meet in church houses and churchyards, to drink ale and indulge in merrymaking and sports, may also have been forerunners of these North Country Walking Days.

SETTING UP THE MAYPOLE, BARWICK-IN-ELMET, YORKSHIRE

Whit Tuesday

Every three years, inhabitants of Barwick-in-Elmet, in Yorkshire, hold on Whit Tuesday an elaborate May festival. The next one should be in 1955.

Barwick's Maypole, which is eighty or more feet high, is renewed as occasion demands; but every three years it is taken down on Easter Monday, repainted and decked with ribbons and artificial flower garlands, which the local Girl Guides make. On Whit Tuesday the Maypole is reset in its old position.

The moving of the Maypole is performed in traditional manner, with the aid of ladders, pitchforks and ropes. The town appoints three pole men to see that the work is properly done.

A popular May Day celebration accompanies the raising of the pole. At one time the festival took place on May Day, but later the time was changed to Whit Tuesday.

* *See* p 102.

THE EASTER CYCLE

RAM ROASTING FAIR, KINGSTEIGNTON, DEVONSHIRE

Whit Tuesday

Kingsteignton still observes the annual ram roasting (or *deer* roasting in recent years) which, according to local legend, originated in pagan times, when the stream which flows through the center of the village dried up, leaving the inhabitants in sore need of water. One story is that on the advice of their priests, the villagers implored the gods for help. Presently they were rewarded by an abundance of water issuing from the land. Since that early drought, Kingsteignton has annually offered a ram as a thank offering. Another version is that the drought ceased when the village people sacrificed a ram on the bed of the dried-out stream.

Formerly, the stream was diverted temporarily from its usual course, and the ram—in deference to the legend—was roasted over a fire built where the waters usually flowed.

In these days, when rams are more costly and harder to come by than in the past, a reindeer is substituted for the traditional animal. Local butchers, in long white coats, turn the spit over a huge pine log fire, while the crowds amuse themselves with May Day festivities and sports which include crowning a queen and winding the May-pole.

In the evening, the deer is cut up and distributed to holders of lucky numbers, since there is not enough meat for everyone to have a portion.

In olden times the ram was decked with flowers and led through the streets before being "sacrificed." Later, the meat was carved and sold to the poor, at moderate price. Sometimes people complain that the modern reindeer is a bit tough; but this does not really matter, since everyone has a fine time at Kingsteignton Ram Roasting!

TRINITY SUNDAY

Pope Gregory IV instituted Trinity Sunday, the Sunday next after Whitsun, about the year 834. Once Trinity was celebrated

241

with mystery plays and elaborate church processions. Now it is a popular occasion for Wakes and Feast weeks, especially in villages where parish churches are dedicated to the Holy Trinity.

One such village is St. Austell, in Cornwall. Religious services, combined with all sorts of secular amusements, mark the ancient dedication feast of the local church, which is noted for its magnificent tower, with carvings of the Twelve Apostles. Throughout the Trinity season the celebration continues. On the Wednesday after Trinity Sunday, villagers perform on the streets a dance, which is somewhat similar to Helston's famous Furry Dance* of the eighth of May.

Trinity, like the other festivals of the Easter cycle, boasts certain traditional foods, which have been restricted, alas, in recent years. At Long Itchington, Warwickshire, where Wakes Week is celebrated at this time, stuffed chine and bread pudding, made with currants, fruit peel, suet, eggs and milk, are customary delicacies, while Cleveland and Stokesley, in Yorkshire, are famous for cheese cakes.

TRINITY FAIR, SOUTHWOLD, SUFFOLK

*Monday, Tuesday and Wednesday
following Trinity Sunday*

Southwold's ancient three-day Trinity Fair is still opened each year on Trinity Monday by the mayor and local dignitaries.

The origin of the fair goes back to 1485. Its charter, granted by William IV (the original charter of Henry VII having been destroyed by fire) is read aloud three times by the town clerk, during the opening ceremonies. The first reading usually is from the steps of the merry-go-round in the South Green; the second in the market square; and the third in the High Street, opposite the Crown Hotel.

The mayor, in scarlet robe and gold chain of office, preceded by the mace bearer, heads the official procession of blue robed aldermen, councilmen and other officials to the merry-go-round. The town

* See Furry Day, p64ff.

crier, in his blue and scarlet uniform, summons the crowd to silence by ringing his hand bell. Then the town clerk reads the charter and proclams the fair as duly opened, under authorizations by the Kings of England. "The same fair shall continue," he reads, "during the three days immediately following the Feast of the Holy Trinity and no longer."

The fair starts getting under way when the mayor and dignified town officials mount the merry-go-round horses and take the first whirl around, to the delight of the cheering crowd. Afterwards the official procession once more forms and goes first to the market, then to the High Street. After the charter is read at these points, the fair is properly opened.

CORPUS CHRISTI

Protestant England no longer celebrates to any extent the Feast of Corpus Christi, or the Body of Christ, which was instituted in the Middle Ages. The festival was a great ecclesiastical holy day in pre-Reformation times, when the Host, enclosed in a magnificent silver pyx, and carried under a cloth-of-gold canopy, was borne in stately procession through the streets of such ancient cities as Chester, York, Durham and Coventry.

In old Catholic England, members of the various trades' guilds, each with characteristic banners and emblems, followed the hundreds of priests, torch-bearers and officials of church and state, who walked in the Corpus Christi processions. Each guild portrayed a religious drama built about a biblical theme, such as the Slaughter of the Innocents, the burial of Christ, or the Last Judgment.

The plays were performed from high partitioned carts, called *pagiante,* from which the name *pageant* is derived. The guilds drew up the carts at various stations during the course of the processional march. The players dressed on one side of a partition and acted on the other, before huge audiences assembled in the streets. Participants in the plays were great in number, often totaling several hundred in a single performance.

Although the sumptuous Corpus Christi processions belong to England's past, vestiges of the accompanying miracle plays survive in the crude dramatic performances of morris dancers and Christmas mummers, of guisers and soulcakers who, as already seen, still enact their traditional roles in many of England's obscure hamlets and picturesque villages.

PART III
FOR FURTHER REFERENCE

REGIONS AND COUNTIES

NORTHERN	Cumberland	Northumberland
	Durham	The Lakes
	Lancashire	Westmorland
	Yorkshire	

MIDLAND	Bedfordshire	Nottinghamshire
	Cheshire	Rutland
	Derbyshire	Shropshire
	Herefordshire	Staffordshire
	Leicestershire	Warwickshire
	Northamptonshire	Worcestershire

EASTERN	Cambridgeshire	Lincolnshire
	Essex	Norfolk
	Huntingdonshire	Suffolk

LONDON

SOUTHERN	Berkshire	Middlesex
	Buckinghamshire	Oxfordshire
	Gloucestershire	Surrey
	Hampshire	Sussex
	Hertfordshire	Wiltshire
	Kent	

WESTERN	Devonshire	Cornwall
	Dorsetshire	Somerset

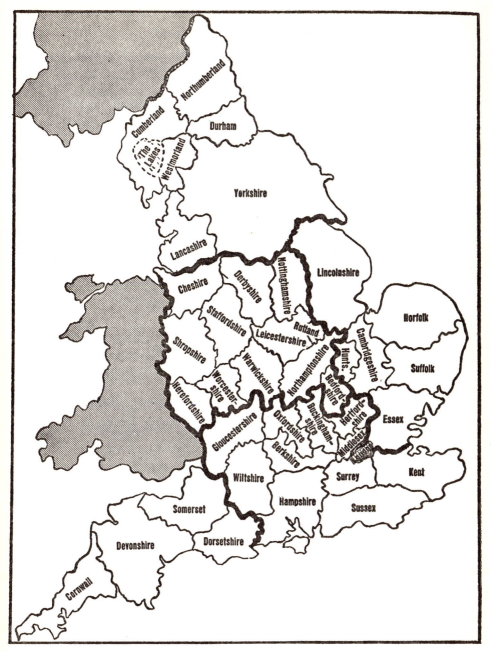

This map indicates the counties in outline. The heavy lines show the grouping of counties **as** used in this book. These groupings correspond with references in the text to the Northern, **Midland,** Eastern, Southern and Western Counties. The Lake region, which actually comprises **a part of** Cumberland, Lancashire and Westmorland, is given simply as The Lakes, because of the **similarity** of customs and ceremonies throughout the area.

ENGLAND'S "TWO" CALENDARS

England really has "two" calendars, the official New Style of civil life, and the Old Style Julian calendar which still persists in some places where some aspects of life have changed little since William the Conqueror's time. As already seen, many country people, continuing to think in terms of *Old* Candlemas, *Old* Lady Day, or *Old* Michaelmas, still celebrate their fairs, revels and village wakes on the same Old Style dates as their ancestors. Even weather rhymes and predictions that aged people quote usually refer to the Old Calendar—still the "right" way to reckon time in parts of Somerset, Herefordshire, Worcestershire and some other counties.

If we are to understand the multiplicity of dates that appear in popular customs, we must think back to England's calendar reform of 1752, which, in some places, never has been wholeheartedly recognized. But we must really go back still further to account for England's reluctance to accept the "new" system of reckoning time.

Julius Caesar instituted the Julian calendar in 46 B.C. Owing to error in the computations of ancient astronomers (who abolished the old Roman lunar calendar and regulated the civil year by the sun's movements), the new solar year was too long by eleven minutes and fourteen seconds. Although the error appears slight, in the course of a hundred and twenty-eight years, it crept up to a day; and in a few centuries the spring equinox, which fell on March 25 in Caesar's day, had gradually slipped back towards the year's beginning. By 1582 the agricultural world had gone completely topsy-turvy, because the spring equinox had retrograded to March 11!

To the pious farmer who for centuries had tilled his land and sowed his seed in accordance with the festivals of the Christian Church, all signs had failed. Seasons had become erratic. Even sun and moon no longer fulfilled their appointed tasks. Agriculture and religion were at odds. Something *had* to be done!

249

At this crucial point Pope Gregory XIII, in consultation with the most learned astronomers of his day, finally harmonized the astronomical and civil calendars by adding ten days, and changing the date of October 5, 1582, to October 15.

All Roman Catholic countries promptly adopted the Gregorian, or New Style, calendar Rome now issued. Protestant Great Britain and the English colonies in America, however, regarded this papal reform with suspicion and dislike. Stubbornly refusing to recognize the change, they continued beginning their year on March 25, in accordance with the Julian, or Old Style, calendar.

The deadlock persisted (the Continent recognizing one calendar, Great Britain the other) until September 1752, when George II was king. Only then did Great Britain and the American colonies finally adopt the "New Style" of computing and distributing time, and begin their years on January 1. By this time, however, an eleven-day variation had developed between the two styles.

This variation continues in some British high days and holy days which, as already seen, are still celebrated eleven days later than the modern calendar. For instance, January 5, Twelfth Night and Epiphany Eve, is also Old Christmas Eve, the "true" night of Christ's birth according to West Country folk. January 6, Twelfth Day and Epiphany, is likewise Old Christmas, while January 17 is Old Twelfth Night, and January 18 Old Twelfth Day. These and many similar date discrepancies are confusing and make it difficult to avoid a margin of error in reporting old observances. The variations prove, however, that while it is one thing for a nation to accept a new calendar system it is quite another to induce simple rural folk to change their age-old holy day dates!

MOVABLE DAYS OF THE EASTER CYCLE

SEPTUAGESIMA SUNDAY (or *Lost Sunday*)
The third Sunday before the beginning of Lent.

QUINQUAGESIMA SUNDAY (or *Shrove Sunday*)
The Sunday before the beginning of Lent, or the Sunday preceding Shrove Monday.

SHROVE MONDAY (or *Collop Monday*)
The Monday preceding Shrove Tuesday.

SHROVE TUESDAY (or *Pancake Tuesday*)
The last day before Lent.

ASH WEDNESDAY
The first day of Lent.

LENT
The forty days that immediately precede Easter, or the first of the forty-six days before Easter.

MOTHERING SUNDAY (or *Mid-Lent Sunday*)
The fourth Sunday in Lent.

CARLING SUNDAY (or *Passion Sunday, Care Sunday*)
The fifth Sunday in Lent.

PALM SUNDAY
The Sunday immediately preceding Easter.

MAUNDY THURSDAY
The Thursday immediately preceding Easter.

GOOD FRIDAY
The Friday immediately preceding Easter.

HOLY SATURDAY
The Saturday immediately preceding Easter.

EASTER MONDAY AND TUESDAY
The Monday and Tuesday immediately following Easter.

LOW SUNDAY
The Sunday immediately following Easter.

ROGATION SUNDAY

> The fifth Sunday after Easter, or the Sunday immediately preceding Ascension Thursday.

ROGATION DAYS

> The Monday, Tuesday and Wednesday immediately preceding Ascension Thursday.

ASCENSION DAY

> The fortieth day after Easter. Ascension Day always falls on a Thursday.

WHIT SUNDAY (or *Pentecost*)

> The fiftieth day after Easter.

WHIT MONDAY

> The fifty-first day after Easter.

WHITSUNTIDE

> The Pentecostal season, or the entire week, beginning with Whit Sunday. Popularly, Whit Sunday and Monday only.

TRINITY SUNDAY

> The fifty-seventh day after Easter.

CORPUS CHRISTI

> The Thursday following Trinity Sunday.

LITURGICAL COLORS: SYMBOLISM AND USE

WHITE: *Life. Typical of innocence and purity, glory and joy.*
All Saints *(November 1)*
Christmas *(December 25)*
Circumcision *(January 1)*
Easter*
Feast of the Annunciation *(March 25)*
Feast of the Purification *(February 2)*
Feasts of the Saints who were not Martyrs
Nativity of St. John the Baptist *(June 24)*
Trinity*

RED: *Fire and blood. A reminder of burning charity and the sacrifice of martyrs.*
Corpus Christi*
Elevation of the Cross *(May 2)*
Feasts of the Apostles and Martyrs
Finding of the Cross *(September 14)*
Holy Innocents *(December 28)*
Whitsunday or Pentecost*

GREEN: *Hope of eternal life, being the color of plants and trees.*
All Sundays which are not specific festivals

VIOLET: *Affection and melancholy.*
Advent *(the four weeks preceding Christmas)*
All Penitential Days, except Good Friday
All Souls *(November 2)*
Lent*
Rogation*

BLACK: *Mourning. Reminiscent of the sorrow of death and the soberness of the tomb.*
Good Friday*

* Movable days.

253

TABLE OF EASTER DATES

And Movable Days of the Easter Cycle to 1984

Year	Shrove Monday	Shrove Tuesday	Ash Wednesday	Mothering Sunday	Carling or Passion Sunday	Palm Sunday	Maund Thursd
1954	March 1	March 2	March 3	March 28	April 4	April 11	April
1955	Feb. 21	Feb. 22	Feb. 23	March 20	March 27	April 3	April
1956*	Feb. 13	Feb. 14	Feb. 15	March 11	March 18	March 25	March
1957	March 4	March 5	March 6	March 31	April 7	April 14	April
1958	Feb. 17	Feb. 18	Feb. 19	March 16	March 23	March 30	April
1959	Feb. 9	Feb. 10	Feb. 11	March 8	March 15	March 22	March
1960*	Feb. 29	March 1	March 2	March 27	April 3	April 10	April
1961	Feb. 13	Feb. 14	Feb. 15	March 12	March 19	March 26	March
1962	March 5	March 6	March 7	April 1	April 8	April 15	April
1963	Feb. 25	Feb. 26	Feb. 27	March 24	March 31	April 7	April
1964*	Feb. 10	Feb. 11	Feb. 12	March 8	March 15	March 22	March
1965	March 1	March 2	March 3	March 28	April 4	April 11	April
1966	Feb. 21	Feb. 22	Feb. 23	March 20	March 27	April 3	April
1967	Feb. 6	Feb. 7	Feb. 8	March 5	March 12	March 19	March
1968*	Feb. 26	Feb. 27	Feb. 28	March 24	March 31	April 7	April
1969	Feb. 17	Feb. 18	Feb. 19	March 16	March 23	March 30	April
1970	Feb. 9	Feb. 10	Feb. 11	March 8	March 15	March 22	March
1971	Feb. 22	Feb. 23	Feb. 24	March 21	March 28	April 4	April
1972*	Feb. 14	Feb. 15	Feb. 16	March 12	March 19	March 26	March
1973	March 5	March 6	March 7	April 1	April 8	April 15	April
1974	Feb. 25	Feb. 26	Feb. 27	March 24	March 31	April 7	April
1975	Feb. 10	Feb. 11	Feb. 12	March 9	March 16	March 23	March
1976*	March 1	March 2	March 3	March 28	April 4	April 11	April
1977	Feb. 21	Feb. 22	Feb. 23	March 20	March 27	April 3	April
1978	Feb. 6	Feb. 7	Feb. 8	March 5	March 12	March 19	March
1979	Feb. 26	Feb. 27	Feb. 28	March 25	April 1	April 8	April
1980*	Feb. 18	Feb. 19	Feb. 20	March 16	March 23	March 30	April
1981	March 2	March 3	March 4	April 1	April 8	April 12	April
1982	Feb. 22	Feb. 23	Feb. 24	March 21	March 28	April 4	April
1983	Feb. 14	Feb. 15	Feb. 16	March 13	March 20	March 27	Marc
1984*	March 5	March 6	March 7	April 1	April 8	April 15	April

* Leap Year

TABLE OF EASTER DATES

And Movable Days of the Easter Cycle to 1984

ood riday	Easter	Rogation Sunday	Ascen- sion	Whit Sun- day or Pentecost	Whit Monday	Trinity	Year
ril 16	April 18	May 23	May 27	June 6	June 7	June 13	1954
ril 8	April 10	May 15	May 19	May 29	May 30	June 5	1955
rch 30	April 1	May 6	May 10	May 20	May 21	May 27	1956*
ril 19	April 21	May 26	May 30	June 9	June 10	June 16	1957
ril 4	April 6	May 11	May 15	May 25	May 26	June 1	1958
rch 27	March 29	May 3	May 7	May 17	May 18	May 24	1959
ril 15	April 17	May 22	May 26	June 5	June 6	June 12	1960*
rch 31	April 2	May 7	May 11	May 21	May 22	May 28	1961
ril 20	April 22	May 27	May 31	June 10	June 11	June 17	1962
ril 12	April 14	May 19	May 23	June 2	June 3	June 9	1963
rch 27	March 29	May 3	May 7	May 17	May 18	May 24	1964*
ril 16	April 18	May 23	May 27	June 6	June 7	June 13	1965
ril 8	April 10	May 15	May 19	May 29	May 30	June 5	1966
rch 24	March 26	April 30	May 4	May 14	May 15	May 21	1967
ril 12	April 14	May 19	May 23	June 2	June 3	June 9	1968*
ril 4	April 6	May 11	May 15	May 25	May 26	June 1	1969
rch 27	March 29	May 3	May 7	May 17	May 18	May 24	1970
ril 9	April 11	May 16	May 20	May 30	May 31	June 6	1971
rch 31	April 2	May 7	May 11	May 21	May 22	May 28	1972*
ril 20	April 22	May 27	May 31	June 10	June 11	June 17	1973
ril 12	April 14	May 19	May 23	June 2	June 3	June 9	1974
rch 28	March 30	May 4	May 8	May 18	May 19	May 25	1975
ril 16	April 18	May 24	May 28	June 7	June 8	June 14	1976*
ril 8	April 10	May 16	May 20	May 30	May 31	June 6	1977
rch 24	March 26	May 1	May 5	May 15	May 16	May 22	1978
ril 13	April 15	May 21	May 25	June 4	June 5	June 11	1979
ril 4	April 6	May 12	May 16	May 26	May 27	June 2	1980*
ril 17	April 19	May 24	May 28	June 7	June 8	June 14	1981
ril 9	April 11	May 16	May 20	May 30	May 31	June 6	1982
ril 1	April 3	May 8	May 12	May 22	May 23	May 29	1983
ril 20	April 22	May 27	May 31	June 10	June 11	June 17	1984*

GLOSSARY OF ENGLISH FESTIVAL TERMS

ADVENT

The term meaning the "coming of the Saviour," which is applied to the four weeks preceding Christ's birth. Advent is the recognized period of preparation for Christmas, just as Lent is for Easter.

ADVENT SUNDAY

The Sunday nearest to the Feast of St. Andrew (November 30), whether it falls before or after.

ALE-DRINKING

A festival of merrymaking, when ale was the beverage drunk. See also *Church-Ale*.

ALL FOOLS' DAY

April 1, when it is customary to play various good-natured tricks and jokes on friends and neighbors.

ALL HALLOWS' EVE (In secular British usage, All Hallow E'en; in American usage, Halloween)

The night of October 31, the Eve or vigil of All Saints or All Hallows.

ALL SAINTS' DAY

November 1, the feast to commemorate all the saints. The early English Church called the feast All Hallows, meaning All Holies. All Saints' is the Eve of All Souls' Day.

ALL SOULS' DAY

November 2, originally a solemn feast day in commemoration of, and prayer for, the faithful who remain in Purgatory.

ANNUNCIATION

March 25, the anniversary of the Angel Gabriel's announcement to the Virgin Mary of the mystery of the Incarnation. See also *Lady Day*.

GLOSSARY

ASCENSION

The fortieth day after Easter. This is the anniversary of Christ's ascension into heaven, forty days after his resurrection. The Feast of the Ascension, reputedly the oldest of the Christian Church, is said to have been kept since 68 A.D.

ASH WEDNESDAY

The first day of Lent in most Christian countries. The name is derived from the old custom of sprinkling ashes on the head in the penitential service of the day.

BANK HOLIDAYS

The days when banks and shops are closed and everyone takes a holiday. British Bank Holidays are Good Friday, Easter Monday, Whit Monday, the first Monday in August, Christmas, and the first week-day after Christmas.

BEARINGS

The support or frame on which various emblems of rushes are made for the traditional Lake country rushbearing ceremonies. See also *Rushbearing*.

BEATING THE BOUNDS (Also called *Perambulation*)

A service, usually celebrated during Ascension week, when vicar, churchwardens and parishioners of a community walk about the boundaries. The custom, which developed before the days of modern surveying, is to preserve in the minds of parish inhabitants an accurate recollection of the boundaries.

BOXING DAY

December 26, the day after Christmas. The day gets its name from the ancient custom (which is still observed) of giving and receiving gifts of money or articles of wearing apparel. The "Christmas Box" once denoted the receptacle used to receive money presents.

CANDLEMAS (Also called *Purification of the Virgin, Presentation of Christ*)

February 2, the fortieth day after Jesus' birth. The name Candlemas originated in the custom of blessing candles in the church on this day and distributing them to worshippers. See also *Presentation of Christ.*

CARLING SUNDAY (often called *Passion, Carlin,* or *Care Sunday*)

The fifth Sunday in Lent. On Carling Sunday it was the custom to eat the traditional carlings, or peas, which were soaked, fried, and seasoned with salt and pepper.

CARNIVAL

The term applied to the period of feasting and merrymaking which immediately precedes Lent and is thought to help compensate for the forty days of Lenten abstinence and self-denial. The word carnival is derived from the Latin *carne vale*, meaning, "farewell meat."

CHILDERMAS See *Holy Innocents' Day*

CHURCH-ALE

An occasion of merrymaking, when specially-brewed ale was drunk, on the anniversary of a church holy day. There were Easter, Whitsun, and other Church Ales, when churchwardens brewed the ale and parishioners contributed provisions. The ale and food were sold in the church or parish house. Profits from the collections were applied to sanctuary repairs, disbursements to the poor, and general charitable causes.

CIRCUMCISION

January 1, one week after the Nativity. This feast commemorates the naming of Jesus and his formal admission into the membership and privileges of the Temple of Israel.

COLLOP MONDAY (Also called *Shrove Monday*)

The Monday preceding Shrove Tuesday, or the Monday before the beginning of Lent. The name comes from the ancient custom of dining on this day on eggs and collops, or slices of fried bacon.

GLOSSARY

COMMONWEALTH

The official designation of the existing form of government in England from the abolition of the monarchy, February 1649, after the execution of Charles I, until the establishment of the protectorate by Cromwell, December 1653.

CORPUS CHRISTI

The Thursday following Trinity Sunday. The day commemorates the institution of the Eucharist and celebrates the doctrine of transubstantiation. Before the Reformation the festival was celebrated with ceremonial processions and the performance of elaborate mystery plays at Chester, York, Coventry, Durham and other wealthy religious centers.

DAY OF ST. PETER IN FETTERS (See *Lammas*)

DAY OF THE INVENTION OR DISCOVERY OF THE HOLY CROSS (Also called *Saint Helena's Day*)

May 3, the day which commemorates the discovery of the "true Cross," in 326 A.D., by Saint Helena, mother of Constantine the Great.

DOOS

Little pastry or gingerbread images which, in Durham and other northern counties, are baked at Yuletide for the children. Usually the small figures have hands crossed in front. Features and buttons are of raisins. Often Doos are made from left-over pastry dough.

EASTER

The Sunday the Christian Church has set aside in memory of Christ's resurrection from the dead. According to the Council of Nice, Easter always is reckoned in the Gregorian calendar as the first Sunday after the Paschal full moon of the vernal equinox (March 21). Should the full moon fall on a Sunday, Easter is on the Sunday following. This holy day never comes *before* March 22, or after *April* 23.

EASTER MONDAY AND TUESDAY

The first and second days immediately following Easter Sunday.

EASTER SEPULCHRE

A recess, or sometimes, a canopied tomb, placed in the north wall of the church chancel, to represent the tomb of Christ. In medieval times it was customary on Good Friday to place Host and crucifix in the tomb. They were guarded until their removal early Easter morning, in symbol of Christ's burial and resurrection.

FAIRING

A present purchased or given at a fair. The term is applied popularly to a cake or goody made for, and sold at, a particular fair. Notable fairings are: Fair Buttons, made for the Great Yarmouth Fair; Barnstable Gingerbread, for the Barnstable Fair; Brandy Snaps, specialty of Nottingham Goose Fair. These and many other fairings are made according to prized traditional recipes.

FIG SUNDAY (also called *Fig Pie,* and *Mothering Fig Pie Sunday*)

The popular name applied to the fourth (sometimes the fifth) Sunday in Lent, when fig (or fag) pies are the traditional food specialty. There is disagreement, according to locality, regarding the proper date of Fig Sunday. In the parish of Draycot-le-Moors, Staffordshire, for example, as in parts of northern Lancashire, the fourth Sunday in Lent (also called Mid-Lent or Mothering Sunday) is known as Fig Pie, or Mothering Fig Pie Sunday; in Northamptonshire and Herefordshire, on the other hand, Palm Sunday, or the sixth Sunday in Lent, is properly called Fig Sunday, after the barren fig tree Christ was supposed to have cursed when making his triumphal entry into Jerusalem.

FOURSES

Plain harvest cakes, made for farm hands during the harvest season, especially in the vicinity of Leisten and Debenham, in East Suffolk. The name *fourses* is thought to have arisen from the fact that the cakes were baked round or square, then cut across twice at right angles, thus making four equal portions. See also *Harvest Cakes.*

GLOSSARY

FRUMENTY

Also called *furmety, frumerty,* etc., from the Latin *frumentum.* A special dish, traditional to Christmas, Mothering Sunday and certain village festivals. Frumenty is made by steeping whole wheat grains in water overnight, then boiling the mixture in milk and flavoring with sugar and spice.

GOOD FRIDAY

The Friday preceding Easter. The day commemorates Christ's Passion.

GUISERS (or Guysers)

Bands of fantastically garbed performers who go about the neighborhood, usually at Christmas time, performing all sorts of antics and singing songs. Usually people reward the guisers with money gifts and plenty of goodies.

GULES OF AUGUST See *Lammas*

GUY FAWKES'S DAY

November 5, anniversary of the discovery of the plot to blow up the Houses of Parliament on November 5, 1605. Guy Fawkes, appointed to set off the gunpowder, was found in hiding by British soldiers.

HALLOWE'EN

See All Hallows' Eve.

HARVEST CAKES

Harvest cakes that are made "off the bread," that is, from bread dough to which sugar, raisins and extra shortening are added, to give a richer loaf. Harvest cakes are baked into round, or square flattish buns, and cut across lightly to make four portions. It was customary on old farms to give each farm hand one bun, measuring between four and four-and-a-half inches across. Often Harvest Cakes and Fourses were served at the same table. The farm workers, sitting at the lower end of the kitchen table, received the plainer Fourses, while the farmer and his family, presiding over the upper end, ate the enriched Harvest Cakes.

261

ENGLISH FESTIVALS

HOCKTIDE

The second Monday and Tuesday after Easter Sunday. The two days go by the name of Hocktide. At this season, in olden times, it was customary to trip people up and bind them for the enforced payment of rents or other dues. Hungerford, in Berkshire, still celebrates Hocktide.

HOLY INNOCENTS' DAY (Also called *Childermas*)

December 28, the anniversary of the slaughter of Bethlehem's innocent children by Herod, who wished to make certain of killing the Infant Jesus.

HOLY-ROOD, or HOLY-CROSS DAY (Also called *Elevation of the Cross*)

Observed on September 14. This festival commemorates the miraculous vision of the cross by Constantine, in 312 A.D., when the Emperor was about to fight Maxentius. According to some authorities, Constantine himself instituted the feast in honor of the Holy Cross which appeared in the heavens with the words, *In hoc signo vinces,* "By this sign you will conquer."

HOLY SATURDAY

The Saturday immediately preceding Easter.

KATTERN CAKE

A special Bedfordshire caraway seed cake, always served for the lacemakers festival on St. Catherine's Day (November 25). See also *Tandra Cake.*

LADY DAY

In addition to its religious significance, Lady Day is a popular term or quarter day. See also *Annunciation.*

LAMB'S WOOL

The term applied to the wine or ale, combined with sugar, nutmeg, ginger and roasted apples, which were used in the wassail bowls of olden times. See also *Twelfth Night.*

262

LAMMAS (Also called *Gules of August, Day of St. Peter in Fetters*)
August 1. In early days Lammas was the time of thanksgiving for the corn harvest. Later the day became identified with customs and usages pertaining to land tenure and rights of pasture. Some people think the name *Lammas* comes from the early Lamb Mass of August 1, when feudal tenants of York's Cathedral of St. Peter in Vinculis (St. Peter in Fetters) used lambs at High Mass. Lammas is a popular term or quarter day.

LENT
The name given to the annual period of fasting and preparation preceding the Easter feast. Lent begins on Ash Wednesday and continues for the forty week days coming before Easter. The six Sundays during the Lenten period are not included, since Sundays always are regarded as feast days.

LOST SUNDAY See *Septuagesima Sunday*

LOW SUNDAY
The Sunday after Easter. The day is so-called because it is of less importance than Easter.

MARTINMAS
November 11, the Feast of St. Martin. Formerly the day was characterized by feasting, drinking and merrymaking. Roast goose is the traditional food of the day. Martinmas is a popular term, or quarter day, especially in the Lake district.

MAUNDY THURSDAY (or *Holy Thursday*)
The Thursday preceding Easter. The day sometimes is called *dies mandati*, Mandate, or Maundy Thursday, because Jesus washed his disciples' feet on this anniversary and commanded his followers to do likewise.

MAY DAY
May 1, the ancient Druidic Feast of Bel. Prior to the Restoration, the advent of the merry month of May was celebrated with all kinds of amusements, the crowning of May

Queens, dancing, singing and "going a-Maying." Although many of the old May customs are still observed, they are largely revivals, and are not celebrated on the first of May.

MICHAELMAS

September 29, a popular term or quarter day, important in the settlement of accounts and rent payments. Michaelmas commemorates the feast of the dedication of St. Michael, chief of the archangels. It was customary in olden times, and still is, to some extent, to serve roast goose on this day. For hundreds of years tenants included a goose in the payment of their Michaelmas rents.

MIDSUMMER DAY See *Nativity of St. John the Baptist*

MOTHERING SUNDAY (Also called *Mid-Lent Sunday*)

The fourth Sunday in Lent. According to old custom boys and girls who are away from home visit their parents on this day and present gifts. In many parts of England it is customary for the children to bring nosegays of wild flowers to be blessed in church. Later the flowers are given to the mothers. See also *Simnel Cake*.

MUMMERS

Companies of performers who go from house to house, usually during Yuletide, acting out the traditional play of St. George and the Dragon and receiving gratuities in return.

NATIVITY OF ST. JOHN THE BAPTIST (Also called *Midsummer Day*)

June 24, the day which commemorates the birth of St. John the Baptist. In many communities St. John's Day, always associated with water, is celebrated with well-dressings. See also *Well-Dressings*.

NATIVITY OF THE VIRGIN

A feast celebrated on September 8, in memory of the birth of the Virgin Mary.

GLOSSARY

PACE-EGGING

The custom of giving simple plays or performances by village boys and men, to collect money and eggs for the Easter festivities. Pace-egging used to be celebrated chiefly in the North Countries, where it still survives in limited degree.

PALM SUNDAY

The Sunday immediately preceding Easter. The name Palm Sunday comes from the custom of carrying palms, in memory of the palms waved before Jesus upon his triumphal entry into Jerusalem. In many English communities branches of native sallow (*salix caprea*) and other catkin-bearing willows are used at Palm Sunday services in place of imported palms. Often people wear sprigs of sallow in buttonholes or on their frocks.

PANCAKE DAY (Also called *Shrove Tuesday*)

The Tuesday before Ash Wednesday. Before the Reformation a bell, rung on Shrove Tuesday, reminded people of confession and shriving by the priest. Later, when the bell which once summoned people to church became a signal for making pancakes and participating in all sorts of sports, Shrove Tuesday popularly became known as Pancake Day.

PARKIN

A traditional cake made from oatmeal, treacle, butter and modern additions, such as baking powder and ginger. Parkins are of many different varieties, according to locality. Yorkshire people claim that "true parkins" belong to their county and nowhere else. Throughout England, however, parkin, in one form or another, is the special holiday delicacy for Guy Fawkes's Day (November 5).

PASSION OF CHRIST

The term applied to the sufferings of Christ between the time of the Last Supper and His death on the cross.

265

PENTECOST (Also called *Whitsunday*)

The festival on the fiftieth day after Easter. The festival commemorates the Apostles' reception of the gift of tongues.

PIKELETS

A kind of thick pancake (known in London as the *crumpet*) which is baked on a girdle, or griddle. In the Midlands pikelets are traditional on the five o'clock Christmas Day tea. Although the pancakes are eaten at other seasons as well, they are customary for this occasion.

PLOUGH MONDAY

The first Monday after Epiphany, or Twelfth Day (January 6), and the traditional time for commencing ploughing.

PLOUGH PLAY

A play which is given by plough boys on Plough Monday or, roughly speaking, during the Yuletide season, in Lincolnshire particularly and sometimes in Nottinghamshire, and other northern and northeastern counties.

PLOUGH STOT

The name given to a performer in a Plough Play.

PLOUGH SUNDAY

The first Sunday after Twelfth Day. On this day the plough is blessed in a number of agricultural communities.

PRESENTATION OF CHRIST

February 2, the anniversary of Mary's presentation of her Son at the Temple, forty days after birth. See also *Candlemas*.

REFORMATION

The great sixteenth century religious revolution, resulting in the establishment of the Protestant Church. In England the Reformation led, during Henry VIII's reign, to the abolition of papal supremacy and the liberation of the Church of England from papal control. Under Queen Mary, there was a brief resurgence of Catholicism, but Protestantism became firmly established under Queen Elizabeth.

GLOSSARY

RESTORATION

The term applied to the reestablishment of the English monarchy, with the return of King Charles II, in 1660.

REVEL

Originally the same as a Wake, the day on which a country church was dedicated. See also *Vigil, Wake.*

ROGATION DAYS

The Monday, Tuesday and Wednesday preceding Ascension Thursday. The name is derived from the fact that the Litany of Saints is chanted during the processions of the three days. It is customary for village processions, headed by clergy and church officials, to visit fields, ponds and meadows on the Rogation Days and ask for Divine blessing on all growing things.

ROGATION SUNDAY

The Sunday preceding Ascension Day.

ROGATIONTIDE

The period of Rogation days.

ROGATION WEEK (Also called *Cross Week, Gang Week, Procession Week*)

The week in which the Rogation days occur.

ROUNDABOUT

A circular platform which revolves to music and carries gaily-painted wooden ponies, elephants, carriages, and so on. Roundabouts, which are similar to American merry-go-rounds, are an amusement feature of every English pleasure fair.

ROYALIST

A Cavalier, as opposed to a Roundhead; a supporter of the king and the royal house. Specifically, in English history, a Royalist was a supporter of Charles I and Charles II in the Civil War of the Commonwealth.

RUSH-BEARING (Sometimes called *Hay-Strewing*)
> A religious ceremony consisting of strewing fragrant, freshly cut rushes or hay over the floor of the parish church. Although the custom is very ancient, it has many survivals in rural England.

SEPTUAGESIMA SUNDAY (Also called the *Lost Sunday*)
> The third Sunday before Lent. Sometimes the day is called the *Lost Sunday* because it has no other special name.

SHROVE TUESDAY
> The Tuesday before Ash Wednesday, or the last day before Lent. See also *Pancake Day*.

SHROVE SUNDAY (Also called *Quinquagesima Sunday*)
> The Sunday preceding Shrove Monday, or the Sunday before the beginning of Lent.

SIMNEL CAKE
> A special gift cake for the mother of a family, usually presented by the children on Mid-Lent, or Mothering Sunday (the fourth Sunday in Lent). Most people agree that the name *simnel* comes from the Latin *simila,* meaning fine flour. (See also *Mothering Sunday*).

SOUL CAKES
> Special oval or round buns once distributed at the church door on All Souls' Day (November 2) as a "charity" for departed souls. In a popular sense soul cakes today mean apples, money, goodies of any kind. These things are given to the Soulers, who make village rounds on All Souls' Eve (November 1). See also *Soulers*.

SOULERS
> Bands of singers who go from door to door on All Souls' Day (November 2) singing traditional rhymes and begging for Soul Cakes.

GLOSSARY

STIR-UP SUNDAY

The Sunday next before Advent. Popularly known as Stir-up Sunday from the *Collect* of the day, which begins, "Stir up we beseech thee, O Lord, the wills of thy faithful people." This is the day when housewives traditionally begin to stir up the ingredients for the Christmas plum puddings and mince pies.

TANDER

The name sometimes applied to the lacemakers' feast on November 30, in honor of their patron, Saint Andrew. Feasting, sports, and general merrymaking characterized the celebration.

TANDRA CAKE

A cake which Bedfordshire people serve at the lacemakers' festival on St. Andrew's Day (November 30). Tandra Cake is made from bread dough, enriched with sugar, raisins and lemon peel. See also *Kattern Cake*.

TRINITY

The Sunday next after Whitsunday (or Pentecost), or fifty-seven days after Easter. The feast commemorates the mystery of the union of Father, Son and Holy Ghost in One Godhead.

TWELFTH NIGHT (Also called *Twelfth Day Eve, Old Christmas Eve, Epiphany Eve*)

January 5, the eve of the twelfth day after Christmas. In the Old Style calendar, Twelfth Night is the eve of the anniversary of the "real" Christmas Day. In olden times Twelfth Night was characterized by jovial revels which centered principally in drinking "lamb's wool" and eating Twelfth Cake.

THE TWELVE DAYS

The name popularly applied to the twelve-day period between Christmas and Epiphany. "The Twelve Days" are the "image of the year," according to folk belief. Whatever is done on these days reflects on the good or bad luck of the coming year. This is why people say that for each mince pie eaten during The Twelve Days, there will be a happy month during the next twelve! The Yorkshire housewife declares she rates a happy month for each time during the Twelve Days anyone requests a piece of her Yule Cake.

VIGIL

In popular usage, the same as a Wake. Originally, the time when people kept vigil on the eve of the day of the saint of their parish church. See also *Wake*.

WAITS

The term applied to bands of musicians who go about singing from house to house during Yuletide. The waits receive gratuities in return for their entertainment.

WAKE

Originally, an annual festival kept by an all-night watch (from Middle English *waken*, to watch, or keep vigil) in the parish church, to commemorate its completion and dedication. In early times booths were set up in the churchyard to provide refreshment for the great crowds, which celebrated the following day as a holiday. Eventually, the wake became little more than a fair or market, attended by country people from miles about. In his *Book of Sports*, Charles I especially mentions *wakes* as among the feasts that should be observed.

WAKES WEEK

Once the entire week which included the parish church's dedication day. Different communities enjoy traditional Wakes Week foods. Fairs, markets, folk dancing and all kinds of amusements characterize Wakes Week celebrations, which now have generally lost all religious significance. Almost every community has characteristic Wakes Week festivities, especially in the North Country.

WASSAIL

The toast, or salutation (from Old English *was hal*, meaning, "Be thou whole," or "hale"), in which health is pledged in drinking.

270

GLOSSARY

WELL-DRESSING

A religious ceremony of blessing local village wells, which the inhabitants adorn with flowers, often in the form of flower-mosaic screens. The custom of well-dressing, which survives especially in many Derbyshire and Staffordshire villages, usually is observed on Midsummer Eve (June 23) or Ascension (forty days after Easter) in the former county, at Whitsuntide in the latter. Well-dressing is said to be a Christian adaptation of the *Fontinalia,* or Roman flower festival, to honor the spirits of streams and fountains.

WHITSUNDAY

A festival occurring on the seventh Sunday and the fiftieth day after Easter. Whitsunday commemorates the descent of the Holy Ghost on the Apostles, on the day of Pentecost. The term "whit," according to some, is thought to mean white, in reference to the wearing of white garments by the converts baptized on this day.

WHIT MONDAY

The fifty-first day after Easter. This is a popular Bank Holiday throughout England.

WHITSUNTIDE

The Pentecostal season, or the entire week, commencing with Whitsunday, or Pentecost. Actually, in modern England, Whitsunday and Whit Monday are the only days popularly observed.

WIG

A caraway-filled cake, made from fine white flour and molded into various shapes, round, triangular, or oblong. Wigs are a Christmas specialty in Shrewsbury. In Bedfordshire, they are a delicacy connected with the lacemakers' festival on St. Catherine's Day (November 25). In Bedfordshire, wigs are so-called because they are baked in small round pans (like cup cake pans), and curl over the edges like wig curls. At least, this is the explanation many local inhabitants give!

SOME HELPFUL BOOKS

GENERAL BACKGROUND

Brand, John
Observations on the Popular Antiquities of Great Britain.
London. Bohn, 1849. 3v. Volume 1 gives festivals and
saints' days and their celebration; volumes 2 and 3, omens,
games, charms, customs.

Bunyan, John
Pilgrim's Progress.
See description of Vanity Fair, First Part. Here the Bedfordshire tinker gives an accurate account of the Court of
Pie-powder which once was incident to every fair and administered justice for all commercial injuries suffered at
the fair.

Burton, Alfred
Rush-Bearing. Manchester, Brook and Chrystal, 1891.
Old but standard work. Includes accounts of strewing
rushes, carrying rushes to church, garlands in churches, etc.
Well illustrated.

Chambers, Robert
*The Book of Days: a Miscellany of Popular Antiquities in
Connection with the Calendar.* London, Chambers, 1863-
1864. 2v.

Curtis, Mary I.
*England of Song and Story; a Picture of Life in England
and a Background for English Literature of the 16th, 17th
and 18th Centuries.* Boston, Allyn and Bacon, 1931.
Holidays, manners, customs and dress.

Ditchfield, Peter Hamson

Old English Sports, Pastimes and Customs. London, Methuen, 1891.

Old Village Life; or, Glimpses of Village Life Through All Ages. New York, Dutton, 1920.

Well presented material, from prehistoric to modern times.

Drake-Carnell, F. J.

Old English Customs and Ceremonies. New York, Scribner, 1938.

First-hand accounts of many old holiday customs still observed in modern England. Excellent photographic illustrations.

Folk-Lore: a Quarterly Review of Myth, Tradition, Institution and Custom. London, Glaisher. Publication of the Folk-Lore Society (British).

See index to each volume for counties, customs and high days.

Frazer, James George

The Golden Bough: a Study in Religion and Magic. 3d. ed. London, Macmillan, 1911-1926. 12v.

See name of day or custom in volume 12, *Bibliography and General Index.*

Graham, Eleanor

High Days and Holidays; Stories, Legends and Customs of Red-Letter Days and Holidays. London, Benn, 1932.

Hastings, James, ed.

Encyclopaedia of Religion and Ethics. New York, Scribner, 1908-27, 12v and *Index.*

Consult *Index* under various holiday headings.

Hole, Christina
English Custom and Usage. London, Batsford, 1941-1942.
Descriptions of many traditional customs that survive to
modern times.
English Folklore. London, Batsford, 1940.

Hone, William
Every-day Book and Table Book. London, Printed for
Thomas Tegg, 1826. 3v.

Hull, Eleanor
Folklore of the British Isles. London, Methuen, 1928.
Excellent as background material.

Long, George
The Folklore Calendar. London, Philip Allan, 1930.
Eyewitness accounts of traditional ceremonies and customs.

Miles, Clement A.
Christmas in Ritual and Tradition, Christian and Pagan.
London, Unwin, 1912.

Needham, A.
How to Study an Old Church. London, Batsford, 1945.
Highly recommended to the casual reader as a guide to old
English churches, their customs and lore.

*Shakespeare's England: an Account of the Life and Manners
of His Age.* London, Oxford University Press, 1932, 2v.
Good material on early customs and festivals. See volume 1, chapter XVI, p516-45, for folklore and superstitions; volume 2, chapter XXVII, p334-484, for sports and
pastimes.

Sikes, Wirt
*British Goblins, Welsh Folk-lore, Fairy Mythology, Leg-
ends.* London, Low, Marston, Searle and Rivington, 1880.
"Quaint Old Customs," p250-337.

Thiselton-Dyer, T. F.
British Popular Customs, Present and Past. London, Bell, 1891.

Urlin, Ethel L.
Festivals, Holy Days and Saints' Days. London, Simpkin, Marshall, Hamilton, Kent, 1915.
Descriptions of many festival customs, arranged in order of occurrence.

Walsh, William S. comp.
Curiosities of Popular Customs. Philadelphia, Lippincott, 1925.
Social life, customs, special days, arranged in alphabetical order.

Whistler, Laurence
The English Festivals. London, Heinemann, 1947.
Descriptions of many holy day origins and customs.

Williamson, George C.
Curious Survivals; Habits and Customs of the Past that Still Live in the Present. London, Jenkins, 1923.

Wright, Arthur Robinson
British Calendar Customs; ed. by T. E. Lones. London, Glaisher, published for the Folk-Lore Society (British), 1936-40. 3v. Volume I, "Movable Feasts"; Volume II, "Fixed Festivals" (January-May); Volume III, "Fixed Festivals" (June-December).
Excellent source material on special days and customs. Well indexed by county and subject.

Wright, Elizabeth Mary
Rustic Speech and Folk-lore. London, Oxford University Press, 1913.
Folk rhymes, customs and survivals.

BALLADS, CAROLS AND FOLK RHYMES

Ballads and Legends of Cheshire. London, Longmans, 1867.
Excellent collection of the county's festival songs, rhymes
and legends.

Dearmer, Percy and others, eds.
The Oxford Book of Carols. London, Oxford University
Press, 1928.
Contains over 200 carols, including many unusual English
traditional songs.

Northall, G. F.
English Folk Rhymes. London, Trübner, 1892.
Many folk rhymes of both local and general interest.

Thistelton-Dyer, T. F.
English Folk-Lore. London, Bogue, 1888.
Customs, nature rhymes and ancient lore.

Wright, Elizabeth Mary
Rustic Speech and Folk-Lore. London, Oxford University
Press, 1913.
Folk rhymes and customs.

CHURCH SAINTS AND CUSTOMS

Andrews, William
Curious Church Customs. London, Simpkin, Marshall,
Hamilton, Kent, 1893.
Entertaining material on baptism, marriage and burial cus-
toms; sports in churches, belfry laws and inscriptions, al-
tars, rood lofts and cloisters.

Baring-Gould, Sabine
*The Lives of the Saints . . . with Introduction and Addi-
tional Lives of English Martyrs, Cornish Saints, and a Full
Index.* New revised ed. Edinburgh, Grant, 1914. 16v.
Volume 16 includes "A Celtic and English Kalendar of
Saints." Look up various saints' days and holy days under
month and date.

Duckett, Eleanor Shipley
Anglo-Saxon Saints and Scholars. New York, Macmillan, 1947.

FESTIVE FOODS

Eden, Helen
County Recipes of Old England. London, Country Life, 1929.

Gerish, W. B.
The Folk-Lore of Herefordshire. Bishop's Stortford, 1911. Beliefs and customs connected with Hot Cross Buns, Pope Ladies and other holiday specialties.

Hackwood, F. W.
Good Cheer: The Romance of Food and Feasting. New York, Sturgis and Walton, 1911.
Colorful background of English holiday cakes.

Mead, William Edward
The English Medieval Feast. London, Allen and Unwin, 1931.
Cookery, social customs and background.

Spicer, Dorothy Gladys
From an English Oven. New York, Woman's Press, 1948. Recipes and traditional background of many high day and holy day cakes and breads (simnels, Shrovetide pancakes, pikelets, etc.), that are mentioned in the text of this book.

FOLK DANCING

Sharp, Cecil J. and Macilwaine, Herbert C.
The Morris Book. London, Novello, 1909-13. (Part IV by C. J. Sharp), Part V (by C. J. Sharp and George Butterworth)
Traditional morris dances, descriptions and music.

Mummers

Chambers, E. K.
English Folk-Play. London, Oxford University Press, 1933.
Standard work on Plough Plays, sword dances, morris
dances and related subjects.

Tiddy, Reginald J. E.
The Mummers' Play. London, Oxford University Press,
1923.
Standard work on the subject.

Old Calendar Customs and Nature-Lore

Poor Robin, an Almanack. London, 1665-1740.

*Shepherd's Kalendar; or Citizen's and Countrymen's Daily
Companion.* Published and sold at Three Bibles and Star,
London Bridge, 1680.

Vachell, H. A.
This was England, a Countryman's Calendar. London,
Hodder and Stoughton, 1933.
Contains a wealth of holiday lore, both ancient and mod-
ern.

Wolseley, Viscountess
The Countryman's Log-Book. London, Lee, Warner, 1921.

Regional Material on the Counties

Berkshire
Berkshire Federation of Women's Institutes, comp.
The Berkshire Book. Reading, Berkshire, Federation of
Women's Institutes, 1951, 2d. ed.

Hayden, Eleanor G.
Islands of the Vale. London, Smith, Elder, 1908.

Cheshire
Ballads and Legends of Cheshire. London, Longmans, 1867.

Heath, Robert
Congleton, Past and Present. Congleton, Printed by the Author, 1887.
Colorful descriptions of Congleton and old Cheshire, including such customs as bear baiting, rush bearing, etc.

Hole, Christina
Traditions and Customs of Old Cheshire. London, Williams and Norgate, 1937.

Ingham, Alfred
Cheshire, Its Traditions and History. Edinburgh, Pillans and Wilson, 1920.
Rich traditional material on Cheshire customs.

Cornwall

Harris, J. H.
Cornish Saints and Sinners. London, Lane, 1906.

Jenkin, A. K. Hamilton
Cornish Homes and Customs. London, Dent, 1934.

Derbyshire

Addy, S. O.
"Garland Day at Castleton." *Folk-Lore,* volume 12, 1902, p394-430.

Rix, Michael M.
"A Re-examination of the Castleton Garlanding." *Folk-Lore,* volume 64, 1953, p342-4.

Dorset

Dacombe, Margaret R., ed.
Dorset Up Along and Down Along: a Collection of History, Tradition, Folk-Lore, Flower Names and Herbal Lore, Gathered together by Members of the Women's Institutes. Dorchester, Friary Press, 1951. 3d ed.

Udal, John Symonds
Dorsetshire Folk-Lore. Hertford, Stephen Austin, 1922.
Customs, proverbs, children's games and rhymes.

Herefordshire
  Gerish, W. B.
  The Folklore of Herefordshire. Bishop's Stortford, 1911.
  Leather, Ella Mary
  The Folklore of Herefordshire. London, Sidgewick and Jackson, 1912.
  A valuable source for the customs of this county.

London
  Kent, Williams, ed.
  An Encyclopaedia of London. New York, Dutton, 1937.
  Contains some good descriptions of London's high days and ancient customs.

Shropshire
  Burne, Charlotte Sophia
  Shropshire Folk-lore; a Sheaf of Gleanings. London, Trübner, 1883.
  Webb, Mary
  Precious Bane. New York, Dutton, 1926.
  Authentic picture of Shropshire life and customs of a generation ago. The book—written in southern Shropshire dialect—describes such events as Telling the Bees, the Hiring Fair, Bull-Baiting, Harvest Home, etc. All of the author's books are recommended for their Shropshire folk background.

Warwickshire
  Bloom, J. Harvey
  Folklore, Old Customs and Superstitions in Shakespeare Land. London, Mitchell, Hughes and Clark, 1929.
  Old festivals, foods and customs.

Westmorland
  Tobey, Frances
  "Two Ancient Festival Survivals in 'Wordsworthshire.' "
  "The Grasmere Rush-Bearing." *Poet Lore,* volume 27, 1916, p326-42

SOME HELPFUL BOOKS

Yorkshire
Blakeborough, Richard
Wit, Character, Folklore and Customs of the North Riding of Yorkshire. London, Frowde, 1898.

INDEXES

INDEX OF CUSTOMS

285

INDEX BY COUNTIES

ENGLISH FESTIVALS

290

INDEX BY COUNTIES

ENGLISH FESTIVALS

INDEX BY COUNTIES

REGIONAL INDEX

NORTHERN COUNTIES

DURHAM

LANCASHIRE

NORTHEASTERN COUNTIES

NORTHUMBERLAND

NORTHWESTERN COUNTIES

WESTMORLAND

YORKSHIRE

MIDLAND COUNTIES

BEDFORDSHIRE

CHESHIRE

DERBYSHIRE

REGIONAL INDEX

295

ENGLISH FESTIVALS

WESTERN COUNTIES

DEVONSHIRE—*Continued*

Ceremony of Drinking the Health of Sir Francis Drake (Plymouth), 93

Lammas Fair (Exeter), 98

Ram Roasting Fair (Kingsteignton), 241

Widecombe Fair (Widecombe-in-the-Moor, Dartmoor), 125

DORSETSHIRE

Garland Day (Abbotsbury), 70

Going a-Shroving (Durweston), 195

May Day Festivities (Shillingstone), 82

Pack Monday Fair (Sherborne), 147

Sick Club Procession (Stoke Abbott), 81

SOMERSET

Bridgewater Fair, 135

Burning the Ashen Faggot (Dunster), 178

Candle Auction (Tatworth), 46

Hobby Horse Parade (Minehead), 48

Pilgrimage to the Holy Thorn (Glastonbury), 11

Punkie Night (Hinton St. George), 153

Wassailing the Apple Trees (Carhampton), 24